TO FULFILL THESE RIGHTS

AMAKA OKECHUKWU

TO FULFILL
THESE RIGHTS

Political Struggle Over Affirmative
Action and Open Admissions

COLUMBIA UNIVERSITY PRESS

NEW YORK

Columbia University Press
Publishers Since 1893
New York   Chichester, West Sussex
cup.columbia.edu
Copyright © 2019 Amaka Okechukwu
All rights reserved

Library of Congress Cataloging-in-Publication Data
A complete CIP record is available from the Library of Congress.
ISBN 978-0-231-18308-6 (cloth)
ISBN 978-0-231-18309-3 (pbk.)
ISBN 978-0-231-54474-0 (e-book)
LCCN 2019013978

To the writers within my parents

CONTENTS

LIST OF ABBREVIATIONS

AABL	Afro-Americans for Black Liberation
AASU	African American Student Union
ACLU	American Civil Liberties Union
ACRI	American Civil Rights Institute
AFT	American Federation of Teachers
BAM	Black Action Movement
BAMN	By Any Means Necessary (Coalition to Defend Affirmative Action, Integration, and Immigrant Rights, and Fight for Equality By Any Means Necessary)
BPRSC	Black and Puerto Rican Student Community
BSU	Black Student Union
CAAV	Committee Against Anti-Asian Violence
CCRI	California Civil Rights Initiative
CEO	Center for Equal Opportunity
CEO	Coloradans for Equal Opportunity
CfJ	Californians for Justice
CIR	Center for Individual Rights
CLEO	Council on Legal Education
CoCRI	Colorado Civil Rights Initiative
CSC	California State College; now CSU (California State University)

CUNY	City University of New York
DiA	Diversity in Action
DRUM	Desis Rising Up and Moving
DRUM	Dodge Revolutionary Union Movement
ELC	Eligibility in Local Context program
EOP	Educational Opportunity Program
HBCU	Historically Black college and/or university
IGU	Internal Governance Unit
LLN	Liberal Legal Network
LSA	Literature, Science, and Arts College of the University of Michigan
MALDEF	Mexican American Legal Defense and Education Fund
MAYO	Mexican American Youth Organization
MCRI	Michigan Civil Rights Initiative
MEChA	Movimiento Estudiantil Chicano de Aztlán
MXGM	Malcolm X Grassroots Movement
NAACP	National Association for the Advancement of Colored People
NAACP LDF	National Association for the Advancement of Colored People Legal Defense Fund
NRPB	National Resources Planning Board
PEO	Program on Educational Opportunity
PLP	Progressive Labor Party
SCSC	Students of Color Solidarity Coalition
SDS	Students for a Democratic Society
SEEK	Search for Education, Elevation, and Knowledge program
SFA	Students for Fair Admissions
SLAM!	Student Liberation Action Movement
SOUL	School of Unity and Liberation
SP-1, SP-2	Special Resolution 1, Special Resolution 2
SPM	Student Power Movement
TAFM	Towards a Fair Michigan
THECB	Texas Higher Education Coordinating Board
TIME	The Improvement of Minority Education, Enrollment, Environment, Employment, Essentials, Encouragement, Etc.

TWLF	Third World Liberation Front
UC	University of California
UM	University of Michigan
USSA	United States Students Association
UT Austin	University of Texas at Austin
WE-CAN	Working to Empower Community Action Now!

ACKNOWLEDGMENTS

T O FULFILL *These Rights* represents a long journey from graduate student to faculty member, from dissertation to book, and so I am eternally grateful for the people, spaces, and networks that supported my intellectual growth during this period. I discovered academic research as an undergraduate student at the University of Southern California and would not be a scholar today without the support of the McNair Scholars Program. My mentors during my undergraduate years, especially Lanita Jacobs and Robin D. G. Kelley, continue to model brilliance and a commitment to the development of young Black scholars.

This book would not have been possible without the funding support of the MacCracken Fellowship and Dean's Fellowship from New York University's Graduate School of Arts and Sciences. I am also indebted to the Social Science Research Council-Mellon Mays Graduate Initiatives Fellowship Program for grant support, professionalization resources, and the robust network of brilliant scholars who will be with me for a lifetime. This book was also supported in part by the American Fellowship from the American Association of University Women.

While revising this book and sowing the seeds for my next book project, I had the great fortune to work for my favorite history institutions in Brooklyn: Weeksville Heritage Center and Brooklyn Historical Society. I am forever grateful for those experiences; they taught me, among many things, how to maintain a disciplined writing schedule, and they gave me a mental break from thinking about racial politics in higher education.

I am thankful for the many activists I talked to and formally interviewed from the Student Power Movement, CUNY Coalition Against the Cuts, Student Liberation Action Movement, Diversity in Action, No Name Collective, Students Against Prop 209, and other organizations. Many thanks to Hank Williams, Rob Holleran, David Suker, Stephanie Campos, Ramiro Campos, Orlando Green, Neha Guatam, Lenina Nadal, Jorge Matos, John Kim, Chris Gunderson, Brad Sigal, Kamau Franklin, Jesse Ehrensaft-Sawley, Rachel LaForest, Sabrinne Hammad, Luz Schreiber, Mariano Muñoz, Kazembe Balagun, Camilo Gatson-Greenberg, Amanda Deveka-Rinear, Irini Neofotistos, Jeremiah Hosea, Harmony Goldberg, Sabrina Smith, Ingrid Benedict, and Kahlil Jacobs-Fantauzzi. I am especially grateful for suzy subways and her willingness to visit the archive with me and share her own interviews conducted with SLAMistas. I am additionally thankful to the many archivists, institutional research analysts, and state clerk staff members who assisted me with tracking down obscure documents and answered my questions.

I give thanks to all my mentors, colleagues, and friends who read my work closely and offered incredible feedback. Thank you to Ellen Berrey and the blind readers of this manuscript for feedback that truly clarified my thinking and connected me to other important scholarship. I owe a special thanks to my dissertation chair, Deirdre Royster, who passionately believed in my potential as a scholar, and Jeff Manza, who believed in the potential of this book. I also thank my additional dissertation committee members, Jeff Goodwin, Juan Corradi, and Lisa Stulberg, for their guidance and support throughout this process. Special thanks to my editor Eric Schwartz and the very patient and helpful editorial staff at Columbia University Press, including Lowell Frye and Caroline Wazer.

Thank you to the various formal and informal writing groups of colleagues from New York University, Columbia University, and The Graduate Center of the City University of New York. I give a special

shout-out to Nijah Cunningham for the graduate school accountability structure and your analytical brilliance and to Paula Austin
for your consistent friendship and willingness to review my work in
the most unfinished of states. Thank you to my D.C. writing buddy,
Manissa Maharawal; your friendship has been so important in this
stage of academic life. Many thanks to colleagues at American Sociological Association, Eastern Sociological Society, and Association of
Black Sociologists meetings for useful feedback on different pieces
of this book. And I am appreciative of my kind and thoughtful colleagues in the Department of Sociology and Anthropology at George
Mason University; thank you for modeling what it means to support
and encourage junior faculty.

I am especially grateful for the organizing and community building that I was able to participate in while this book project came
together. Much gratitude to Malcolm X Grassroots Movement, The
Brecht Forum, Boggs Center to Nurture Community Leadership,
Growing Roots, Brooklyn Movement Center, Crown Heights Community Mediation Center, Groundswell: Oral History for Social Change,
and Visionary Organizing Lab. This work, and these relationships,
kept me sane, grounded, and useful to the communities that matter the most to me and pushed me to grow intellectually in ways that
often made the book harder to write! Thank y'all for welcoming my
participation and contribution. In the future, I hope to better integrate the intellectual work and the political work in the service of a
new world.

To family and friends, thank you for your patience, even as life
moved on and I was still in school, and still working on this book.
I am forever thankful for the love and support of my parents, Georgette
Brooks Okechukwu and Iffy Okechukwu. Their example of hard work,
discipline, sacrifice, and faith provided me a road map for making it
through some of the most difficult of times. My brother, Amechi Okechukwu, has always remained eternally optimistic and supportive,
and for that I am grateful. I thank God for my grandparents, especially
Jesse and Laura Brooks, and the rest of my ancestors for instilling in
me a deep faith in God and for always praying for me. To the countless
family and friends across the world who rooted for me, even when
they did not understand what I was doing and why it was taking so

long, I appreciate you lifting me up. To my sisterhood, from the Bay to Brooklyn, thank you for your humor, creativity, wisdom, and encouragement. Special shout-outs go to Ashley Johns, Audrey Davis, Chanel Brown, Divinity Matovu, Courtney Layne, Yvette Osei-Akosa, and DéLana Dameron-John. To Matt Birkhold, you have challenged me to grow—intellectually, emotionally, spiritually—and I am forever grateful for our collective growth and all that we have left to do.

Finally, I give all thanks to God for bringing me through this journey. Making it through graduate school and into the academy has been incredibly challenging to my sense of self, strength, purpose, and community. However, this experience forced me to develop stronger faith and a more meaningful relationship with God, and for that I am especially grateful.

TO FULFILL THESE RIGHTS

INTRODUCTION

[We demand] a goal of 10 percent of the total population in Ann Arbor be made up of Black students by 1973–74. This shall increase yearly until the overall population of Blacks shall approach, if not exceed, the proportion of Blacks in the state. . . . Our efforts will culminate at the March 19 meeting of the Board of Regents at which time the question of our demands must be considered and acted on favorably.

—Black Action Movement, "Demands," University of Michigan, February 5, 1970

Lastly and most importantly, we demand an increase in black representation on this campus equal to 10 percent. We ask that the University understand that we are prepared to do what is necessary at any given moment if these demands are not met. We have heard the University say the phrase "we're listening" since 1970 and we are tired of waiting for a response.

—Tyrell Collier, Black Student Union leader, delivering student demands, University of Michigan, January 20, 2014

IN EARLY 2014, Black students at the University of Michigan (UM) made demands reminiscent of those from another era. Mobilizing in person and online using the hashtag #BBUM (Being Black at University of Michigan), their claims echoed those made by Black students at the university decades earlier. But they were not alone. Throughout 2014 and 2015, students at more than eighty colleges and universities held protests and sit-ins and petitioned their administrations.[1] Central to these Black Lives Matter–inspired mobilizations were calls for greater representation of Black students and racially competent campus climates. As expressed by students from UM, these protests emerged from the unfulfilled promises of racial justice that administrators and, by extension, the State had made in response to the civil rights and Black Power movements.

At a time when the discourse of colorblindness and diversity structured the national conversation about racial inequality, and the law restricted (and in many places banned) race-conscious admissions policies, Black students at UM and across the country rejected shallow declarations of a postracial world. The almost identical demands made by Black students across a period of almost fifty years force us to come to terms with what has not been resolved in the post–civil rights era. Why has so little changed?

In the 1960s, in response to a changing racial climate, as well as the first generation of widespread campus protests over educational access at predominantly White institutions, liberal administrators implemented new admissions policies intended to extend university inclusion to Black and Latino students. Competitive, elite public and private colleges adopted affirmative action. Open admissions emerged as a demand for broad access at less selective institutions, most notably enacted as a compromise to more radical demands by Black and Puerto Rican students in the City University of New York (CUNY) system. At a time when the federal government made modest concessions in response to the civil rights movement and urban rebellions, some political officials openly recognized the need to proactively redress deep-seated racial inequality. In his 1965 Howard University commencement speech titled "To Fulfill These Rights," even President Lyndon Baines Johnson argued for policies that would go beyond "equality as right and theory" to "equality as a result," or equal achievement outcomes among Blacks and Whites.[2]

However, in the decades since, affirmative action and open admissions—or, considered together, race- and class-inclusive admissions—have become targets of conservative mobilization and in many cases have been overturned or significantly revised. Renewed protest among Black college students, inspired by a larger movement against police brutality and White supremacy, affirms that universities are but one site of struggle in a system of racial domination—just as protests by Black students of the 1960s and 1970s emerged in relationship to civil rights and Black Power mobilization. Students challenge the purpose and function of higher education by demanding not only an increased presence of Black and Latino students but also ethnic studies curriculum and social space. Student protests for affirmative action and ethnic studies departments and against campus racism, then and now, push for a fundamentally different world.

Students are correct to point to the persistence of racial inequality in higher education. In 2016, 43 percent of Whites between the ages of twenty-five and twenty-nine had attained a bachelor's degree, but only 23 percent of Blacks had achieved the same.[3] Though scholars have rebutted claims that African American men are more likely to be incarcerated than enrolled in colleges and universities, African Americans of all genders are more likely to enroll in for-profit colleges—predatory institutions that endow their students with more debt, nontransferable credits, and an education that has little value in the job market.[4] Much of the student loan crisis, characterized by the highest loan default rates among borrowers in twenty years, is concentrated among former students of for-profit colleges. Of students who left school in 2011 and defaulted by 2013, 70 percent had pursued degrees at for-profit colleges.[5] Over 28 percent of African Americans enrolled in four-year colleges attend for-profit institutions, as compared to 10 percent of Whites and 15 percent of Latinos.[6] Along with the disproportionate impact of the subprime mortgage crisis on Black families, education is also a site of exploitation, racial disparity, and a mechanism of inherited disadvantage.

For Black students who make it to elite universities, negotiating the campus racial climate, their social and economic status, and the lack of institutional supports, all impact academic achievement and attrition rates.[7] While scholars repeatedly illustrate the significance of college degree attainment for the economic mobility of the socially disadvantaged[8] and the role that social capital from elite universities plays in obtaining employment,[9] it is clear that a historical legacy of systemic racism produces disadvantage in education, employment, and social mobility. Even with important advancements in the educational sphere, including an increase in public university enrollment among all students, persisting educational inequality rooted in systemic race and class disparities indicates that America has failed to live up to its democratic ideals. Thus, interventions in the form of race- and class-inclusive admissions are (and have been) important in addressing race and class inequality in higher education. Affirmative action and open admissions are crucial policies through which to examine the shifting practices and understandings of racial politics in the twentieth and twenty-first centuries.

To Fulfill These Rights traces the adoption and retrenchment of affirmative action and open admissions policies in higher education, centering political struggle over race and class politics. Through political struggle, conservative political actors, liberal administrators, legislators, and radical students define, challenge, and transform racial practice and ideas, upholding and confronting racial hegemony in post–civil rights America. By studying political contestation over affirmative action and open admissions, I contribute insight into how the racial logics of colorblindness and diversity reify racial hegemony. Additionally, I draw attention to the ways in which elite and grassroots mobilization drive racial formation in the twenty-first century.

DEFINING AFFIRMATIVE ACTION
AND OPEN ADMISSIONS

Definitions of affirmative action vary according to the time period, sector, and institution. The varying applications of and legal restrictions on affirmative action have led to much public confusion over its meaning and scope, and opponents have used this inconsistency to generate public hostility toward its use. While I will specify the particular policies in operation at a variety of educational institutions, for the purpose of clarity, affirmative action encompasses policies and programs that provide special consideration to historically excluded groups, such as racial and ethnic minorities and women, in the spheres of education and employment. This special consideration is given to underrepresented groups for the purpose of creating and maintaining diverse campuses and workplaces. In universities, this includes the consideration of race in admissions decisions; however, it also extends to outreach programs, targeted recruitment, scholarships and financial aid awards, retention and matriculation programs, and programs that encourage and support the attainment of advanced degrees. I focus on the consideration of applicant membership in historically excluded or underrepresented racial groups in admission decisions. These historically excluded and underrepresented groups are typically African American, Latino, and Native American students. Importantly, affirmative action in university admissions operates almost exclusively at selective public and private institutions.

Affirmative action's piecemeal adoption emerged within a context of civil rights legislative victories, largely as a progressive remedy to racial discrimination in employment. The history of Black resistance to labor exploitation is as long as Black presence in the New World, however, significant mobilization against employment discrimination in the wartime defense industries by A. Phillip Randolph and the March on Washington Movement in the 1940s created the conditions for the emergence of the civil rights movement of the 1950s and 1960s.[10] While many civil rights demands related to the enforcement of nondiscrimination in employment, education, and public accommodations, affirmative action was a distinct attempt to remedy past (and persisting) discrimination through race-conscious considerations. In the wake of lawsuits and Supreme Court decisions, the only permissible use of affirmative action in universities today is for the creation of diverse student bodies.

In the realm of higher education, affirmative action developed in relation to federal guidelines for remedying discrimination at federally funded institutions (in compliance with the Civil Rights Act of 1964) *and* attempts by liberal administrators and foundations to establish early experimental programs that admitted small numbers of Black students to elite public and private universities.[11] Pursuant to Title VI of the Civil Rights Act of 1964, Congress created the Office for Civil Rights to monitor and enforce nondiscrimination in federally assisted institutions, and established the office in the Department of Health, Education and Welfare (part of which later b U.S. Department of Education). In the early 1970s, the to interpret university compliance with the Civil Right as requiring plans and goals to integrate student bodies among universities with a documented history of explicit discrimination).[12] While the federal government framed these plans as voluntary for institutions without a documented history of discrimination, universities deemed in violation of Title VI of the act risked losing their federal funding.

These remedial prescriptions were reframed as desires for campus "diversity" in 1978, after the Supreme Court decision in *Regents of the University of California v. Bakke* determined that admissions efforts aimed at racial reparation were permissible only in institutions where *specific* illegal discrimination had been documented against individuals and groups. Although societal racial discrimination had been legally taken off the table and racial quotas had been determined to be illegal, Justice Lewis Powell's opinion asserted that campus diversity was a compelling governmental interest and that race could be utilized as a factor, but not the determining factor, in college admissions. Yet even this opinion provided grounds for political conflict: while universities interpreted Powell's opinion as a guideline to inform program development and revision, the split decision of the Court raised questions as to whether his opinion was an actual binding precedent and, thus, whether diversity was legally a compelling governmental interest. This legal confusion further made affirmative action vulnerable to legal challenge.

Affirmative action bans prevent public universities, and other state agencies, from considering race in admission and employment decisions. The following states have passed successful affirmative action bans that amend the state constitution: by ballot proposition, California (1996), Washington (1998), Michigan (2006), Nebraska (2008), Arizona (2010), and Oklahoma (2012); by state legislature, New Hampshire (2011); and by executive order of the governor, Florida (1999). Between 1996 and 2003, the Fifth Circuit Court of Appeals ruling in *Hopwood v. Texas*, which rejected Powell's *Bakke* opinion, temporarily banned affirmative action in Texas, Louisiana, and Mississippi; however, this ban was not enforced in Louisiana and Mississippi because court oversight in those states made affirmative action enforcement mandatory in response to a history of state-sponsored segregation.[13] The Supreme Court decision in *Grutter v. Bollinger* (2003) later superseded *Hopwood v. Texas* and established that race could, in fact, be considered in university admissions. Other universities have quietly ended their use of affirmative action, often in response to the threat of lawsuits.[14] In their analysis of one thousand public and private universities with selective admissions practices, representing 35 percent of all enrolled undergraduates, Dan Hirschman and Ellen Berrey found that universities' public acknowledgment of the consideration of race in admissions declined from 60 to 35 percent over the twenty-year period from 1994 to 2014.[15] Though the use of affirmative action policies has been widespread among selective colleges and universities,[16] persistent legal and electoral challenges reflect an environment hostile to affirmative action.

In contrast to the use of affirmative action at selective universities, *open admissions*, also called open enrollment and inclusive admissions, operates at non-elite, less selective, and/or noncompetitive institutions, where admissions criteria are limited to factors such as a high school diploma and a modest grade point average. Although open admissions policies differ across institutions, standardized testing is typically not required (or is deemphasized); neither is a record of extensive extracurricular activities or additional curricular factors. Open admissions is most often practiced at community colleges.

Prior to the 1940s, many public and private universities effectively operated open admissions policies for White men (and some White women) simply because the demand for college was not high. While admissions officers actively discriminated against applicants of color and White women were often eligible to attend only women's colleges, only small numbers of Americans applied to college.[17] People who attended college often came from wealthy and established families, and they often pursued specialized professional training, such as medicine or law.

After the GI Bill (1944) gave returning soldiers the opportunity and means to attend college, college enrollments ballooned, states established more public universities to meet the demand, and institutions began to apply additional admissions criteria, including standardized test scores, to manage growing enrollments.[18] However, a movement to democratize higher education emerged as part of civil rights and Black Power mobilization. In these demands emerged a call for open admissions. While the policy of open admissions is most associated with the CUNY system, activists across the country demanded it, and many institutions adopted open admissions or programs that targeted Black and Brown students and reduced admissions criteria.[19] Activists who specifically demanded open admissions recognized the ways that institutional racism structured primary and secondary schooling—resulting in fewer college preparatory course offerings, overburdened teachers, and minimal financial allocations for school facilities, textbooks, and educational materials. They argued that engaged and ambitious students should not be barred from college due to circumstances beyond their control. Whereas detractors demanded adherence to meritocracy and high academic standards, activists emphasized the need for public higher education that lived up to the democratic ideals it espoused. Calls for open admissions cannot simply be relegated to the 1960s. The Movement for Black Lives policy platform, the political agenda of a coalition of Black Lives Matter organizations, demands the implementation of open admissions for Black students at all public universities in the United States.[20]

While affirmative action is legally circumscribed by the law, there are no legal restrictions governing open admissions, although it is not practiced widely in four-year undergraduate institutions. In fact, the use of open admissions at CUNY, the largest urban university in the United States, was significant because of the great impact this policy had on the eleven four-year colleges in the system, completely shifting their racial demographics and unraveling the selectivity that had previously been practiced. Open admissions is dependent on robust remedial course offerings so that students can strengthen their academic skills before moving into more demanding coursework. Thus, elimination of remedial courses effectively eliminates the practice of open admissions, as it did in the CUNY four-year colleges. However, colleges of varying ranks enroll students in remedial programs: in 2011, approximately one in four students that attended college the fall after high school graduation had to take remedial courses in their first year of college. Further, community college students are not the only students enrolled in remedial courses: 40 percent attend public or private four-year colleges. And 45 percent of their families are from middle- and upper-income backgrounds.[21] Thus, remedial coursework is not exclusive to colleges that employ open admissions; selective institutions regularly offer some form of remedial courses to undergraduates, and a significant number of students take them.

In this book, I examine cases of political struggle over affirmative action and open admissions because they are both educational-access policies adopted in response to mobilization by Black and Puerto Rican activists across the country in the 1960s and 1970s. Distinctions between these policies are significant, however these dissimilarities reflect the contrasting class and social position of the institutions themselves. What is meaningful to my analysis is that policy adoption *and* retrenchment occurred at the same time, with parallels between the discourse and political action utilized to successfully adopt, protest, and eliminate these policies. Additionally, the relationships between conservative think tanks and advocacy organizations across the cases I consider suggest shared actors, goals, and outcomes. More importantly, an understanding of retrenchment at an institution that has historically assured broad access is necessary in a consideration of educational inequality. Because affirmative action and open admissions are not the same, their differences illustrate a larger story about race and class stratification, elite-driven rollback, and the changing sociopolitical landscape. Challenges to these policies across institution type illustrate the gravity and consistency of the attack on programs that improve education and class outcomes for Black and Latino people, in particular.

THE ROLLBACK OF AFFIRMATIVE ACTION

As of 2018, Harvard College, the University of North Carolina at Chapel Hill, and the University of Texas at Austin all faced lawsuits challenging the consideration of race in their admissions process. In 2017, Princeton University sued the U.S. Department of Education in an attempt to block the release of its admissions records to a litigious anti–affirmative action organization. An internal announcement seeking attorneys within the U.S. Department of Justice framed affirmative action as "intentional race-based discrimination,"[22] suggesting that the elimination of affirmative action is a priority of the department—part and parcel of a groundswell of White nationalism and conservative reactionary governance led by President Donald Trump. That race- and class-access policies emerged as a result of desegregation efforts makes affirmative action, and other civil-rights-era policies, a target of persistent conservative mobilization.

These threats are not new. The first challenges to affirmative action occurred soon after policy adoption. The affirmative action policy at University of California Davis's Medical School had been in place for only five years when Allan Bakke, a White, thirty-three-year-old rejected applicant, filed suit in 1974. The result was the landmark Supreme Court decision in *Regents of the University of California v. Bakke* (1978), which limited the parameters of affirmative action. Backlash to affirmative action emerged not only across the field of higher education but also in the employment sector.[23]

Affirmative action is a highly symbolic issue. Attacks on affirmative action mobilize White claims of unfairness and "reverse racism" and uphold the myth of American meritocracy. Implicit are racial ideas about deservingness and entitlement to opportunity. Since the 1970s, the White working and middle classes have experienced declining wages, occupational instability, and rising unemployment. They have come to perceive relatively minor policies like affirmative action as unjust and, even more, as the reason for their declining quality of life. At the same time, university admissions have grown to be incredibly competitive, elevating once accessible colleges to higher ranks in the higher education hierarchy. Politicians on the Right have exploited White anxieties to consolidate political power.

The Right's track record of dismantling antidiscrimination and race-access policies is well known. The modern consolidation of the American Right is rooted in the rejection of the civil rights movement and subsequent progressive reforms. Liberals who have capitulated to anti–affirmative action campaigns also respond to the precarity of Whiteness in the post–civil rights era, where reference to racial oppression of the past may be acceptable but efforts to address the contemporary manifestations of racism through social policy are seen as going too far. Under neoliberalism, the increasing importance of attaining an elite college degree in the face of a shrinking and unstable job market, paired with a competitive, individualistic outlook, works to magnify the anxieties of Whites about affirmative action. Recent court cases featuring Asian plaintiffs illustrate that this investment in American meritocratic ideals and entitlement to elite university admissions extends beyond White communities and complicates how we understand the practice of diversity in these spaces. Still, the alliance of Asian plaintiffs and their supporters with conservative organizations signals an embrace of a colorblind logic and consent to the rollback of race-access policies.

Challenges to affirmative action in higher education should not be understood in isolation; they are connected to efforts to eliminate affirmative action in employment and contracting,[24] to redraw electoral districts to disadvantage Black and Latino voters,[25] to abolish the Voting Rights Act,[26] and to circumscribe other rights.[27] Attempts to revise the law in the areas of voting, education, and employment assert a vision to reverse civil rights gains, under the veil of colorblindness, "fairness", and historical amnesia. In the age of Trump, these attempts will be incessant, marked by a discourse that is more brash and explicitly White supremacist, though rollback efforts have been evident since the 1970s.

WHAT THIS BOOK IS ABOUT

In the case of affirmative action in higher education, how and why has political struggle persisted for so long? What is the status of race- and class-inclusive admissions policies today? And what does this political struggle tell us about racial politics in the post–civil rights era? *To Fulfill These Rights* addresses these questions through a sociological history of the struggle over affirmative action and open admissions retrenchment in higher education. I begin with the post–World War II expansion of higher education and the impact of the civil rights movement on higher education reform; examine fields of conflict during policy adoption, rollback, and revision; and conclude by considering contemporary political dynamics, which will likely result in the end of affirmative action.

I document post-*Bakke* challenges to affirmative action and open admissions in four regionally distinct sites: the University of California, University of Michigan, University of Texas at Austin, and City University of New York. More specifically, I examine how conservatives successfully challenged affirmative action and open admissions through an analysis of the political opportunities, the vulnerability of these educational-access policies, and the use of *racial political strategy*, or the ways in which race is mobilized in the demands, rhetoric, and tactical decision-making of political actors. These challenges feature the national coordination of resources, shared use of racial political strategy, and, importantly, appropriation of civil rights legal tactics by conservatives to gut and eliminate affirmative action. These confrontations, related to larger attempts to roll back and further restrict access to social, political, and civil rights, provide evidence of a neoliberal racial political landscape, characterized by colorblind and diversity logics. In the field of higher education, this means a reification of racial inequality under the cover of colorblind market logics, using principles such as meritocracy, competition, and elevated standards as justification for the elimination of policies providing broader access.

At sites where conservatives successfully terminated or restricted affirmative action and open admissions, I explore how university administrators and liberal politicians navigated policy revision using a diversity logic, including racial discourse and new policy development. Importantly, what Berrey calls "the organizational infrastructure of diversity"[28] reflects the post-*Bakke* university landscape, where multiculturalism is central to the expansion of student life and curricula aimed at preparing students who are predominately White for a global economy. However, this organizational infrastructure largely obscures and attempts to erase the historical roots of campus inclusion efforts: the radical activism of Black and Latino students. New policy adoption also serves as an example of *defensive innovation*, or the efforts to retain previous policy outcomes with new means. As court decisions and ballot contests have legally restricted the means by which universities can compose racially diverse student bodies, some legislators have used what Lani Guinier and Gerald Torres refer to as "political race" in developing policies that consider the impact of both race and class marginalization and ultimately benefit working-class Whites as well as racial minorities.[29] Importantly, the emerging liberal defense of retrenchment through the promotion of what has been called "class-based affirmative action" also contributes to anti–affirmative action fervor. Thus, I explore the constraints of diversity management in elite public universities.

Though public discourse about these policies typically center the actions of universities and conservative organizations, I came to this project through the examination of student organizing against rollback in the 1990s and 2000s. Through my own involvement in Left organizations, I discovered that political struggle over open admissions and affirmative action served as a training ground for student activists, developing a new generation of organizers, activists, cultural workers, and organizations aimed at fighting various manifestations of oppression and exploitation in the United States and beyond. I focus on mobilization in New York and California, in which students resisted a largely internal attack on open admissions and affirmative action waged by university trustees and, later in California, joined efforts to resist a state ballot initiative. Throughout, I explore the ways in which the post–civil rights racial logics of color blindness and diversity shape the racial political terrain and are manifested in the discourse and activities of conservative political actors, liberal politicians, progressive coalitions, university administrators, and student activists.

The federal government has yet to formally eliminate affirmative action, though the Trump administration has restored the Bush-era "race neutrality" position, an effort that includes the withdrawal of federal guidelines on methods to achieve campus diversity.[30] However, the post–civil rights *racial hegemony*, or the reigning racial hierarchy and common sense that define the post–civil rights period, has produced the social and political conditions in which Americans embrace civil rights rhetoric while rejecting any methods to achieve racial justice. This can be seen in the Right's efforts to reinterpret the term *colorblind*—once used by civil rights activists in their demands for access to opportunities solely afforded to Whites—to mean the rejection of racial equality. It is also evident in conservative declarations that the Reverend Martin Luther King Jr. was, in fact, a conservative, rather than a political radical hounded by the Federal Bureau of Investigation.[31] This post–civil rights period of racial hegemony does not require the complete elimination of civil-rights-era policies to contribute to deepening racial inequality and to undermine social citizenship rights. Ultimately, I consider the prolonged battle to both defend and eliminate race- and class-access policies in higher education to be part of a greater struggle over competing visions for American democracy.

Because this book focuses on political struggle over race- and class-inclusive policies, it does not reproduce the structure or arguments of other texts on affirmative action. It does not review debate over the merits of affirmative action and is not meant to convert opponents of race- and class-access policies. It does not rehash statistics regarding college readiness among Black and Latino students, their retention and matriculation rates in college, or their pathways after graduation. Further, it does not analyze the universities that academically competitive Black and Brown students attend instead of public flagships after the elimination of affirmative action at certain sites. There is rigorous and compelling research already available on these topics (refer to appendix A for a literature review on race- and class-inclusive admissions).[32] Instead, I highlight political struggle over affirmative action and open admissions in higher education as a location to examine how race (and class) is produced.

To be clear, I do not argue that affirmative action is a radical political project. Race- and class-access policies cannot single-handedly restructure the political-economic system, which continues to reproduce racial inequality in the United States. Radical interventions would go beyond the symptoms of systemically entrenched disparity to fundamentally reshape the political-economic system and civil society. Affirmative action will continue to be limited and imperfect because it has functioned through historical and contemporary conditions of racial capitalism. However, affirmative action, a progressive policy intervention, has been successful in providing access to elite higher education to a significant number of people from racially marginalized groups. Open admissions has also been successful in producing substantial class mobility for working-class students of color. Affirmative action and open admissions make an important contribution to the maintenance of a middle class for Black and Latino communities, and for that reason alone, these policies should be supported and maintained.

A POST-CIVIL RIGHTS RACIAL FRAMEWORK

The explanatory agenda of this book is to explore the competing racial logics of colorblindness and diversity as deployed, practiced, and symbolized in political conflict during the post-civil rights period. In this section, I provide a framework for the book by establishing key concepts that shape the political conflict over race- and class-inclusive admissions. *Racial hegemony* refers to the racial "common sense" that reinforces dominance and subordination. *Neoliberalism* is the ideology and structural manifestation of late-stage capitalism, which emphasizes such principles as privatization, state deregulation, and the "individualisation of everyone."[33] *Colorblindness* and *diversity* are the racial logics that constitute racial hegemony under neoliberalism.

RACIAL HEGEMONY

Drawing on Antonio Gramsci's theorization of hegemony, which describes the cultural dominance of the ruling class over the masses, race scholars Michael Omi and Howard Winant argue that racial hegemony constitutes a cultural and structural racial hierarchy that accompanies outright racial dominance. Race is a socially constructed category that structurally and symbolically organizes society. However, the manner in which race organizes society shifts according to the ways that the state and civil society attach meaning to race,[34] and these meanings and practices change over time. Implicit and explicit to racial hegemony is racism: actions that reproduce racial domination and exploitation.[35] Whereas force is central to the ways that many understand racism, racial hegemony produces the racial "common sense" that is less visible, but no less threatening, to society and is central to the reproduction of racial difference and hierarchy.

Prior to the civil rights movement, outright racial domination characterized American racial hegemony. This domination was enforced through coercion of the racially marginalized; segregation and exclusion, lynching and other extralegal violence, and genocide of Native Americans are all examples of coercive domination. Omi and Winant argue that the civil rights movement disrupted this deployment of power, constituting a "racial break," with most racially marginalized groups granted access to formal political and social citizenship rights. The operation of power in the racial order could no longer primarily depend on outright force as political movements pushed for major reforms that formally dismantled segregation and exclusion and gave marginalized groups access to rights promised by the Constitution. To maintain social order and racial stratification, the racially marginalized had to be allowed some moderate amount of power.[36] Additionally, political and economic elites appropriated and reinterpreted racial discourse that had been developed by the progressive and radical political movements.

In this book, I demonstrate how conservative elites have appropriated civil rights discourse in order to dismantle race- and class-inclusive admissions. I also illustrate how the state has transformed the principle of racial redress into that of diversity in university admissions after early resistance to affirmative action. While forms of coercive racial domination and social control persist during this period of racial hegemony (see mass incarceration, police brutality, forced separation of undocumented families in immigrant detention centers, and drastic health disparities across race and class lines, for example), and are perhaps more visible in the Trump era, the "manufactured consent" of colorblindness and diversity has dominated the ways that the powerful engage in racial discourse and practice in the post–civil rights neoliberal era.

NEOLIBERALISM

The neoliberal political-economic context is critical to understanding challenges to race- and class-inclusive admissions and the conditions for changing racial politics. In the 1970s, the welfare state and the economic liberalism it supported, including raised wages, lowered unemployment rates, an increased demand for consumer goods, and high state spending on social services, began to face crisis. High inflation and economic stagnation meant incredible economic instability: the unemployment rate drastically increased (more than doubling from 3.6 percent in 1968 to 7.7 percent in 1976), the federal deficit from Vietnam War spending worried international investors, and the 1973 oil crisis negatively impacted weakening economic conditions even more, with calls for gas rationing and long lines at gas stations angering the public.[37] This "stagflation" also greatly affected the wealth of business elites and the affluent. Neoliberalism emerged as a way for the wealthy, who had expanded enterprise greatly during the mid-twentieth century but resented the tax burden, to reverse this economic downturn and gain greater control over the political-economic system.[38]

Neoliberalism is organized by a few ideas that most scholars can agree on: minimal state intervention in the market, strong private property rights, an emphasis on free enterprise and individual rights (rather than the collective public good), and the redefinition of citizens as consumers. Economic rationality is extended into social and cultural fields, and industries are created, developed, and expanded in areas that were not seen as profitable before, such as public schooling, water, and the administration of highways, ports, hospitals, and public transportation.[39] This is the context in which workers' wages increased by less than 5 percent and CEO salaries increased by 400 percent on average by the 1990s.[40] The state's role in neoliberalism is to protect and preserve the ideology and practices of this form of advanced capitalism, in which unregulated market competition is the foundation of society.

Neoliberalism informs the racial landscape, particularly given the power of the public sector in transforming the opportunities racial minorities have been able to access. When social welfare policies, designed to guarantee a minimum level of social rights for all citizens, are dismantled, the socially marginalized are the most materially impacted. When economic crisis occurs, as it inevitably does under capitalism, neoliberal principles that emphasize individualism and meritocracy obscure how inequality grows and how the poor and racially marginalized become scapegoats for social and economic problems.

In relation to public higher education, neoliberal governance has decreased both federal and state levels of university funding, resulting in steeply rising tuition and fees for students.[41] Additionally, universities have adopted corporate management styles, increased investments in university-based business ventures and corporate-public partnerships, and solicited privately funded conservative think tanks, departments, and fellowships on campuses, suggesting a wholesale privatization of public education.[42] Programs in economically productive fields such as business, science, and technology have expanded while devalued programs such as those in Black and ethnic studies, the humanities, and the social sciences have been downsized or eliminated. Still, selective universities embrace diversity as a marker of their progressive, competitive education. The neoliberal story of race claims the absence of racial inequality while signifying the minimal inclusion of racial minorities into power . In this book, I examine political struggle over race- and class-inclusive admissions in order to illustrate how colorblindness and diversity serve as the dominant racial logics of the neoliberal period.

COLORBLINDNESS

On its surface, colorblindness promises that color, or racial identity, will not interfere in the practice of democracy. The Civil Rights Act of 1964 puts forth a legal framework of nondiscrimination, though legal authorities had claimed a colorblind Constitution since at least the late nineteenth century.[43] The Act prohibits discrimination on the basis of race, color, sex, national origin, and religion. When civil rights activists demanded the removal of societal racial barriers, they spoke from the experience of living in the apartheid Jim Crow system, in which the state barred African Americans from social and political citizenship.

Conservatives have twisted these demands and appropriated the language of colorblindness to call for the removal of policies and programs created to address race and class disparities in the post–civil rights period.[44] Colorblindness calls for institutions and individuals to ignore race, especially in decision-making and resource allocation.[45] Thus, the colorblind logic is best represented by Supreme Court Chief Justice John Roberts's plurality opinion regarding a voluntary school desegregation plan in Seattle: "The way to stop discrimination on the basis of race is to stop discriminating on the basis of race."[46] This example conveys one way in which the colorblind logic is established as legal common sense: by calling for the end of efforts to monitor and address discrimination and pointing to the potential victimization of Whites when colorblindness is not maintained. Colorblindness is the primary racial logic deployed in attempts to dismantle affirmative action.

Race scholars have long examined the role of colorblindness in the law, discourse, social relations, and more.[47] Appropriately, many race scholars refer to colorblind ideology as colorblind racism.[48] Until power relations are restructured in ways that eliminate racial hierarchy, a colorblind racial logic will continue to maintain racial oppression. Ultimately, colorblindness is the language of racial backlash. However, colorblindness contends with the logic of diversity in the post–civil rights neoliberal period.

DIVERSITY

Diversity generally refers to discourse and practice that celebrate racial and ethnic inclusion. However, diversity's ambiguity has grown to include gender, sexual orientation, and disability, and "diverse ideas" and "diverse people" are vague categories used on university campuses, in workplaces, and throughout organizations. As scholars have noted, diversity does not aim to challenge institutional racism but instead facilitates racial tokenization, stalls racial reform, and can be a shallow symbol of corporate goodwill.[49] As sociologists Wendy Leo Moore and Joyce Bell argue, institutional pushes for diversity often mask an abandonment of racial redress efforts, particularly in the desertion of poor and working-class African Americans.[50]

Once an innocuous term and goal, diversity has now become a contentious issue on university campuses, with students demanding more racially supportive environments and with administrators defensively renaming affirmative action programs as diversity and inclusion efforts. The ubiquity of diversity as a catchphrase, racial logic, and discourse frame in the post–civil rights era is directly related to its use in the law and its subsequent embrace by universities in their defense of affirmative action programs. The split decision of the Supreme Court in *Regents of the University of California v. Bakke* (1978) outlawed racial quotas while asserting the legitimacy of diversity. Diversity here included race and ethnicity, along with variations in region and class, disciplinary interests, and special talents. As a defensive measure, universities revisited their affirmative action programs and revised them in accordance with "diversity" principles, rather than racial remedy. Although universities interpreted the *Bakke* precedent as a legal defense of affirmative action, the split decision produced legal uncertainty regarding the governmental interest of diversity. Later legal defenses of campus diversity focused on the benefits that White students received from interacting with people from different backgrounds, and the amicus curiae briefs filed in these cases by corporations argued that success in a global economy requires an embrace of racial and ethnic diversity.

Though political conservatives disparaged diversity (and "political correctness") and challenged affirmative action programs, they also engaged in racial tokenism for the purpose of political legitimacy. As diversity is now a dominant racial logic and accusations of racism could even limit the political aspirations of Republicans, as it did (albeit temporarily) for Jefferson Sessions's failed campaign for district court judge in 1986 and Trent Lott's resignation from Senate leadership in 2002, Republicans, too, engage in attempts to racially diversify their spokespersons. Many Republicans hoped for a Colin Powell presidential run in the 1990s,[51] and Michael Steele, Clarence Thomas, Bobby Jindal, Elaine Chao, and Ben Carson are prominent racial-minority spokespersons that the Republican Party has relied on to appear tolerant.

Colorblindness and diversity characterize the post–civil rights period in ways that provide opportunities and constraints for both conservatives and liberals. The saturation of colorblindness in the law and civil society made challenges to race- and class-inclusive policies advantageous for conservatives. However, the widespread acknowledgment of diversity's merits provided important openings for defenders of these policies as well. Colorblind and diversity logics persist throughout each political struggle over affirmative action and open admissions policies and steer the development of offensive and defensive strategies in this conflict.

SITES OF CONTENTION

This book utilizes the events at four universities to examine political conflict and the production of racial meaning. The qualitative and interpretive research design centers fields of conflict and movement stages—early political mobilization and policy implementation, later political mobilization and policy retrenchment, and new policy development—occurring over a fifty-year period (refer to appendix B for a discussion of research methodology).

As political conflict is the object of study, I selected four sites where conservatives successfully targeted affirmative action or open admissions: the University of California (UC), University of Michigan, University of Texas at Austin (UT Austin), and City University of New York. UM, UT Austin, and multiple campuses of the UC system regularly appear in rankings of the top ten and top twenty public universities in the United States.[52] These are selective and elite institutions with international reputations for academic excellence, robust alumni networks, and influence in a variety of professional fields. These institutions were also the most important sites for battles over affirmative action in the 1990s and early 2000s. CUNY is a less selective university system that serves working-class students in New York City. Its graduates lead in social mobility, or the ability of students in the bottom economic quintile to reach the top fifth of income distribution.[53] CUNY is the most important site at which to examine the political conflict over open admissions because it was the largest system to employ open admissions in four-year undergraduate colleges. Overall, conservatives targeted public universities because they are particularly open to outside influence: public universities are driven by a public mission, local and state politicians often influence their governance, and tax dollars serve as their economic base.

As explained in table I.1, challengers utilized various tactics to dismantle affirmative action, though they were not always successful. Filed by the Center for Individual Rights in 1992, the *Hopwood v. Texas* case, which concerned the affirmative action policy utilized at UT Austin's Law School, is the first significant challenge to affirmative action post-*Bakke*. The Fifth Circuit Court of Appeals decision in this case banned affirmative action in Texas only three years after court supervision of the state's higher education system (the consequence of a history of state-sponsored segregation) ended.[54] This ban persisted until 2003, when the *Grutter v. Bollinger* decision, concerning the affirmative action policy at UM's Law School, superseded *Hopwood*. In *Grutter v. Bollinger*, the Supreme Court decided that the consideration of race in the individual review of law school applicants was constitutional. At the same time, the Court, in *Gratz v. Bollinger* (2003), ruled that the point system UM used in admitting undergraduate applicants (which allotted twenty points for membership in an underrepresented minority group) was unconstitutional, though diversity could be legitimately considered in the individualized review of applicants.

After *Grutter*, UT Austin reintroduced the consideration of race into its undergraduate admissions procedures through individualized review. Between 1996 and 2003, liberal Texas legislators had also developed an automatic admissions policy that guaranteed admittance to Texas universities, including the flagship UT Austin, to a fixed percentage of high-performing state high school graduates (starting with the top 10 percent). This Ten Percent Plan (later reduced to the top 7 percent) maintained moderate representation of Black and Latino students without specifying race. However, the reintroduction of race in filling the non–automatic admission seats provided the opportunity for Edward Blum and the Project on Fair Representation to file *Fisher v. University of Texas* (also known as *Fisher I*), which challenged this consideration of race. The Fifth Circuit Court of Appeals determined that UT Austin's use of race was permissible under the Constitution, and the plaintiffs petitioned the Supreme Court to review that decision. The Supreme Court

TABLE I.1 Challenges to race- and class-inclusive admissions

Year	Challenge	Tactic	Site
1995	The University of California Board of Regents eliminates affirmative action in admissions and hiring	Trustees	University of California system
1996	*Hopwood v. Texas* eliminates affirmative action in Texas (until *Grutter* in 2006)	Legal	Federal courts
1996	Proposition 209 eliminates affirmative action in university admissions, state hiring, and public contracting throughout California	Ballot proposition	California
1999	The City University of New York Board of Trustees eliminates open admissions in senior colleges	Trustees	City University of New York
2003	*Gratz v. Bollinger* declares University of Michigan's undergraduate affirmative action plan unconstitutional	Legal	Federal courts
2003	*Grutter v. Bollinger* declares University of Michigan Law School's affirmative action plan constitutional	Legal	Federal courts
2006	Proposal 2 eliminates affirmative action in university admissions, state hiring, and public contracting throughout Michigan	Ballot proposition	Michigan
2013	In *Fisher I*, the Supreme Court remands the case to the Fifth Circuit to review using "strict scrutiny"	Legal	Federal courts
2016	In *Fisher II*, the Supreme Court upholds the University of Texas at Austin's undergraduate affirmative action program.	Legal	Federal courts

determined that the Fifth Circuit had not used the legal standard of strict scrutiny in reaching its decision and sent the case back to the lower court. The Fifth Circuit again concluded that UT Austin's consideration of race was constitutional, and the Supreme Court again heard the case, as *Fisher II*, and ultimately upheld the affirmative action policy at UT Austin.

In 1995, the UC Board of Regents eliminated affirmative action in the UC system. The following year, a few months after *Hopwood*, a conservative-led anti–affirmative action ballot proposition (Proposition 209) succeeded in California, eliminating affirmative action in university admissions, state hiring, and federal contracting throughout the state. In 1999, the CUNY Board of Trustees, influenced by the conservative think tank the Manhattan Institute for Policy Research, ended open admissions in CUNY's four-year colleges. Soon after *Grutter*, activists involved in *Grutter*, *Gratz*, and Proposition 209 banded together and launched an anti–affirmative action ballot proposition in Michigan, which voters passed in 2006. These activists also mounted successful efforts to pass ballot initiatives banning affirmative action in Washington, Nebraska, Arizona, and Oklahoma, but similar campaigns failed in Colorado and Missouri. I include a secondary analysis of the failed conservative elite mobilizations in Missouri and Colorado to examine why a largely successful tactic (the ballot referendum) failed in these two states, though it succeeded in the majority of cases. Several anti–affirmative action lawsuits, concerning Harvard University, the U.S. Department of Education (in preparation for a Princeton University lawsuit), and the University of North Carolina at Chapel Hill, are pending in federal courts.

FORWARDING A THEORIZATION OF SOCIAL MOVEMENTS AND RACE

To Fulfill These Rights provides a theoretical contribution to social movement and race scholarship by advancing an understanding of concepts that mediate racial formation and political mobilization and explain the precarious state of affirmative action and open admissions in the United States. Because the theoretical and empirical interventions of this book intersect with fields and disciplines such as race, social movements, law and social policy, critical race theory, higher education, Black studies, American studies, political science, and history, *To Fulfill These Rights* expands an understanding of race- and class-inclusive admissions beyond higher education policy. It provides evidence on how social movement actors develop racial political agendas, produce racial political strategies and accompanying tactics, experience success and failure according to their ability to translate racial ideas, create and revise policy in line with dominant racial logics, and cultivate counterhegemonic race- and class-oriented resistance. Its five chapters offer insight on how social actors produce race through political struggle.

Chapter 1, "A Right of Postwar Citizenship: The Emergence of Mass Higher Education and Race- and Class-Inclusive Admissions," situates the adoption of affirmative action and open admissions within the emergence of mass higher education and the civil rights movement's mandate for Black inclusion in American citizenship. Civil rights movement mobilization and federal policy prescriptions encouraged (and forced) many university administrators to desegregate their campuses, but the desire for crisis management in response to campus protest sometimes led to more aggressive compensatory programs. This analysis advances an understanding of policy adoption and revision that centers not only the agency of the federal government and university administrators, but also grassroots resistance. A greater racial landscape shaped by the civil rights movement and urban rebellions provided favorable conditions for the success of campus-level mobilization.

Chapter 2, "Legal Mobilization: Racial Political Strategy and Affirmative Action Retrenchment in the Federal Courts," utilizes the framework of *racial political strategy*, or the deployment of race in a plan for collective action, to explore how conservative think tanks and legal defense organizations mounted legal challenges to affirmative action in Texas and Michigan. Through racial political strategy, I examine how racial practice and ideas operate in relationship to social movement goals, demands, discourse framing, arenas, and tactical repertoires. Appropriating civil rights legal tactics and discourse, conservative elites asserted a colorblind social world in which Whites became victims of discrimination. In challenging diversity as a legitimate state interest, as well as the means by which universities produced diverse classes, conservatives utilized White female plaintiffs to mobilize gendered vulnerability in their quest to construct White victims of affirmative action. This consideration develops a mechanism of racial projects—racial political strategy— through which elements of social movements can be specified and assessed. Conservative elites worked to socially and legally define Whiteness as victimized in the post–civil rights period.

Chapter 3, "Board Votes and Ballot Initiatives: Racial Political Strategy in Trustee Decision-Making and State Elections," documents how conservatives projected colorblind and meritocratic ideals in their internal challenges (via university boards of trustees) and external challenges (via ballot propositions) to affirmative action and open admissions in California, Michigan, and New York. This chapter investigates the role of conservative think tanks, faculty, racial-minority spokespersons, anti–affirmative action federal plaintiffs, and civil rights discourse and symbolism in the political struggle over race- and class-inclusive admissions.

Using racial political strategy to explain how conservatives successfully eliminated affirmative action and open admissions in these cases, I revisit Stuart Hall's concept of *articulation*[55] and Omi and Winant's use of *rearticulation* to explore why mobilization against affirmative action failed in Colorado and Missouri. Omi and Winant argue that rearticulation, or the appropriation and reinterpretation of civil rights principles by the powerful in order to support racial hegemony, accompanied the incorporation of activists and small numbers of racial minorities into power.[56] I show how the failure of rearticulation played a role in the defeat of the anti–affirmative action ballot propositions in Colorado and Missouri. This contribution complicates understandings of elite mobilization through an analysis of why elite challengers succeed and fail.

Chapter 4, "A Force of Nature: Student Resistance to Policy Elimination," explores how student activists in New York and California resisted policy retrenchment through a critique of colorblindness and diversity and through radical protest. Student activists' resistance employed race and class solidarity, coalitions, and the building of a national network of young activists. Although student activists were unable to stave off policy elimination, their political organizing cultivated lifelong activism among many participants. This chapter contributes to a broader understanding of protest in defense of race- and class-inclusive admissions by highlighting grassroots resistance and national relationships between affirmative action and open admissions activists. Grassroots organizing challenged the racial discourse of authorities on both sides of policy retrenchment.

Chapter 5, "The Limitations of Diversity: Defensive Innovation After the End of Affirmative Action and Open Admissions," examines the *defensive innovation* of university administrators, or the development of methods and discourse that support campus diversity in the wake of affirmative action policy elimination, in California, Michigan, and Texas. Legally barred from considering race in admissions but committed to maintaining moderate diversity, university administrators expanded recruitment and individualized review of applicants, increased scholarship offers, and/or implemented percent plans. They also publicly framed their commitment to diversity as an expression of selective liberal arts education and, ultimately, a practice of democracy. CUNY's elimination of open admissions was part of a greater strategic plan, and this chapter explores how and why administrators and city authorities abandoned efforts to publicly and internally commit to broad educational access. This analysis offers insight into how administrators defensively create diversity in university policy and discourse. As universities are the primary locations that define diversity, this chapter has implications for how diversity is practiced and understood across the racial political landscape.

Finally, the conclusion looks to the precarious persistence of affirmative action, highlighting renewed campus demands for racial inclusion, pending anti–affirmative action lawsuits, and a shifting racial political regime under the Trump administration. The protracted battle over affirmative action has implications for how we understand the emergence of a new racial regime and the methods by which elites legislate social change. The deployment of White victimization and entitlement frames, the measured strategies of conservative elites in relationship to political opportunity, and the tactical repertoire of legal mobilizations and ballot propositions may emerge to further advance a Republican policy agenda in the Trump era.

The theoretical and empirical implications of this political struggle extend beyond the field of education. Through contestation, we gain insight into how elite and grassroots mobilizations propel racial formation in the post–civil rights neoliberal period, how the seemingly contrasting logics of colorblindness and diversity work to uphold racial hegemony, and how these logics shape the conditions for the emergence of unveiled reactionary White supremacy in the twenty-first century.

1

A RIGHT OF POSTWAR CITIZENSHIP

The Emergence of Mass Higher Education and Race- and Class-Inclusive Admissions

---

But freedom is not enough. You do not wipe away the scars of centuries by saying: Now you are free to go where you want, and do as you desire, and choose the leaders you please. You do not take a person who, for years, has been hobbled by chains and liberate him, bring him up to the starting line of a race and then say, "you are free to compete with all the others," and still justly believe that you have been completely fair. Thus it is not enough just to open the gates of opportunity. All our citizens must have the ability to walk through those gates. This is the next and the more profound stage of the battle for civil rights. We seek not just freedom but opportunity. We seek not just legal equity but human ability, not just equality as a right and a theory but equality as a fact and equality as a result.

—President Lyndon Baines Johnson, Commencement Address at Howard University, June 4, 1965

THE CIVIL rights movement transformed the American landscape by redefining the moral terms of democracy, forcing the country to grapple with its national identity. That an American president from the segregated South would embrace the discourse of civil rights and acknowledge the racial barriers to equality conveys how successful the civil rights movement was in gaining concessions from the State. What President Johnson referenced in the speech quoted in the epigraph to this chapter goes beyond nondiscrimination through its recognition of structural obstacles and the need to implement corrective policy. Many understood this speech to be an endorsement of affirmative action, providing a framework for ensuring "equality as a result" through special programs that consider a person's race in employment and university admissions decisions.

From 1964 to 1978, the State encouraged the private and public sectors to establish affirmative action programs as a means of desegregation and racial redress. Access to low-cost public higher education became a primary factor in the growth of the American middle class after World War II, but such mass higher education emerged in a segregated context. The civil rights movement demanded equal educational access, and university administrators at elite public universities soon developed experimental, voluntary affirmative action programs that admitted small numbers of Black and Latino students. Student protests against persisting campus racial inequality and the slow speed of reform often compelled more aggressive affirmative action policies, as did federal oversight of universities that resisted integration. The State and the field of higher education adopted affirmative action for the purpose of racial redress, yet its adoption as a means of crisis management made it vulnerable to challenge once disruption was no longer a threat to the political system. The split decision in the Supreme Court case *Regents of the University of California v. Bakke* (1978) rendered racial redress an illegal justification for affirmative action while preserving diversity as a governmental interest. The logic of diversity became a central feature of selective public universities and contributed to the persistence of affirmative action, even in the face of significant legal challenges. Still, the policy remains politically vulnerable.

In this chapter, I explore the development of affirmative action within the context of mass higher education. First, I examine the development of mass higher education as an expansion of the American citizenship regime. Then I detail the civil rights movement's legal challenge to segregated education and the adoption of the federal Civil Rights Act of 1964, leading to the emergence of voluntary and mandatory affirmative action policies in universities. I provide a synopsis of the political struggle over federal desegregation enforcement under President Nixon, followed by a discussion of the emergence of campus-level race- and class-inclusive admissions and student protest over racial politics at the University of Texas at Austin, University of California Berkeley, University of Michigan, and City University of New York. I conclude the chapter by considering the institutionalization of affirmative action and the diversity logic in selective universities after the first significant legal challenge to the policy in *Regents of the University of California v. Bakke* (1978).

THE EXPANSION OF AMERICAN PUBLIC HIGHER EDUCATION: SOCIAL CITIZENSHIP RIGHTS IN AN ERA OF RACIAL DOMINATION

Sociologist T. H. Marshall conceptualized citizenship as encompassing three groups of rights: civil citizenship, which includes freedom of speech and faith, the right to justice, and the ability to own property; political citizenship, or the right to participate in the political process; and social citizenship, or the right to enjoy a level of economic welfare and security. His analysis of the development of the twentieth century citizenship regime in the United Kingdom led him to argue that Western social citizenship rights mitigated the inevitable inequality produced by capitalism.[1] Marshall believed that, rather than undergoing societal transformation through revolution, the State could counterbalance the market by providing social welfare, thereby ensuring the livelihood of its citizens where the market failed. In the mid-twentieth century, nations incorporated social citizenship rights into many citizenship regimes in response to the devastation of the worldwide Great Depression in the 1930s and World War II in the 1940s.[2] Nation states developed public health care, unemployment insurance, and social protections for elderly people and those with disabilities. Many Western nations also established and expanded public education, including university-level education, as technology and knowledge production became more integral to economic development under advanced capitalism.

Educational access remains an important element of social citizenship and thus reinforces citizenship more broadly. One cannot fully exercise civil or political citizenship without access to social citizenship rights. When segments of the nation are systematically barred from access to quality education, social disenfranchisement and second-class citizenship remain their realities. As the attainment of higher education continues to correlate with greater economic opportunities for social mobility, it is necessary to examine the development of public higher education in relationship to the social citizenship regime and the system of racial oppression in the United States. In the twentieth century, higher education persisted as a site of race and class stratification while becoming a significant site for social movement mobilization.

PUBLIC HIGHER EDUCATION IN THE UNITED STATES BEFORE 1944

Major expansion of postsecondary education in the United States did not occur until after World War II, with the advent of the GI Bill and the growth of the welfare state; however, the federal government had established many public universities through statutes passed nearly a century before. The Morrill Acts of 1862 and 1890 provided federal lands and funds for the development of public colleges, mainly in the western and midwestern United States, where ample land was available. Whereas early private colleges focused largely on religious and legal training and served as central sites for the socialization of elite White men, the State's interest in expanding the economy molded land-grant colleges into training grounds for agriculture, science, and industrial technology.[3]

The Morrill Act of 1890 concentrated on former Confederate states and consented to the racial caste system by requiring that states establish separate colleges for Black students, leading to the founding or state sponsorship of many historically Black colleges and universities (HBCUs), such as Southern University, Lincoln University, and Florida Agricultural and Mechanical University. During the Reconstruction era, religious missionary societies and the Freedman's Bureau had established other HBCUs—many of them private colleges, such as Spelman College, Morehouse College, Howard University, and Hampton University—in order to educate formerly enslaved people.[4] The passage of the Morrill Acts marked the first time that the federal government, rather than the states, committed a significant amount of public resources to university-level education.

The land-grant colleges, and other public universities that emerged during this period, provided the foundation for the modern research universities that would expand at an extremely rapid rate in the post–World War II era.

Other early public colleges were established as civil corporations, in which a group received a charter from the state legislature to establish a school on behalf of the state or through municipal tax funds and donations from wealthy benefactors.[5] Because many of these institutions emerged during slavery, Reconstruction, or soon thereafter—when the apartheid system of Jim Crow structured opportunity in the United States—most Black students did not begin to enter these colleges until after World War II. In fact, many did not enroll until two or more decades later, during the height of the civil rights movement. Prior to this time, Black students who had the opportunity to advance educationally largely attended HBCUs, which educated much of the Black elite through the 1960s.[6]

Elite private and public colleges have respected reputations as meritocratic institutions, but their high social standing often belies the historical nature of their admissions and their construction of "merit" as a reflection of power relations. Until the mid-twentieth century, admissions offices at Ivy League institutions such as Harvard, Yale, and Princeton reserved large numbers of freshman class seats for graduates of northeastern elite boys' boarding schools. Ivy League institutions were important spaces that socialized White wealthy men, and legacy status and graduation from elite feeder schools were such determining factors in admissions that admissions directors in the 1950s and 1960s aimed to *raise* academic standards by widening the recruitment pool. WASP ancestry, athletic prowess, elite connections, and the ability to pay tuition shaped what Ivy League admissions committees considered to be "character," and character often carried more weight than academic scores, as scholastically mediocre students could be admitted with reservations.[7]

Elite admissions committees often rejected high-performing Jewish students, determining that they did not have suitable "character" and thus did not rank high enough in their elite admissions structure.[8] Many Ivy League institutions maintained Jewish quotas, admitting only a limited number of Jews; the rest flocked to other

elite institutions that would admit them, including public universities.[9] The Ivy League's required courses and admissions tests were
drawn directly from the curricula of elite boarding schools, so high-
performing students at public secondary schools often did not have
the coursework necessary to be considered for admission. As the educational sociologist Jerome Karabel states in his comprehensive text
on the history of Ivy League admissions, "the particular definition
of 'merit' at any given moment expresses underlying power relations
and tends, accordingly, to reflect the ideals of the groups that hold
the power of cultural definition."[10] Unlike some European nations,
the United States never had a tradition of college admissions based
solely on high grades and test scores. Thus, "merit" is not (and has
not been) a straightforward or consistent measurement; rather, it
has been historically constructed according to the aims and desires
of the institutions themselves.[11] The admissions offices at selective
institutions seek to construct a student body that reflects the universities' respective institutional identities. In public institutions, which
have historically featured more economic diversity and lower tuition
and are culturally less patrician than their private peers, the concept
of merit has also shifted over time.

Between 1870 and 1944, American universities surfaced and disappeared at a rapid rate. Admissions criteria were vague and not
strongly enforced, except in the case of banning racial minorities and
women and limiting Jewish students. Most Americans did not aspire
to higher education during the nineteenth and early twentieth centuries, and colleges struggled to fill classrooms and pay instructors;
thus, many of their students were those who could afford to attend,
not those who were the most intellectually promising. Enrollments
increased, however, as higher education facilitated the elevation of
many professions, with positions in fields such as engineering, medicine, economics, and public administration requiring more scholarly
training. By the turn of the twentieth century, universities began to do
the work of public relations, creating interuniversity sports leagues,
building sports stadiums, and serving as a source of entertainment
for the towns and cities in which they were located.[12]

The four regionally distinct universities at the center of this book
reflect similar patterns of emergence. When Michigan adopted a state

constitution in 1835, it was the first state to embrace a Prussian model of education, in which the state administered and funded the system of primary, secondary, and university-level education.[13] Though historians trace the founding of the University of Michigan to 1817, it educated only small groups of secondary students until the Ann Arbor campus opened and the first college students enrolled in 1841.[14] The University of Michigan and University of Texas (established in 1883 by Texas's seventh constitution) were both established as civil corporations during the period in which the states were granted statehood.[15] In 1868, a partnership between California's governor and the trustees of a fledgling private college established the University of California as a land-grant college, modeled after the University of Michigan.[16] A popular statewide referendum in 1847 established the Free Academy in New York as a school for immigrants and the poor, supported by municipal taxes and wealthy benefactors.[17] It was later renamed City College, the first institution of the system that would eventually become the City University of New York.

   Though three of these universities had enrolled their first Black students by the 1880s (University of Michigan in 1853, University of California in 1881, and City College in 1884), most of these students enrolled at the graduate level, having already received undergraduate degrees from HBCUs. Additionally, at the time, these students were always the singular non-White student at their institution.[18] The University of Texas at Austin did not admit its first Black student until 1950, when the U.S. Supreme Court forced the institution to desegregate its graduate and professional schools in the *Sweatt v. Painter* decision. The university did not admit Black undergraduates until 1954, and campus housing and social activities did not desegregate until 1964.[19] Black students did not enter any of these universities in significant numbers until after the civil rights movement.

EDUCATION AS PUBLIC GOOD: THE WELFARE STATE AND PUBLIC UNIVERSITIES, 1944–1973

The Servicemen's Readjustment Act of 1944, better known as the GI Bill of Rights, contributed greatly to the expansion of higher education in the twentieth century. The National Resources Planning

Board, a group created to advise President Franklin Roosevelt on long-range planning, predicted a bleak reality for GIs and the U.S. economy in the readjustment period after World War II—8 to 9 million unemployed workers. Past American Legion Commander Harry Colomery, one of the primary architects of the GI Bill, expressed fears of massive revolts by returning servicemen in his testimony to the House Committee on World War Veterans Legislation.[20] President Roosevelt asked Congress to pass a variety of veterans' benefits in 1943, including unemployment insurance and educational assistance, on the grounds that veterans "must not be demobilized into an environment of inflation and unemployment, to a place on a bread line or on a corner selling apples."[21] Providing benefits was not simply the right thing to do, as Americans rightfully felt obligated to take care of their military veterans; it also assuaged politicians' fears about unemployed, militarized men and the role this population played in the rise of totalitarianism in Europe.[22] Additionally, as technological innovation advanced, the GI Bill promoted the development of new, management-oriented labor force skills, new industries, and new war technology. The United States emerged from World War II economically dominant, and the State envisioned providing veterans' benefits as a way to further stimulate the economy and promote American economic and cultural hegemony throughout the world. Higher education figured prominently in achieving these objectives.

The GI Bill, signed into law by President Roosevelt in 1944, provided a number of benefits to returning military personnel, including low-cost loans to start businesses and purchase homes in the suburbs, unemployment insurance, access to newly built Veterans Administration hospitals, job counseling, and vocational training. Importantly, the GI Bill also paid for college tuition, a family stipend (to cater to nonworking spouses), and incidentals for college enrollment.[23] The Veterans' Preference Act of 1944 gave disabled and nondisabled veterans, their wives, and widows of veterans an extra five to ten points on the civil service exam; provided explicit preferences for veterans who passed the exam (they were to be moved to the top of the list of those eligible for civil service jobs); and set aside for veterans such working-class service jobs as elevator operator and messenger.[24] The GI Bill and Veterans' Preference Act operated as explicit, uncontroversial preference programs that were developed and enacted prior to any ameliorative race-conscious social policy.[25] Scholars argue that the GI Bill constituted an early form of affirmative action, for White working-class men, because of its active exclusion of African Americans and women and its abundant benefits for returning White male soldiers.[26]

The U.S. military, Veterans Administration, U.S. Employment Service, and Federal Housing Administration denied Black GIs access to their benefits, including new educational, residential, and occupational opportunities. As a result of the racist practices of military offices in the South, African Americans were disproportionately given dishonorable discharges, which disqualified them from receiving veterans' benefits.[27] For the Black GIs honorably discharged, the U.S. Employment Service actively discriminated against them, distributing information regarding only menial jobs with low pay and excluding their applications outright.[28] Public universities actively rejected large numbers of Black veteran applicants; by 1947, fifteen thousand Black soldiers who could not gain entry to overcrowded HBCUs were denied entry to historically White educational institutions.[29] Women's units were not considered part of the military, and, thus, they were also ineligible for GI benefits.[30] The GI Bill, which supported the expansion of the middle class for the White working-class family, structurally reinforced White male supremacy by functionally excluding African Americans and women. Thus, the GI Bill effectively served as a wide-scale program of preferential treatment.

The GI Bill did much to expand the welfare state by providing an incentive to attend college, creating a demand for university education, and propelling further legislation that would expand higher education on a mass level. Under the GI Bill, the number of degrees awarded by colleges and universities doubled between 1940 and 1950, and classrooms in public and private universities became crowded with veterans.[31] The GI Bill initiated mass higher education and led to other legislation that allotted funds for the building of more campuses, the recruitment of more instructors, and the development of more student services. The state extended the GI Bill three more times in order to accommodate Korean War and Vietnam War veterans, as well as personnel serving during peacetime.[32] During this period, Americans embraced higher education as a key to economic growth and an important weapon in the arsenal to win the Cold War.[33]

Along with mass college enrollment came the expansion of university infrastructure and bureaucracy. A quickly growing student body necessitated more professors, staff, administrators, classrooms, dorms, and student spaces. Academic concentrations began to expand, and remedial programs to assist underprepared veterans and other students became essential to the large public university.[34] The Johnson administration passed the Higher Education Facilities Act of 1963 and the Higher Education Act of 1965, which dedicated more federal funds to the construction of new university buildings and campuses and to the establishment of scholarships, educational grants, and low-interest loans for students in need. School fees were low, often less than $50 a semester, and if students could not secure scholarships or grants, they often could maintain a part-time job and pay for their education.[35] The growth of the student population also led to the establishment of larger university admissions offices. During the 1960s, admissions offices began to require applicants to take aptitude tests, such as the Scholastic Aptitude Test (SAT). The University of California system, for example, began a slow adoption of the SAT, experimenting with out-of-state applicants in 1960 and making the SAT a requirement for admission in 1968. The SATs did not truly begin to be determinative in its eligibility decisions until 1979.[36]

Beginning in the 1960s, states began to shape their public higher educational institutions (community colleges, four-year colleges, and research universities) into tiered systems in which different categories of students could move through and receive a range of educational experiences from vocational training to a PhD. The case of California is a notable example. In 1959, a research team and Clark Kerr, then president of the University of California system, anticipated the increasing enrollment of baby boomers. They developed a plan, the *Master Plan for Higher Education in California*, which created a linked, coherent three-tier system of postsecondary education in the state, consisting of the California Community College system (CCC), the California State College system (CSC, now CSU), and the University of California (UC). This plan delegated academic research to UC, making it the primary awarding institution for master's and doctoral degrees, though California state colleges could also award master's degrees and doctoral degrees jointly with the UC system. Community colleges would issue associate's degrees and vocational training certificates, and the California state colleges and UC schools would issue bachelor's degrees.[37] This structure was intended to provide broad educational access to California residents.

The plan guaranteed all graduating high school seniors admission to any of the community colleges, the top one-third admission to the CSC system, and the top 12.5 percent admission to the UC system.[38] Graduates of the community colleges would be guaranteed a transfer to a California State College or UC campus in order to complete a bachelor's degree. In the eyes of the California legislature, and Kerr himself, this plan created a system that provided wide access to higher education and remarkable educational quality.[39] Many credit this plan with the emergence of one of the world's high-reputation public university systems and with the heightened economic productivity of California in the second half of the twentieth century. Kerr's master plan and his further success at the UC system earned him the cover of *Time* magazine in 1960 and influenced other states to develop similar systems for higher education.[40]

Kerr also provided another contribution to the modern university— the term *multiversity*, a neologism used to describe the modern university systems emerging at the time. Rather than replicating the model of the old university structure—a small community of teachers and students focused on graduate professional education (particularly law and medicine)—the multiversity was a large, multifunctional institution that consisted of students, teachers, nonacademic staff, administrators, alumni, and a variety of academic fields across undergraduate and graduate schools. Kerr insisted that the multiversity would be more responsive to solving societal problems and creating a more economically productive citizenry.[41] The multiversity—represented more and more by large university systems with multiple campuses, specializations, and degrees—came to represent a more efficient, bureaucratic way of organizing mass high education. In the period between 1950 and 1975, the UC system added four campuses (Riverside, San Diego, Santa Cruz, and Irvine); the University of Texas added and absorbed four campuses (Dallas, San Antonio, Tyler, and Permian Basin); the University of Michigan added two campuses (Dearborn and Flint); and the City University of New York consolidated six senior colleges, six community colleges, and two graduate programs into a unified system. By 1973, students enrolled in public higher education represented 79 percent of all American college students.[42]

The United States' economic abundance during this period, dependent on its exploitation of the Third World and its monopoly over industry while war-torn European countries sought to rebuild, funded this massive expansion of higher education. The government and civil society embraced beliefs that higher education led to a more productive population and promoted the public good.

THE CIVIL RIGHTS CHALLENGE:
FIGHTING FOR SOCIAL CITIZENSHIP RIGHTS

Educational access had a prominent role in the civil rights movement's fight to gain social citizenship rights. Black Americans had always understood the value of education: slave codes made it illegal to teach enslaved people to read and write, and the efforts of many to learn in spite of oppressive laws were significant acts of resistance. During Reconstruction, Black legislators and citizens played a central role in the establishment of public education in various states, expanding the social citizenship rights of poor Whites and Blacks, only to later have these rights taken away.[43] This section explores the civil rights legal challenge to discrimination in education and the federal concessions adopted in response to this mobilization. As a result of these challenges, affirmative action emerged as both a mandatory and a voluntary means for universities to accomplish campus desegregation.

Charles Hamilton Houston, litigation director of the National Association for the Advancement of Colored People (NAACP), was the primary architect of the legal strategy utilized to dismantle segregation in the United States. Houston, and later Thurgood Marshall, implemented the "equalization" legal strategy, which first attacked the lack of enforcement of the "equal" in the "separate but equal" doctrine of *Plessy v. Ferguson* (1896). Houston built the equalization strategy on a variety of assumptions—the primary one being that states could not afford to provide equal quality educational accommodations for Black and White students, as the resource chasm between Black and White schools was profound. If states were legally forced to provide separate *and* equal education, segregation would legally implode under the financial burden. Houston believed that this equalization strategy could be utilized by the scores of Black lawyers whom he had trained at Howard University Law School and who were located throughout the South. He thought that successful cases would stimulate local backing, building a support structure and leading to more sustained grassroots organizing.[44]

Thus, Houston proposed a series of lawsuits that would attack (1) the unequal distribution of school funds and (2) the unequal salaries of Black and White teachers. The decisions rendered in these cases served as legal precedents that ultimately culminated in *Brown v. Board of Education* (1954), the case that dismantled legal segregation and successfully challenged *Plessy v. Ferguson* (1896). Once Houston's equalization strategy established numerous legal precedents, including the Supreme Court case *Sweatt v. Painter* (1950), which dismantled segregation in the graduate schools at the University of Texas, Marshall mounted an all-out attack on the constitutionality of segregation.[45] These legal challenges were able to effectively highlight the economic contradictions inherent in "separate but equal," as well as the social consequences of segregation in education, asserting the benefits of interaction among diverse students.[46] In the important precedent cases *McLaurin v. Oklahoma State Regents* (1950) and *Sweatt v. Painter* (1950), the NAACP legal teams established the "intangible considerations" of university education, going beyond the quality of institutional facilities and library offerings to include the role of classroom deliberation and student networks in education. These considerations, which would later serve as primary justifications for maintaining diversity on campuses in defense of affirmative action, would also be applied to public primary and secondary schools in *Brown v. Board of Education* (1954).[47]

The NAACP legal team used these strategies in *Murray v. Pearson* (1935), *Missouri ex rel. Gaines v. Canada* (1938), *Sipuel v. Board of Regents of University of Oklahoma* (1948), *Sweatt v. Painter* (1950), and *McLaurin v. Oklahoma State Regents* (1950)—five cases that challenged segregation in public universities and served as significant precedents for *Brown v. Board of Education*—as well as hundreds of other cases.[48] NAACP lawyers successfully challenged White voting primaries, racial restrictive covenants, and segregation on buses and trains. But their strategy largely focused on schools; thus, *Brown* became the final (unanimous) decision that legally dismantled segregation in schools and public accommodations. Still, higher education was slow to implement desegregation, with many universities refusing outright to implement the Court's ruling.[49] Additional Supreme Court decisions had to reinforce *Brown*,[50] and civil rights direct action and federal deployment of the National Guard were needed to compel universities in Mississippi and Alabama to desegregate.[51]

The passage of the Civil Rights Act of 1964, a landmark piece of civil rights legislation, outlawed racial, gender, religious, and ethnic discrimination in the United States. Still, many civil rights activists viewed the Civil Rights Act of 1964, a colorblind law, as an incomplete compromise. Activists insisted that protection against police brutality and the ability for the U.S. Justice Department to introduce desegregation and discrimination lawsuits were necessary stipulations excluded from the 1964 act.[52]

Nevertheless, the Civil Rights Act did grant a range of protections, including the prohibition of discrimination in public accommodations and the establishment of the Office for Civil Rights within the Department of Health, Education, and Welfare (HEW) to assess the existence of discrimination and protect civil rights in federally assisted entities such as educational institutions.[53] Although there were struggles to include quotas and preferential treatment for Black people in the Civil Rights Act, it was passed without reference to either, and affirmative action (a term yet to be defined) was mentioned only in relationship to employment plans.[54] However, the Office for Civil Rights interpreted Title VI of the Civil Rights Act to require plans and goals to diversify faculty and student bodies in order to stimulate desegregation—this became known as affirmative action.[55] Whereas the State framed these plans as voluntary, the Civil Rights Act gave HEW enforcement power, and universities deemed in violation of Title VI risked losing their federal funding.[56] Still, HEW did not provide clear guidelines for the implementation of affirmative action, leaving the institutions themselves to develop their own approximations to remain in compliance.

Civil rights reforms did not only benefit African Americans; the Equal Pay Act of 1963 and Title VII of the Civil Rights Act were huge victories for all women. For years, many women professors had complained about university discrimination and unequal salaries; they researched the employment rates of women PhDs, drafted resolutions at professional association meetings, and wrote to their elected officials.[57] Ironically, the inclusion of women as a protected class in the Civil Rights Act occurred as an act of sabotage. Conservatives had attempted to add sex discrimination to each title of the civil rights bill in order to divide support and tank the legislation. In the case of Title VII, Congressman Howard K. Smith, a Dixiecrat from Virginia, moved to include sex during the House debate in order to defeat the entire bill. Instead, the House passed the amendment in less than two hours and authorized the entire act two days later.[58] Black people organized and fought for access to each element of citizenship rights during the civil rights movement, but these rights were extended to the whole of society.

Still, by the end of the 1960s, many states had not enforced desegregation in higher education. In 1969, HEW informed nineteen states[59] that their university systems were at risk of losing federal funding and directed them to develop desegregation plans.[60] President Richard Nixon then fired the director of the Office for Civil Rights, Leon Panetta, for attempting to enforce desegregation.[61] However, the NAACP soon sued HEW for not enforcing the Civil Rights Act. In that case, *Adams v. Richardson* (1973), the court decided that HEW had to reinforce requests for desegregation plans, thus conveying that ending de jure segregation was not enough. States had to demonstrate their efforts made to end segregation through plans, timelines, and goals—or mandatory affirmative action.[62] The higher education systems for these nineteen states faced court supervision over these mandatory affirmative action plans, and in the 1980s, these states entered into consent decree settlements, in which they agreed to continue implementation of affirmative action in exchange for terminating court oversight.[63] Thus, at the same time that the Supreme Court's plurality opinion in *Regents of the University of California v. Bakke* (1978) outlawed racial quotas, although it was interpreted to support diversity as a governmental interest, almost 40 percent of states were legally required to implement affirmative action as a consequence of documented segregation, creating what Matthew Shaw terms a "parallel development" of mandatory and voluntary affirmative action.[64]

Various studies suggest that the State developed affirmative action as a means of "crisis management" or pacification in relationship to urban riots and social movements, which were spreading across northern cities in the mid- and late 1960s.[65] President Johnson could not understand why so many cities erupted into flames after the passage of the Civil Rights Act of 1964. Civil rights leaders could not explain (or stop) these riots, and a crisis of legitimacy over civil rights leadership emerged. President Johnson began to convene legislators, business elites, and civil rights leaders together to develop solutions to prevent riots.[66] The National Advisory Commission on Civil Disorders, also known as the Kerner Commission, organized to investigate the causes of urban riots (centering on the Watts Rebellion of 1965, Chicago Rebellion of 1966, and Newark and Detroit Rebellions in 1967), found that the federal and state governments were not providing sufficient housing, education, and social services to inner-city Black neighborhoods. The commission's report asserted a need for grander policy directives to combat poverty, even in the wake of Johnson's Great Society programs. Though the report did not specify many solutions, it did suggest race-conscious affirmative action in law enforcement and the National Guard, acknowledging that many of the riots emerged in response to police brutality. Additionally, the report suggested that diversifying the media would work to demobilize urban rebellions, as the investigation determined that contemporary media did not represent the ideas and actions of the Black community.[67]

President Johnson encouraged both business elites and educational administrators to develop policies that would intentionally target Black applicants in order to diversify workplaces and campuses, keep institutions in compliance with federal law, and demobilize rioting and protesting. Affirmative action policies emerged out of the need for political expediency in resolving discrimination in employment and higher education. Yet because the federal government did not establish clear and comprehensive affirmative action guidelines for higher education, leaving institutions to independently develop their own plans, a variety of questions regarding measurement and design of the programs remained: How does one measure "equality"? Should public universities aim to enroll minority students in the same proportion as that minority's representation in the state population? Or should institutions enroll more minority students to account for past discrimination? Is admitting minority students enough, or do universities have to account for the graduation rates of these students in the measurement of equality? Ultimately, how do reform policies, meant to serve short-term outcomes without restructuring the state, economy, or society, remedy hundreds of years of systemic oppression?

Most administrators and policy makers could not answer these questions when crafting affirmative action programs. And although the Civil Rights Act suggested goals and plans for desegregation, it existed as a colorblind law that specified nondiscrimination rather than equality-seeking remedies for past discrimination. The absence of a federal model on which to base program design led to inconsistent applications of affirmative action in both education and employment. Thus affirmative action was inherently vulnerable to later challenges. The numerous anti–affirmative action federal lawsuits did more to delimit its boundaries than did any federal guidelines or legislation. The haphazard and inconsistent development of the programs in response to crisis doomed affirmative action from the outset.

THE ARRIVAL OF CAMPUS-LEVEL
AFFIRMATIVE ACTION

University administrators developed affirmative action policies in two phases. The first phase was characterized by mild policies that centered on recruitment and admissions, while the second phase consisted of more aggressive policies that utilized goals, timelines, and quotas. Campus-level plans emerged in the 1960s, before the federal government began instituting nondiscrimination policies in the employment sector.[68] Northern Ivy League institutions established most of the early campus plans between 1961 and 1964. Sociologists Lisa Stulberg and Anthony Chen demonstrate that among northern elite universities (including the University of Michigan, UC Berkeley, and UCLA), affirmative action policies appeared before the urban rebellions in the late 1960s and were strongly correlated with response to the March on Washington and civil rights mobilization in Alabama in 1963. They argue that these policy developments arose as a result of liberal northern administrators reconciling the Black southern civil rights movement's moral appeal against racism with their own beliefs about justice in the university context.[69] Stulberg and Chen's argument counters the crisis management thesis of affirmative action implementation; however, nonviolent civil rights protest also served as a disruption to the American social and political landscape. Civil rights protest influenced administrators and inspired the small numbers of students—mostly Black but also Latino, Asian, and White. It is possible that administrators aimed to control potential and actual campus protest through the further development of early affirmative action programs as social movement concessions. Nonviolent protest, urban rebellion, federal agencies, and university administrators all shaped the environment in which affirmative action programs were developed and implemented in selective institutions.

Most private and public elite institutions developed the first-phase mild affirmative action programs by the late 1960s. A few of these programs were partially funded by foundations.[70] A variety of foundations and education associations began to study the accessibility of higher education, concentrating on Black enrollment. In the mid-1960s, institutions such as the Rockefeller Foundation, Carnegie Corporation, Sloan Foundation, and the Ford Foundation began to fund early "compensatory programs," which focused on recruitment, tutoring, financial assistance, and precollege summer programs. At the University of Michigan and University of California, the Ford Foundation contributed financial aid to new Black students.[71] Most

of these kinds of programs prioritized the recruitment and cultivation of undergraduate students of color; fewer resources targeted the
scarcity of racial minorities and women in graduate and professional
schools or in the professoriate. These first-phase affirmative action
programs recruited small numbers of racial minorities. Southern
universities, such as the University of Texas, notoriously lacked serious enforcement of nondiscrimination policies until federal agencies threatened them with action.[72]

The following pages explore the adoption of campus-level affirmative action and open admissions at the University of Texas at Austin
(UT Austin), the University of California Berkeley (UC Berkeley), the
University of Michigan (UM), and the City University of New York
(CUNY). In response to campus unrest led by students admitted
under first-phase affirmative action programs, community support
for protesting students, and ensuing pressure to enact nondiscrimination policies on campuses, universities began to institute more
aggressive policies. These second-phase affirmative action policies
included targeted numerical admissions and hiring goals, quotas,
and the formal inclusion of race and gender in admissions decisions.[73] Black and Latino students in New York City, who were overwhelmingly concentrated at underperforming high schools that did
not prepare students for college, demanded that the racial demographics of students enrolled in the city's public colleges match
those of the students enrolled in the city's public high schools. They
received open admissions policies that provided wider admissions
criteria and remedial programs. Open admissions policies have historically advanced the same goal as affirmative action, although they
were instituted to serve largely working-class Black and Brown communities and do not articulate the consideration of race.

Many of the first-phase policies yielded minimal results. Enforcement from the Office for Civil Rights was weak. Small numbers of
Black and Brown students mobilized around the slow progress; the
need to include Black, Third World, and ethnic studies in the curriculum; and the goal of making universities more responsive to the needs
of racially marginalized communities. Student revolt pressured universities to adopt more aggressive second-phase policies and become
more proactive in enrolling and graduating students of color.

UNIVERSITY OF TEXAS AT AUSTIN

UT Austin was founded as one of the state's two flagship public universities in 1883 and has since come to be regarded as one of the best public research universities in the country, classified as a "public ivy."[74] For much of the twentieth and twenty-first centuries, the oil industry contributed greatly to the university: UT Austin's ownership of millions of acres of oil reserves supports its endowment, and oil executives have served on the UT system's Board of Regents.[75] As in other southern states, Jim Crow structured Texas institutions until the federal government passed civil rights legislation. UT Austin remained a Whites-only institution until the Supreme Court forced it to desegregate in 1950.

In 1946, as part of the NAACP equalization legal strategy, Heman Sweatt, a mail carrier and NAACP member, volunteered to apply to the University of Texas Law School in Austin to test the application of "separate but equal." Other than his race, he met all eligibility requirements.[76] When the law school rejected his application, he filed suit against the university, claiming that the institution violated his right to equal protection under the law by refusing him admission on the basis of race. In order to uphold racial segregation (and avoid admitting Sweatt), Texas quickly formed a law school for African Americans in Houston, the School of Law of the Texas State University for Negroes, to open in 1947.[77] In response, Sweatt refused to attend because the law schools were not of equal quality. This civil rights test case went to the Supreme Court, where NAACP lawyers, led by Thurgood Marshall, successfully highlighted the unequal accommodations between the two schools and the substandard educational quality of the newly formed law school. The Supreme Court decided this landmark case in Sweatt's favor on the same day that it rendered a favorable judgment in another civil rights test case, *McLaurin v. Oklahoma State Regents*, which desegregated graduate schools at the University of Oklahoma. Together, these decisions desegregated graduate education in the United States.

The decision in *Sweatt v. Painter* required the integration of the graduate and professional schools at UT Austin, but still permitted racial segregation of undergraduate students, as Black

undergraduates could seek the same course of study at the historically Black institutions Texas State University and Prairie View A&M.[78]
Though the *Supreme Court's* decision forced UT Austin to integrate its
graduate schools in 1950, it was slow to obey, and the Supreme Court
had to reinforce its decision in 1954. UT Austin did not open its doors
to Black undergraduate students until 1954, when *Brown v. Board of
Education* eliminated segregation at all educational levels, and even
then, it continued to deny Black students housing and exclude them
from participation in extracurricular activities until 1964.[79] Students
actively protested this exclusion, picketing the Board of Regents and
staging campus sit-ins.[80]

In 1967, when the Office for Civil Rights began instructing universities to collect racial demographic information from registered students, less than 1 percent of the more than 29,700 UT Austin students
reported "Negro."[81] In the following year, the regents authorized the
first affirmative action program at the university, the Program on
Educational Opportunity (PEO). Financially supported in part by the
Ford Foundation, the program admitted Black and Latino students
under special admissions procedures that required supplementary
materials such as recommendations, biographical letters, and interviews. In its inaugural year, the program accepted thirteen Black and
twelve Mexican American students; these students were able to gain
access to support services such as financial aid, tutoring, and a special orientation. Regent Frank Erwin, adamantly against affirmative
action, encouraged the Board of Regents to issue a statement in the
summer of 1970 reiterating that no students or faculty "shall solicit or
recruit for admission to that institution any person who cannot meet
the usual requirements for admission to that institution."[82] The university soon revised the program to accept students on a provisional
basis only during the spring and summer terms, thus placing them
on a different time line than other freshmen and making matriculation more uncertain.[83]

Black and Mexican American students, with the support of sympathetic faculty and student government funds, initiated the first
recruitment program in the late 1960s, named Project Info. Project
Info sent integrated teams of students and faculty to Texas high
schools, where they informed high school students about the benefits

of the university. These volunteers also advised potential applicants about the educational preparation required to fulfill admissions criteria. As a result of student protest, President Hackerman and Dean Silber transferred Project Info to the Admissions Office; however, once institutionalized, the program received only slightly higher funding than the school mascot. President Hackerman and Dean Silber also initiated the Ethnic Studies program during this period, as a result of campus protest.[84]

Action led by Regent Erwin eventually terminated the Black and Mexican inclusion program, PEO, and an accompanying program, CLEO (Council on Legal Education Opportunity), for law students. In 1971, a team from the Office for Civil Rights came to conduct a routine review and concluded that UT had been "derelict" in its minority recruitment.[85] The team critiqued Project Info for not doing more; after control of the program had been transferred from students to the administration, Project Info had not been spending its allocated funds.[86] A campus group called The Blacks, formerly Afro-Americans for Black Liberation (AABL), organized a protest to demand 13 percent Black enrollment, the addition of a Black studies program, an increase in scholarship funds for Black students, and the renaming of the library after Malcolm X.[87] The Blacks, the Mexican American Youth Organization, the Action Group for Action, and other students formed a multiracial coalition called TIME (The Improvement of Minority Education, Enrollment, Environment, Employment, Essentials, Encouragement, Etc.). They organized protests, spoke at Board of Regents meetings, and wrote political editorials in the *Daily Texan*, the student newspaper.[88] In 1973, likely in response to court supervision of the Texas higher education system, the Board of Regents finally agreed to authorize a $1.5 million minority aid program designed to admit three hundred minority students per year for four years. The university established the Achievement Scholars Program to disburse these funds.[89] However, Black enrollment did not reach 3 percent until the late 1980s (table 1.1).

While the Supreme Court deliberated over the landmark affirmative action case *Regents of the University of California v. Bakke* in 1977, the Office for Civil Rights found that Texas had yet to sufficiently eliminate the effects of segregation and demanded a more ambitious

TABLE 1.1 University of Texas at Austin undergraduate demographics (%)

	1975*	1982	1990	2000	2010	2014
White	82.2	82.9	72.1	63.7	51.7	46.1
Black	1.7	2.8	3.9	3.4	4.8	4.7
Latino**	5.9	8.7	12.4	13.5	19.4	21.8
Asian	0.5	1.9	7.6	14.9	17.8	18.8

Source: *University of Texas Statistical Handbooks*, Office of Institutional Reporting, Research, and Information Systems.

Note: Percentages do not total 100 percent. In addition to rounding, the categories American Indian, Foreign, and "Other" are not included.

*UT Austin did not begin collecting racial demographic data until 1972 and did not begin organizing these data by graduate/undergraduate level until 1975.

** Collected by Spanish surname at the time.

affirmative action plan that included goals for minority enrollment and the admission of students who did not meet typical admissions criteria. Litigation between UT Austin and the Office for Civil Rights continued sporadically over a twenty-year period. The Office for Civil Rights claimed that UT Austin had yet to do enough to desegregate its campus into the 2000s.[90]

In the case of UT Austin, student mobilization and federal oversight were key to the development of more aggressive affirmative action policies. Following court-ordered desegregation, UT Austin admitted small numbers of Black and Brown students. Student mobilization focused on challenging the Board of Regents and developing student-led recruitment. Struggles between students and administrators resulted in the institutionalization of the student-led recruitment program and then the subsequent institutional abandonment of this program and early compensatory programs. Court-ordered supervision forced a greater institutional commitment to affirmative action. The remnants of de jure racial segregation actively framed the implementation of race-inclusive policy. Of the four universities featured in this book, UT Austin was the last to implement a meaningful race-conscious admissions plan. Significantly, it was also the first of the four to experience the loss of affirmative action.

UNIVERSITY OF CALIFORNIA

Clark Kerr's 1960 *Master Plan for Higher Education in California* served as a model for the expansion and organization of postwar mass higher education across the country, but it also had a perhaps unanticipated effect on Black college students in the state. The tiered education system—organized into open enrollment community colleges, the California State College system for the top 33 percent of high school graduates, and the University of California system for the top 12.5 percent of high school graduates—resulted in a kind of tracking system in which Black students were largely consigned to the community colleges. Beginning in the 1960s, the inclusion of the SAT in the admissions decision-making process also negatively shaped these racial consequences. California state colleges, which formerly admitted the top 70 percent of high school graduates and often accommodated older adult students, now reserved seats for the top 33 percent of high school graduates.[91]

A decade after *Brown v. Board of Education*, Blacks and Latinos were virtually absent from the professional schools at UC Berkeley and had very little presence in the undergraduate schools.[92] In 1966, the UC system institutionalized the Educational Opportunity Program, or EOP (founded in 1964), which waived standard admissions requirements for 2 percent of incoming students. Faculty initially organized the program mainly to attract musicians and athletes who had demonstrated academic talent but had been denied education opportunities in secondary schools largely because of their low-income status.[93] The program provided financial aid, tutoring, academic counseling, and other support services to its students. UC Berkeley had instituted some version of this program prior to the 1960s; after World War II, between 35 and 45 percent of admissions to UC Berkeley and UCLA were filled by "special admission" GIs, who did not meet standard admissions requirements.[94] By 1964, the Board of Regents restricted this special admissions category to 4 percent and then in 1979 to 6 percent, after the decision in *Regents of the University of California v. Bakke* (1978).

EOP served a variety of students who did not meet standard admissions requirements, not only underrepresented racial minorities.

However, it was the primary mechanism by which UC Berkeley administrators attempted to include underrepresented minorities; in 1968, the program included 918 Blacks, 500 "Mexicans," 217 "Orientals," 16 American Indians, 150 unidentified, and 147 White students.[95] This special admissions process, previously reserved for athletes and musicians, began to include racial minority students after Black students pushed for their own inclusion. Similar to what occurred at UT Austin, Black students at UC Berkeley recruited Black high school students to apply prior to admissions officers taking on this responsibility.[96] As affirmative action developed out of this special admissions process, it always occurred through the individual review of applicants at the Berkeley campus.

Although students were key to placing pressure on the UC campuses to recruit more Black students through EOP, much campus organizing emerged around establishing a Black studies department and a Third World college to encompass Black studies, Chicano studies, and Asian American studies at UC Berkeley. Following their peers at San Francisco State College—whose five-month strike led to the first Black studies department at a four-year college in the country—the Third World Liberation Front (TWLF), a coalition of Black, Chicano, and Asian American student organizations at UC Berkeley, organized a strike at the beginning of 1969.[97] Prior to the strike, the African American Student Union had been negotiating with the university for nine months for the establishment of a Black studies department.[98] In addition to demanding ethnic studies, TWLF students requested minority faculty appointments, minority control over ethnic studies departments, and additional admission seats for minority students.[99]

The strike—supported by faculty and administrators of color, Local 1570 of the American Federation of Teachers (representing teaching assistants), the Student Senate, and eventually the Academic Senate—lasted three months. Over 150 students were arrested and thirty-six students suspended; police brutality was rampant, and Governor Ronald Reagan called in the National Guard to end the strike.[100] However, the strike won major victories: in the fall semester of 1969, the Department of Ethnic Studies began classes for programs in Afro-American studies, Chicano studies, Asian American studies, and Native American studies. By the spring semester of 1970, the Black Studies program offered thirty courses.[101]

Although the racial demographics at UC Berkeley did not shift greatly after this period, the California legislature issued resolutions in 1974 and 1984 calling for the UC system, and for California public higher education institutions generally, to increase the percentage of underrepresented students to match their percentage in the state population. UC Berkeley and UCLA never reached these goals.[102] The UC Board of Regents had increased the special EOP admissions percentage to 6 percent by the end of 1970s, but the 1978 *Bakke* decision compelled the president of the UC system to make race-conscious admissions separate from the 6 percent special admissions percentage.[103] *Regents of the University of California v. Bakke*, a landmark Supreme Court case regarding the use of affirmative action in admissions to the UC Davis Medical School, determined that achieving a diverse student body was a compelling interest of the State, allowing a limited consideration of race in admissions, yet it outlawed the use of racial quotas. Though UC Berkeley had not utilized quotas for any racial group, the *Bakke* decision placed all universities on notice regarding their inclusion of Black students. By 1979, the freshman class at UC Berkeley was 3.9 percent Black and 4 percent Latino.[104]

Increasing admissions competition began to draw public attention to UC Berkeley's admissions practices. In 1975, the university accepted 77 percent of freshman applicants, but by 1990, it accepted only 38 percent of freshman applicants.[105] In the early 1980s, in response to complaints from Asian applicants claiming an Asian enrollment cap, the Office for Civil Rights (now a part of the U.S. Department of Education) began to investigate UC Berkeley's and UCLA's admissions practices (to be discussed in chapter 3). Although the UC leadership issued apologies to Asian students, they admitted no wrongdoing. In 1989, the Admissions and Enrollment Committee of the Berkeley Division of the Academic Senate, headed by Professor Jerome Karabel, released a report that detailed the changing admissions policies at UC Berkeley. Although the new policies did not significantly change the demographics at the university, they aimed to diversify the student body by adding the consideration of socioeconomic status and older nontraditional students, and raising

TABLE 1.2 University of California Berkeley undergraduate demographics (%)

	1993	2000	2010	2014
White	33.3	30.4	30.3	26.6
Black	5.4	4.3	3.4	3.3
Latino	13.6	9.6	11.7	13.5
Asian	36.5	40.2	39.6	38.9

Source: Fall Enrollment Data and Common Data Set, Statistical Summary of Students and Staff, Office of Planning and Analysis, UC Berkeley.

Note: Percentages do not total 100 percent. In addition to rounding, the categories American Indian, Nonresident alien, and Race/ethnicity unknown are not included.

academic standards by increasing the percentage of students admitted solely on academic achievement from 40 percent to 50 percent (the latter echoing UC-wide admissions policies from the 1970s).[106] By the early 1990s, UC Berkeley's Black undergraduate population had reached 5 percent (table 1.2).

Even though *Bakke* emerged as a significant challenge to affirmative action, UC Berkeley never enrolled the state share of Black or Latino students before the state banned affirmative action in the 1990s. Student mobilization did more to compel the adoption of ethnic studies than did the increased representation of Black and Latino students. *Bakke*, attention from the U.S. Department of Education, and state political pressure encouraged UC Berkeley to revisit admissions practices, which eventually led to moderate increases in underrepresented student populations. However, UC and UM would experience crushing blows to their affirmative action policies in the 1990s and 2000s in the form of anti–affirmative action ballot initiative campaigns.

UNIVERSITY OF MICHIGAN

UM, established in 1817, remains one of the most prestigious and selective public universities in the country. Though it admitted its first two Black students in 1868, there were fewer than twenty minority students on campus at a time before World War II. Black students could not afford to attend the university, as student jobs went to White students. By 1954, two hundred Black students attended UM, though roommate assignments and fraternity membership remained segregated. In 1962, a federal investigation concluded that there was racial bias in hiring at UM and encouraged integration in the areas of employment and student enrollment.[107] University administrators established the Opportunity Awards program in 1964 to recruit minority students and provide them support services, including financial aid. Opportunity Awards students had a different admissions process than mainstream students, in that letters of recommendation and academic "promise" outweighed numerical scores.[108] Although Opportunity Awards aimed to serve disadvantaged students overall, and thus also admitted White students, 85 percent of these students admitted between 1964 and 1968 were Black.[109] Though figures from that period differ, by 1969 the student population of 32,000 students was between 3 and 4 percent Black.[110]

As was the case on other historically White campuses of that era, Black students at UM protested the lack of Black representation in the student and faculty bodies and demanded support services and a Black-oriented curriculum. In 1968, shortly after the assassination of Martin Luther King Jr., a group of Black students occupied the UM administration building to protest the lack of Black representation on campus. In response, the administration established a scholarship fund in King's name and appointed a few Black administrators. The discussions that emerged between students and administrators during this period led to the creation of the Center for Afro-American Studies in fall 1969.[111]

In spring 1970, Black students formed the Black Action Movement (BAM) and demanded an increase in Black enrollment to 10 percent of the student body, which would make it proportional to the Black population in the state of Michigan.[112] In addition to this central demand, students called for the hiring of more recruiters for Black students, the expansion of the Martin Luther King Jr. scholarship, tuition waivers for poor students, the establishment of a Black student center, the hiring of more Black faculty, and an increase in the minuscule Latino student population. In response to the administration's refusal of their terms, students called a strike, pulling hundreds of books off the shelves of the university library (thereby shutting it down), interrupting classes, blockading the Michigan Union snack bar, and organizing multiple demonstrations. In response, new UM President Robben Wright Fleming tentatively announced 10 percent Black enrollment as a goal of the administration, saying that other demands might be granted if funding could be gathered.[113]

The protesting students pledged to shut the campus down until all of their demands were taken seriously. White student groups like Students for a Democratic Society joined their protest in solidarity. Many students, unwilling to cross the picket line, stopped attending classes, and some professors and teaching assistants canceled their classes in support of the strike.[114] The university newspaper reported that by the fifth day of the strike, class attendance dropped to 40 percent in the Literature, Science, and Arts College, 40 percent in the School of Public Health, and 10 percent in the School of Social Work.[115] After about a week, the administration and students reached an agreement: the university agreed to dedicate money to reaching the 10 percent Black enrollment goal by 1973–1974, in addition to funding recruitment programs and support services. However, the rest of the students' demands were ignored.

The administration soon abandoned the plan, and by 1975, the 10 percent goal had still not been reached.[116] In response, BAM II launched and demonstrated.[117] Among its many demands were calls for the university to meet the following demographic characteristics: 4 percent Asian American, 3 percent Native American, 8 percent Mexican American, and 16 percent Black American.[118] In 1970, African Americans composed 11.2 percent of the population in Michigan, though nearby Detroit was 43.7 percent Black, 1.79 percent Latino, and 0.3 percent Native American.[119] Full Hispanic demographics were not available until 1980, when the U.S. Census added "Hispanic origin" to the long-form census.

In 1976, UM met its goal of 10 percent African American students, but by the early 1980s, Black enrollment began to decline (table 1.3). By 1983, the Black population at UM stood at 4.9 percent.[120] Further, a university study conducted in 1980 reported that 85 percent of Black students had experienced racial discrimination from their peers.[121]

TABLE 1.3 University of Michigan undergraduate demographics (%)

	1968	1973	1980	1990	2000	2010	2014
White	96.5	90.4	89.8	79.4	67.6	70.7	66.3
Black	2.5	7.02	5.2	6.7	8.2	4.7	4.4
Latino	0.1*	0.72*	1.1	3.2	4.3	4.6	4.6
Asian	0.7	1.6	2.5	8.1	12.5	12.3	13.5

Source: U.S. Office for Civil Rights University Reports; University of Michigan Ethnicity Reports, Office of Registrar.

Note: Percentages do not total 100 percent.In addition to rounding, the categories Native American and Unknown are not included. Some students selected more than one category.

* Collected by Spanish surname at the time.

In 1987, BAM III emerged from Black students' rejection of the hostile racial climate on campus. Its many demands included a $5 million five-year initiative dedicated to the recruitment and retention of Black students, tenure for Black faculty, and an endowment for the multicultural center.[122]

In response to BAM III, UM President James J. Dunderstadt announced a multiyear affirmative action plan called the Michigan Mandate, which aimed to diversify the student and faculty bodies. The Michigan Mandate set target goals, reserved funds to increase scholarships for Black and Latino students, developed more ethnic studies programs, and established a multimillion-dollar center for African American studies.[123] Decades later, Dunderstadt's Michigan Mandate honored many of the original BAM student demands. However, this more aggressive plan produced the conditions under which a conservative backlash would emerge, particularly in the *Gratz v. Bollinger* and *Grutter v. Bollinger* Supreme Court cases, which challenged affirmative action policies at UM.

In the case of UM, administrators developed mild affirmative action policies, students demanded more aggressive policies, and through persistent student struggle, affirmative action goals and commitments became institutionalized. As on other campuses, calls for stronger affirmative action policies were made in tandem with demands for Black studies and Black institutional spaces.

CITY UNIVERSITY OF NEW YORK

City College, the first college of what would eventually become the CUNY system, was established in 1847, at a time when most Americans did not attend college. Its mission to educate the children of immigrants and the poor was remarkable in an era when most colleges were the private bastions of elites. As a result of Ivy League universities' use of quotas to limit Jewish enrollment, City College (and other municipal colleges such as Hunter, Brooklyn, Queens, and Baruch colleges) attracted a large population of Jewish students and remained majority-Jewish until the post–World War II boom in college enrollment.[124] These public colleges in New York City were also a hotbed of openly radical political activity—fueled by socialist and communist students and faculty in the 1930s and 1940s and by early Students for a Democratic Society and Friends of SNCC chapters that emerged in the 1960s.[125] During this period, City College's high academic reputation garnered the nicknames "Harvard of the Proletariat" and "Harvard-on-the-Hudson."[126]

Only a high school diploma and New York City residency were necessary for admission until 1924, when, for the first time, there were more applicants than seats. That year, administrators instituted a 72 percent high school grade point average requirement for admission. With a spike in applicants to the newly unified CUNY system in 1961, the required grade point average rose to 85 percent at Hunter and Queens Colleges and to 87 percent at Brooklyn College by 1963.[127]

The CUNY senior (four-year) colleges were virtually all White: in 1964, Black undergraduate students made up less than 2 percent of the combined student bodies, and there were only thirty Black full-time tenured faculty members out of three thousand in the senior colleges. These dismal numbers were directly related to the inferior education that Black New York high school students received: in 1968, the attrition rate was 50 percent for Black students, in contrast to 13 percent for White students.[128] A 1971 study by the CUNY Institute for Social Research determined that only 16 percent of Black graduates from New York public schools achieved grade point averages of 80 percent or above, in contrast to 50 percent of White graduates from the same school system.[129] Educational inequality at the primary and secondary levels was preventing Black students from entering colleges—not just in New York City, but also across the country.

In response to outrage from Black legislators and editorials in the *New York Amsterdam News*, the city's Black newspaper, the CUNY Board of Higher Education (renamed the Board of Trustees in 1979) initiated recruitment programs, namely SEEK at City College and College Discovery in the CUNY community colleges. The program, Search for Education, Elevation, and Knowledge (SEEK), established as an affirmative action program, recruited Black and Puerto Rican students who showed academic promise but who had lower high school grade point averages than those typically admitted. Instead of admitting students solely on the basis of their grade point averages, as was the case with the rest of the student body, SEEK also utilized recommendations from teachers and community leaders in selecting students. By 1966, SEEK had become a university-wide operation, though it made the biggest impact at City College. By 1968, the SEEK program consisted of 600 Black and Puerto Rican students at City College, about 6 percent of the student population—an improvement but still a small percentage, as City College was located in Harlem, famed capital of Black America.[130] SEEK students were not full members of the university community; they were not allowed to vote in student government elections or play on athletic teams.[131] The SEEK students—politicized by their experiences as students and community members, and many already radical activists in their own right—decided to organize themselves to protest the lack of racial progress within CUNY. Although CUNY (and the schools that preceded the organization of CUNY in 1961) had always promoted mass educational access in its mission, Black and Brown students' experiences of racial discrimination propelled them to fight for an educational system that included their communities in the curriculum and on campus.

In February 1969, Black and Puerto Rican students at City College occupied the office of the president and presented five demands to the college administration: that Black and Puerto Rican studies programs be established, that Black and Puerto Rican history courses and Spanish-language courses be mandatory for education majors, that a separate orientation program be created for Black and Puerto

Rican students, that students be given greater power in the administration of SEEK, and that the number of minority freshmen reflect the 40–45 ratio of Blacks and Puerto Ricans in the New York City public school system.[132] A few weeks later, as a result of campus agitation by the Black and Puerto Rican Student Community (BPRSC) over budget cuts to SEEK, the lack of administrative action regarding the five demands, and police brutality against protestors, BPRSC occupied and shut down the South Campus of City College for two weeks, renaming it the University of Harlem.[133] Supported by faculty members such as SEEK advisor and poet Toni Cade Bambara, sympathetic community members who delivered food to the striking students, and activists and public figures such as Betty Shabazz, Kathleen Cleaver, James Forman, and Adam Clayton Powell Jr. who visited the campus, BPRSC gained media attention and initiated a public conversation among faculty, administrators, legislators, and everyday New Yorkers about educational access.[134]

The 1969 student strike led to the establishment of the open admissions policy—a compromise made by the CUNY Board of Education in order to make the university system more accessible without alienating White middle-class students and their families.[135] Though Black and Puerto Rican students did not get the proportional representation they requested, now every high school graduate in New York City (including White working-class students) would be able to attend one of CUNY's four-year, tuition-free colleges. Population demographics at CUNY shifted dramatically (table 1.4). Prior to the open admissions strike, the Board of Education had planned to slowly phase in a less radical admissions plan, to begin six years later—assigning most high school graduates to community colleges. However, student protest forced CUNY to expand access to the four-year colleges to a wider population of students and to begin implementation almost immediately.

Remedial programs were the foundation of the open admissions policy; without support services dedicated to the eager but underprepared students, open admissions would not be possible.[136] The impact of this policy is unparalleled: CUNY became the largest degree-granting institution for Black and Latino students in the United States.[137] Significantly, the first-phase mild affirmative action

TABLE 1.4 City University of New York undergraduate demographics (%)

	1967	1970	1980	1992	2000	2010	2014
City College							
White	87.3	68.3	33.7	14.0	12.3	19.3	20.0
Black	4.2	16.4	31.3	42.1	39.4	23.2	20.3
Latino	1.9*	5.7*	23.6	27.0	32.0	34.6	32.6
Asian**	n/a	n/a	10.2	16.5	16.0	22.8	27.0
Hunter College							
White	88.6	74.7	60.7	43.7	40.7	41.9	38.2
Black	4.5	12.4	20.3	22.3	20.4	12.5	12.0
Latino	2.1*	6.4*	13.4	21.4	22.5	19.7	20.6
Asian**	n/a	n/a	4.7	12.4	16.1	25.7	29.0

Source: *City University of New York Student Data Books*, Office of Institutional Data.
Note: Percentages do not total 100 percent.In addition to rounding, the category American Indian is not included.
* Categorized as "Puerto Rican."
** Asian categories were not sufficiently collected until after 1970.

policies that emerged in the development of SEEK transitioned into a more aggressive second-phase policy with the adoption of open admissions. Though CUNY did not adopt affirmative action per se—open admissions existed as a policy that did not articulate race—it attempted to accommodate the race and class politics at a larger, less selective, working-class college system in the biggest, most racially diverse city in the country.

THE INSTITUTIONALIZATION OF AFFIRMATIVE ACTION AT SELECTIVE UNIVERSITIES

By the end of the 1970s, selective universities had fully embraced affirmative action in university admissions. Political scientist Daniel N. Lipson argues that three types of institutional isomorphism—that is, institutional homogeneity in policy adoption—were at work in the institutionalization of affirmative action in public universities:

coercive, in that federal and legal support existed for the establishment of affirmative action policies; normative, in that the embrace
of diversity among educational professionals was widespread; and
mimetic, in that campus officials learned and borrowed from each
other in the development of affirmative action plans and admissions
procedures.[138] Normative and mimetic isomorphism largely shaped
the institutionalization of affirmative action policies, as state review
and enforcement of affirmative action policies has been uneven.

In the challenge to affirmative action in *Regents of the University of
California v. Bakke* (1978), Allan Bakke, a White male applicant to the
medical school at UC Davis, sued the university system because he
was not admitted. He claimed that the affirmative action plan used
by the medical school violated his right to equal protection under the
law, resulting in "reverse racism" against Whites. In the unclear, and
controversial plurality opinion, five justices agreed that racial quotas
violated the Civil Rights Act of 1964, while four justices agreed that
race was a compelling state interest. Justice Lewis Powell, who agreed
with both decisions, casted the deciding vote to admit Bakke to UC
Davis, but also affirmed the principle of diversity.[139] Yet the lack of
clarity in *Bakke*'s split, plurality opinion (in which the justices agreed
on the result, but there was no majority agreement on the rationale
for the result) made affirmative action vulnerable to future legal
challenges (see chapter 2). However, the *Bakke* decision did make
clear that racial redress was an illegitimate and illegal justification
for the persistence of affirmative action programs. Justice Powell's
opinion, which many (including university administrators) interpreted as the reigning ruling in this split-decision case, importantly
cites Harvard University's inclusion of race in its admissions plan as
a model for universities to replicate.[140]

Harvard University's plan, which was dependent on the individual review of each application, considered race as a "plus factor" in
admissions, though not the primary factor, and did not use racial
quotas or strict goals. The commendation of this Harvard plan contributed to normative and mimetic isomorphism in regard to affirmative action in universities across the country: Ivy League universities
already commanded the highest respect among institutions of higher
education, and their stance on campus diversity would reinforce the

persistence of the diversity logic across the academy. Later, when public universities' affirmative action policies were challenged in the federal court system, Ivy League institutions filed amicus curiae briefs, pledging their support of diverse campus environments. Powell's opinion laid the groundwork for the legal inclusion of diversity in university admissions policies, though vaguely underspecifying the role of diversity goals in relationship to racial quotas. Because the term *affirmative action* became yoked to ideas of racial quotas and reparations, universities began to rename their affirmative action programs and associated student affairs work as diversity and inclusion programs.[141] Ultimately, the consideration of campus diversity in admissions plans became institutionalized in the field of higher education after the elimination of the principle of racial redress and the eradication of the practice of racial quotas.

However, even with the logic of diversity framing affirmative action's persistence and even with the continuation of mandatory affirmative action plans as part of desegregation in southern states, affirmative action remained threatened and unstable due to its adoption primarily as political concession. Law and social policy are interpretive concepts; legislators and pressure groups (such as think tanks and lobbyists) can influence the application or repeal of law as time, skill, and opportunity allow.[142] Although this is true for all policies, affirmative action was incorporated unevenly, was interpreted differently across institutions, and lacked federal models for implementation or measurement, making it particularly vulnerable to legal and political challenge. As affirmative action, along with civil rights policies more generally, was adopted at the federal level, direct vote processes did not factor into its adoption or implementation. When the political context changed, commitment to affirmative action waned among policy makers, some university professionals, and the larger public. The political context of the 1960s, pushed leftward by radical movements and urban rebellions, was a highly important factor in the adoption of affirmative action across the field of higher education. As understandings of race and racial inequality changed and as the influence of the Right on American political culture grew, tolerance for these race- and class-inclusive admissions policies shifted.

Overall, the adoption of race- and class-inclusive admissions policies should be understood within the context of the expansion of American citizenship rights in the twentieth century. Though GI Bill benefits expanded public educational access to White working-class men, these rights were not immediately extended to women and Black people. In fact, these groups were systematically shut out of public higher education through policies that favored White male veterans. The civil rights movement's grassroots and institutional challenge to the racialized restrictions on a range of civil, political, and social citizenship rights forced the desegregation of public education and prompted a new federal commitment to policies that defended all federally protected groups against discrimination. Affirmative action aimed to address institutionalized discrimination and its impact on employment and university admissions.

The federal adoption of affirmative action as a means of crisis management in response to the civil rights movement and urban rebellions rendered it susceptible to changing understandings of racial politics over time. Although the Civil Rights Act of 1964 encouraged both mandatory and voluntary affirmative action as a means to desegregate educational institutions, it was a colorblind law that specified nondiscrimination (rather than racial redress) and encountered political shifts that limited enforcement.

The campus-level adoption of affirmative action, prompted by the federal government in some cases and by liberal university administrators in other cases, began with mild, first-phase affirmative action policies focused on targeted recruitment and minimal admission of racial minorities. However, in response to campus protest as well as federal and state oversight, university administrators adopted more progressive second-phase affirmative action policies. The normative embrace of diversity as a lawful educational imperative, as evidenced through shared practices among administrators, established diversity management as a legitimate, widespread arrangement in higher education. However, affirmative action at public universities remained particularly vulnerable due to the penetrability of state institutions.

In the late twentieth and early twenty-first centuries, public figures such as politicians, trustee members, and nonstate political elites contested and shaped the legitimacy of diversity and colorblindness in selective higher education. The institutional autonomy of public universities can be undermined due to their public mission, the role of public elected officials in their governance, and their institutional funding by tax dollars. The racial political landscape of the post–civil rights era would shape the conditions under which affirmative action and open admissions would be repealed in several important locations. The particular post–civil rights racial logics of diversity and colorblindness would both clash and cohere in ways that would unravel the legislative gains of the civil rights movement.

2

LEGAL MOBILIZATION

Racial Political Strategy and Affirmative Action Retrenchment in the Federal Courts

My goal was through the courts to restore the original vision of the civil rights movement. And that vision . . . was that your race and your ethnicity should not be a factor that is used to help you in some way or harm you in some way. . . . Heman Sweatt [plaintiff in Sweatt v. Painter (1950), which successfully challenged segregation in Texas] didn't want his race to be used as a factor to harm him obviously. But he didn't want his race to be used as a factor to help him either. He didn't want the bar raised and he didn't want the bar lowered. Abigail Fisher basically made the same argument. She didn't want the bar raised for her because she was White, she didn't want it lowered either. I think that that arc that connects Heman Sweatt to Abigail Fisher is the founding principle of the civil rights movement and for forty years that principle has evolved in ways that are hard to recognize from the time that my mother and father and so many advocated for desegregation in the '50s and '60s. So to the degree that I can provide cases that will continue to restore that original vision then that's what I hope to do.

—Edward Blum, 2014, conservative legal strategist and organizer

THE ORIGINAL VISION

In the 1990s and 2000s, it became common for conservative elites to claim moral and political descent from the civil rights movement. In the epigraph to this chapter, conservative legal strategist Edward Blum speaks about his passion for restoring the "original vision" of the civil rights movement in the contemporary period. Yet he has made it his business to challenge the consideration of race in the formation of majority-minority electoral districts,[1] fight the organization of electoral districts according to total population, in favor of voting eligible population,[2] and reverse Voting Rights Act protections.[3] The policies that Blum has successfully challenged once protected and enfranchised African American citizens in particular. In conservatives' rewriting of American racial history, Blacks and Whites have faced the same obstacles. Their fictional accounts make no distinction between the ordeal of an African American activist who encountered threats to his life while desegregating the University of Texas Law School and the journey of a White, upper-class University of Texas legacy applicant who was rejected due to her academic record. The "original vision" that conservatives have fixated on focuses on colorblindness—a racial ideology that borrows the language, but betrays the spirit, of the civil rights movement. Pairing colorblindness with ideas of meritocracy, conservatives have organized legal challenges to the use of affirmative action in public university admissions.

In this chapter, I examine how conservatives utilized legal tactics in their efforts to challenge affirmative action. First, I introduce *racial political strategy*, a framework that specifies how race is deployed in political conflict. I then explore the development of the conservative network of support behind anti–affirmative action legal mobilization. Then I analyze conservative racial political strategy in the following cases: *Hopwood v. Texas* (1996), *Gratz v. Bollinger* (2003), *Grutter v. Bollinger* (2003), *Fisher v. University of Texas* (2013), and *Fisher v. University of Texas* (2016). In these court challenges, conservatives deployed a racial political strategy of White victimhood, which rearticulates White subjectivity as being victimized by affirmative action.

RACIAL POLITICAL STRATEGY

In order to analyze conservative political mobilization, I draw from both social movement and race scholarship to capture the racial dimensions of political strategy. Although social movement scholars have yet to reach consensus regarding a singular definition of strategy, a number of them define *strategy* as "a plan of collective action intended to accomplish goals within a particular context."[4] The study of strategy explores the kinds of strategies available (and why); the interrelated decision-making regarding tactics, sites, frames, and demands; strategy implementation at various aggregate levels; and the duration necessary for strategy execution.[5] But what about racial strategies? In what ways do political actors' choices about tactics and strategy communicate racial meanings? In their approach to the historically contingent nature of race, Michael Omi and Howard Winant define racial projects (the engines of racial formation) as those that link racial representation to the material distribution of resources.[6] Racial projects shape both racial ideology and the racial opportunity structure. I define racial political strategy as the deployment of race in a plan for collective action—specifically, the goals, targets, and tactics employed in mobilization.

Racial political strategy specifies how social movement actors deploy race in political conflict. By drawing attention to the discursive articulation of race, through language and cultural symbols, we see how conservatives strategically frame themselves as victimized and shape legal and public notions of colorblindness, diversity, merit, and racial justice in the post–civil rights period. Additionally, we gain insight into how conservatives frame Black and Brown students, universities, and the State in relationship to race and power. When we focus on the mobilization of race in social movement tactics and in relationship to political opportunity, we see how conservatives appropriate the civil rights legal tactical repertoire in federal court challenges.

Racial political strategy allows us to examine how racial concepts and practices are projected in the midst of political mobilization. Through an assessment of racial political strategy, we can pinpoint if and how the post–civil rights racial logics of colorblindness and diversity are reflected and deployed in the mobilization of conservative elites. In this way, I draw attention to discursive practices and tactical actions.

Conservative mobilization against race- and class-inclusive admissions provides an opportunity to examine racial political strategy and processes of *rearticulation*. Omi and Winant suggest that groups produce new subjectivity by discursively reframing familiar themes.[7] With new subjectivity, groups are able to forge a new politics. In the civil rights movement, activists rearticulated Black subjectivity by reframing Black religious themes and other Black cultural markers to move from survival and accommodation to political resistance.[8] In mobilizing against affirmative action and open admissions, conservatives utilized rearticulation in their appropriation of racial justice language and symbols. They redefined White racial subjectivity as being victimized, and this new subjectivity was then deployed to buttress the need for colorblind political practice.

THE NETWORK

Court and ballot challenges to affirmative action emerged in relationship to a larger conservative network of support. Conservative organizations began to more strategically organize themselves in the post–World War II period. American cultural and political upheaval during this period caught many in the economic and political elite by surprise. Not only were people rebelling in the streets, but they were also forcing concessions from the State and shifting what the mainstream considered to be socially acceptable. As a result of this political activity, government regulation over business grew in the 1960s and 1970s, resulting in laws regarding consumer protection, employee safety, air and water quality, and antidiscrimination in workplaces and educational environments. Activists openly spoke about challenging capitalist exploitation and embracing socialism, and universities were hotbeds for political debate over class repression and racial oppression. Though members of the business community grew panicked over the impact of these regulations and anticorporate attitudes on their bottom line, initially they were not particularly organized.[9]

As Steven Teles documents, progressive movements of the midtwentieth century were supported by a "liberal legal network": the liberal lawyers, academics, and public interest law firms that coordinated the legal arm of mobilization.[10] Anchored by organizations such as the National Association for the Advancement of Colored People Legal Defense Fund (NAACP LDF) and the American Civil Liberties Union (ACLU), this network paved the way for a "constitutional law revolution," which provided opportunities for further rights-based legal challenges.[11] Emerging in the New Deal period, this network not only contributed to victories in civil and women's rights but also trained a generation of lawyers that moved law schools and the courts to the Left, transformed legal aid into an instrument of social change, and invented the field of public interest law. The liberal legal network excelled in selecting cases, introducing legal precedent, raising funds from organizations such as the Ford Foundation, and formulating legal ideas and strategy. Even with the financial and political resources of the wealthy, conservative elites lacked coordinated legal tactics, relevant ideology, and mass media influence.[12]

However, the Powell memo signified a change. In 1971, corporate attorney Lewis F. Powell penned a confidential memorandum to his friend Eugene B. Sydnor Jr., chair of the Education Committee of the U.S. Chamber of Commerce. The memo, titled "Attack on American Free Enterprise System," served as a clarion call for business elites to organize themselves to collectively counter the attack on capitalism (which Powell understood to include proposals to limit corporate tax breaks and the appointment of socialist professors in universities). He suggested aggressive coordination among business interests to target the media, the courts, universities, and knowledge production more generally. He proposed to uphold capitalist and conservative virtues by expanding the role of business schools, appointing conservative faculty, creating speakers' bureaus, evaluating and creating textbooks for college and high school students, and encouraging more scholarly work to promote business interests and the system of free enterprise.[13] The Powell memo also contained calls for ideological influence over television, politicians, and political consultants and staffers and for renewed attention to the courts. As Powell stated regarding the law,

As with respect to scholars and speakers, the Chamber [of Commerce] would need a highly competent staff of lawyers. In special situations it should be authorized to engage, to appear as counsel amicus in the Supreme Court, [sic] lawyers of national standing and reputation. The greatest care should be exercised in selecting the cases in which to participate, or the suits to institute. But the opportunity merits the necessary effort.[14]

Powell, also a board member for Phillip Morris as the tobacco industry fought to conceal the link between smoking and lung cancer, was two months from being nominated to the Supreme Court by President Richard Nixon.[15] Years later, his opinion in the *Regents of the University of California v. Bakke* Supreme Court case shaped the terms of affirmative action. Powell wrote that diversity is a compelling state interest but that quotas cannot be utilized to construct diverse environments; further, racial identity can be only one factor in admissions decisions, equally weighted against many other factors. Although the plurality opinion in this case later created confusion as to whether Powell's opinion was actually law, universities interpreted his opinion as a defense of affirmative action. Powell's opinion was heralded as the saving grace of affirmative action, providing a legal precedent to support diversity, while his ideas about strategically countering the Left were taken up by the conservative movement and would later be used to undermine affirmative action—illustrating how diversity itself does not necessarily challenge racial inequality in the post–civil rights era. Diversity logics can be utilized to support conservative political activity.

The Powell memo circulated among business elites, reflecting what many of them were already thinking and saying. When William Baroody Sr., president of the neoconservative think tank American Enterprise Institute (AEI), gained access to the Powell memo, he reworked some of its elements in a speech he then gave to CEOs in 1972, designating AEI (rather than the Chamber of Commerce) as a key institution in the political consolidation of the Right.[16] The Powell memo provided a framework for expert fund-raising pitches for conservative think tanks. While conservative elites continued to contribute directly to political campaigns, they now directed their attention to building libertarian and conservative institutions, such as foundations, think tanks, academic disciplines, scholarly journals, public interest law firms, and media outfits focused on spreading conservative ideology and making policy interventions.

Benefiting from income tax law that provided incredible incentives for charitable giving, the wealthy had become accustomed to establishing private family and corporate foundations since the 1920s, when Richard Mellon, a wealthy philanthropist (and U.S. treasury secretary) secured the passage of revenue acts that slashed tax rates. However, instead of giving only to museums, local beautification projects, animal cruelty prevention, and their low-paid employees, conservative elites began to direct their money into shadow institutions, such as Richard Mellon Scaife's Carthage Foundation, the Heritage Foundation, Charles Koch's Cato Institute, and more.[17] Long-established organizations like AEI suddenly found more financial support, and other long-standing foundations, such as the Smith Richardson Foundation, Lynde and Harry Bradley Foundation, and Olin Foundation, shifted their mission to support free markets and other conservative causes. Elites succeeded in shielding themselves from taxes through the formation and growth of the modern conservative movement and ultimately wielded more power than individual politicians.

Conservative foundations, such as the Olin Foundation, Lynde and Harry Bradley Foundation, Carthage Foundation, Smith Richardson Foundation, JM Foundation, Donner Foundation, and DonorsTrust, provided financial resources to politicians and organizations central to ballot initiatives, court challenges, and board of trustee decision-making concerning the elimination of affirmative action and open admissions (table 2.1). Think tanks and public interest law firms that were key to elite mobilization against affirmative action and open admissions, such as the Manhattan Institute for Policy Research, Hoover Institution, Center for Individual Rights, and American Civil Rights Institute, also maintained relationships with larger, national support organizations such as the National Association of Scholars, American Enterprise Institute, and American Council of Alumni and Trustees. This conservative network provided the financial resources, policy reports, media framing, and sustained relationships needed nationally to challenge policies in regional and national contexts. This network became particularly powerful with the ascendance of the Reagan administration in 1981.

TABLE 2.1 Networks of support for anti–affirmative action and open admissions challenges

Foundation	Organization	Tactic/Location
Olin Foundation	Claremont Institute	Ballot measure/CA
	Hoover Institution	
	American Civil Rights Institute	Ballot measure/MI
	Manhattan Institute	Trustees/NY
	American Council of Alumni & Trustees	
	American Enterprise Institute	Legal/TX
Lynde and Harry Bradley Foundation	Claremont Institute	Ballot measure/CA
	Hoover Institution	
	American Civil Rights Institute	Ballot measure/MI
	American Council of Alumni & Trustees	Trustees/NY
	Empire Foundation	
	Center for Individual Rights	Legal/MI
	American Enterprise Institute	Legal/TX
	Project on Fair Representation	
Scaife Foundation	Claremont Institute	Ballot measure/CA
	National Association of Scholars	
	Center for Individual Rights	Legal/MI
	Manhattan Institute	Trustees/NY
	American Enterprise Institute	Legal/TX
Smith Richardson Foundation	Hoover Institution	Ballot measure/CA
	National Association of Scholars	Legal/MI
	Manhattan Institute	Trustees/NY
	American Enterprise Institute	Legal/TX
Castle Rock Foundation	Claremont Institute	Ballot measure/CA
	National Association of Scholars	Legal/MI
Koch Family Foundation	Center for Individual Rights	Legal/MI
DonorsTrust	Project on Fair Representation	Legal/TX

THE REAGAN REVOLUTION: CONSERVATIVE DOMINANCE IN THE FEDERAL COURT SYSTEM

The Reagan and George H. W. Bush administrations greatly shaped the legal conditions under which affirmative action would be challenged. The administrations' influence on the federal court system directly contributed to the political opportunities conservatives had to challenge affirmative action in the courts and to the legal precedent established by successful challenges to affirmative action in employment and federal contracting. Conservative think tanks and foundations played a major role in the construction of the Reagan administration and the explosion of conservative ideology during this period. While organizations like the Washington Legal Foundation and Mountain States Legal Foundation influenced public discourse and legal cases, no foundation exerted greater influence than the Heritage Foundation. Ten days into Reagan's presidency, the foundation circulated the *Mandate for Leadership* report, a twenty-volume proposal for conservative governance, to Reagan's transition team. By the end of Reagan's first year, 60 percent of the think tank's recommendations had been implemented. No champion of affirmative action, the Heritage Foundation encouraged the U.S. Justice Department to make challenges to affirmative action a major priority.[18] However, during the Reagan administration, these challenges to affirmative action focused on the employment sector.

Republicans of previous eras, including Presidents Nixon and Gerald Ford, supported affirmative action as a means of political expediency during a period in which racial redress was still the prominent way of dealing with racial reform.[19] In contrast, the Reagan administration worked to legally and culturally establish colorblindness as the only legitimate way to engage in racial politics. During the 1980s and 1990s, conservatives began to frame compensation obtained through class-action race discrimination lawsuits as "reverse discrimination" against Whites, and redress for plaintiffs began to occur primarily through cases involving individuals.[20] Thus, the Reagan administration's legal constraints on the use of affirmative action made it a remedy only for specific discrimination against individuals and not for discrimination against groups.

Before these changes, a person could sue a company for employment discrimination, provide statistical evidence regarding underrepresentation of federally protected groups, and claim disparate impact of the company's practices with respect to those protected groups. The disparate impact argument, informed by an understanding that employment practices may result in discrimination even without organizational intent, was critical to the ways that discrimination cases had previously been decided. After the judgment in *Wards Cove Packing Co. v. Atonio* (1989), conservative federal judges interpreted remedies for underrepresentation and disparate impact as illegal quotas and rejected the implementation of new affirmative action plans.[21] Plaintiffs now had to prove that companies employed a hiring or promotion process that *intentionally* discriminated against protected class employees, rather than one that routinely disadvantaged those employees. Legislators and educational institutions developed affirmative action plans to address disparate impact in college admissions, but the justification and legal precedent supporting this ameliorative practice at the group level had now been eliminated. This foreclosed the opportunity for racially disadvantaged groups to collectively make claims on the State, rendering assertions of persisting structural racial inequality illegitimate. The Reagan administration also falsely equated the practice of affirmative action with the sole use of quotas, effectively shaping discourse about affirmative action that persists into the contemporary period.

The proposed Civil Rights Act of 1990, sponsored by Senators Edward Kennedy and Augustus Hawkins, aimed to protect affirmative action plans in employment, limit lawsuits that challenged court-sanctioned affirmative action plans, and allow the use of disparate impact in court cases. However, it was vetoed by President George H. W. Bush, labeled a "quota bill," and dubbed the "Civil Rights Sham of 1990" by the *New York Times*.[22] Because Reagan and Bush appointed so many conservative federal district and circuit court judges during their presidencies (about 475), they effectively tilted the court rightward and influenced the legal environment in which affirmative action lawsuits and appeals would be considered.[23] In the 1980s, the Supreme Court rendered some favorable decisions regarding employers' affirmative action plans;[24] however, it rejected many more plans and placed limits on the damages that could be awarded.[25] According to legal scholar Barbara A. Perry, by the mid-1990s the Supreme Court's stance on affirmative action cases could be characterized as "deciding not to decide" because it rejected these cases on appeal, allowing the lower court decisions to stand.[26] By 1992, 60 percent of federal judges with life appointments had been appointed by Reagan or Bush, and this makeup of the courts persisted for years to come.[27] The conservative federal courts provided the opportunity for anti–affirmative action challenges.

The Reagan and Bush administrations also contested civil rights policy by making conservative appointments to key supervisory bodies and by effectively eliminating the enforcement of these policies through budget cuts. Reagan gutted the U.S. Commission on Civil Rights, a key federal body tasked with gathering facts and making recommendations regarding discrimination and civil rights issues. His administration cleared the commission of liberals and moderate Republicans and replaced its leadership with White and Black ultraconservatives; the new commission explicitly rejected affirmative action and embraced the goal of a "colorblind society."[28] It is not surprising that this shift occurred after that very commission documented that Reagan's Justice Department impeded the enforcement of civil rights laws.[29]

Reagan also slashed funding for the Civil Rights Division of the Justice Department and the Equal Employment Opportunity Commission (EEOC). During Clarence Thomas's chairmanship of the EEOC, the agency abandoned affirmative action goals and timelines. It also did not enforce back pay for large discrimination cases, such as that in which General Motors was accused of discrimination against Black, Latino, and female employees; the company eventually settled the case for $42 million.[30] In addition to rejecting affirmative action, Reagan and his appointees ended forced and voluntary busing,[31] refused to sanction universities that discriminated,[32] and vetoed the Civil Rights Restoration Act of 1987.[33] Black politicians even accused Reagan's Justice Department of waging a campaign of harassment and scrutiny of Black elected officials.[34] The Reagan and Bush administrations greatly shaped the legal and political conditions of affirmative action, decimating its practice in employment and creating political opportunities for conservatives to legally challenge affirmative action in public universities.

RACIAL POLITICAL STRATEGY
IN THE FEDERAL COURTS

Mounting legal challenges to the consideration of race in university admissions may be the most recognizable tactic utilized by conservative elites. A federal rejection of affirmative action would dismantle the policy at every higher education institution that receives federal funding; thus, Supreme Court challenges had the potential to restructure higher education nationally, at both public and private institutions.

These court challenges relied on a White victimhood racial strategy, deployed through the use of White female plantiffs and legal arguments using the equal protection clause of the Fourteenth Amendment. In these legal cases, conservative organizations presented plantiffs as victims of government-sanctioned diversity gone too far. The legal tactics utilized in cases involving the University of Texas at Austin and the University of Michigan, organized by the Center for Individual Rights and later the Project on Fair Representation, appropriated civil rights methods by developing class-action lawsuits and using them as test cases. Conservative legal strategists established precedents and built upon these test cases, chipping away at affirmative action through the law, just as the civil rights movement did in challenging legal segregation in the courts. Through these cases, conservative legal strategists put forth a vision of universities as colorblind meritocracies; the consideration of race in admissions violated this vision. Although this legal tactic has yet to result in a wholesale federal rejection of affirmative action, it has further elevated the most stringent legal standard, strict scrutiny, in deciding affirmative action cases. This shift has created a more hostile legal environment for the persistence of affirmative action at universities.

HOPWOOD V. TEXAS: THE START OF A REVOLUTION

After the *Bakke* case, more than a decade passed before another challenge to affirmative action in universities was heard. Prior to its participation in *Hopwood v. Texas* (1996), the Center for Individual Rights (CIR), a libertarian, nonprofit public interest law firm dedicated to eliminating progressive race-, gender-, and class-oriented policies, had primarily pursued free speech cases in which it defended White professors and students accused of speech or acts offensive to women and African Americans. It represented White men who had published statements that Blacks were inferior to Whites, made sexually explicit comments in class lectures, and students who had dressed up in blackface and tattered clothing as "slaves."[35] These were relatively minor cases that did not reach beyond the federal district courts. CIR, which represented clients at no cost, claimed to defend the "individual liberties" of Americans from the "aggressive and unchecked authority of federal and state governments" and clearly identified the federal government as its target.[36] Using the equal protection clause of the Fourteenth Amendment—which grants every citizen equal protection under the law—as the justification for a colorblind society, CIR claimed White victimhood as a result of the State's overreach. According to this logic, affirmative action denied Whites equal protection under the law.

CIR's founders, Michael McDonald and Michael Greve, had previously worked at the Washington Legal Foundation, a conservative public interest law firm that also intervened in court cases, filed amicus briefs, brought original cases, and regularly partnered with think tanks such as the Heritage Foundation and the Koch brothers' Cato Institute.[37] In 1992, Steven W. Smith, a lawyer at the conservative Texas Legal Foundation, was contemplating a run for the Texas Supreme Court. Smith filed a request under the Texas Open Records Act in order to view the affirmative action policy at his alma mater, the University of Texas at Austin (UT Austin) Law School.[38] After concluding that the law school's admissions procedures resulted in "reverse discrimination," he solicited potential plaintiffs by sending letters to thirty-one White applicants rejected by the UT Austin Law School and later sought support from CIR. Cheryl Hopwood was one of nine who responded and one of four included in the lawsuit. CIR saw this as the perfect opportunity to challenge affirmative action and establish legal precedent.[39]

Described as the "start of a revolution" by CIR, *Hopwood v. Texas* was an important test case for conservative elites' attempts to end affirmative action in higher education.[40] Prior to the *Hopwood* case, the UT Austin Law School had produced more Black and Mexican graduates combined than any other historically White institution; only the historically Black university Howard University had produced more Black lawyers. The UT Austin Law School utilized an index system that took into account undergraduate grade point average (GPA), Law School Admission Test (LSAT) score, and other factors such as letters of recommendation, socioeconomic background, "hardships overcome," and racial background. A quota did not exist, as the numbers of accepted Black and Mexican students varied from year to year and their numbers never reached the proportion of Blacks and Mexicans in the state population.[41] The only quota the law school used was that for Texas residents, who filled 80 percent of the law school's seats. Admission was offered to White applicants who had the same Texas index scores as many Black and Mexican admits, however more Black and Mexican students with lower-range index scores had been admitted than other groups. Also, in 1992, the law school had created a separate committee to review the minority candidates' applications.[42] The *Hopwood* attorneys successfully framed this separate pool of students as a racial quota. Equating a variety of policies, including point systems, grid systems, individualized review, and the use of multiple admissions committees to quotas was central to the legal tactic across cases.

Hopwood, lead plaintiff in the case, has been described as the perfect candidate to challenge the UT Austin Law School policy.[43] The law school defended its rejection of Hopwood and the other three plaintiffs on the basis that they all had "weak majors at weak undergraduate institutions" (Hopwood graduated from California State University Sacramento after completing community college with a major in accounting). However, Hopwood was the ideal sympathetic White female victim. She was raised in a single-parent household, worked part-time while attending college, and supported her family as an accountant while taking care of her Air Force officer husband and a child with cerebral palsy.[44] It was easy for CIR to present her as a deserving applicant, victimized by a policy that considered race, rather than drawing attention to policies that privileged state residency requirements or rigorous undergraduate coursework. After the *Bakke* decision in 1978, White female lead plaintiffs were used in every federal challenge to affirmative action in universities until 2016 and thus have been central to this legal tactic. Even though scholars have pointed to the ways that White women have benefited from affirmative action,[45] this legal tactic uses the patriarchal and racist frames of White female fragility to argue that affirmative action policies render Whites as victims.

CIR and its four plaintiffs—Hopwood, Douglas Carvell, Kenneth Elliott, and David Rogers—filed a lawsuit seeking a declaration that the law school's use of affirmative action was unconstitutional, elimination of the policy, and monetary damages for being rejected.[46] Utilizing the equal protection clause of the Fourteenth Amendment, they argued that the use of affirmative action denied Whites equal protection under the law. In short, they were victims of "reverse racism." The UT Austin Law School defended its affirmative action policy, maintaining not only that providing a diverse learning environment was a compelling state interest but also that its program existed in order to remedy segregation at UT Austin. The U.S. Department of Education had actively supervised the affirmative action plans utilized in Texas due to this past discrimination. However, Texas had entered into a consent decree with the federal courts to end court supervision; under this agreement, court supervision ended three years before Smith and CIR sued UT Austin.[47]

When the trial began in 1994, CIR argued that the *Bakke* decision had been "implicitly overruled" as a result of what its lawyers framed as inconsistent decisions rendered in employment affirmative action cases.[48] When it became clear that Judge Sam Sparks would not accept a challenge to *Bakke*, CIR then argued that the two-committee system (framed as a dual-track system, which *Bakke* linked to quotas) was unconstitutional.[49] While the judge agreed that the two-committee system was unconstitutional, he upheld the pursuit of diversity and the constitutionality of affirmative action at the UT Austin Law School. His decision was representative of a judicial trend since *Bakke*: courts constrained the means to diversify campuses but upheld the objective of diversity.[50]

CIR appealed to the Fifth Circuit Court of Appeals, a conservative branch of the federal courts.[51] In 1996, the Fifth Circuit rendered its controversial decision, declaring that *Bakke* was no longer the law—and perhaps never had been (because *Bakke* was a split-decision case). The court also determined that diversity was not a compelling state interest and that affirmative action could be used only to remedy specific racial discrimination identified at the UT Austin Law School, rather than racial discrimination in the greater society.[52] This decision eliminated affirmative action throughout the Fifth Circuit's jurisdiction of Texas, Louisiana, and Mississippi, though Louisiana and Mississippi, still under court supervision due to their histories of segregation, were required by the federal government to maintain their affirmative action programs.[53] The UT Austin Law School petitioned the Supreme Court for a writ of certiorari so it could review the decision, but the Supreme Court refused to hear the case, allowing the appellate decision to stand.

This refusal was historic. In the first challenge to affirmative action in universities since *Bakke*, the courts rejected diversity *and* the means to ensure it. While *Grutter v. Bollinger* (2003) later reversed the decision in *Hopwood*, for a time conservative elites succeeded in ending affirmative action (in programs, scholarships, and admissions processes that considered race) in the public universities of Texas. Shortly after *Hopwood*, Smith (who was little known before the case) unsuccessfully ran for a position on the Texas Supreme Court, though he was later elected to the court in 2002.[54] His role in the *Hopwood* case became the primary means by which he was identified in local media throughout election coverage.[55] By recruiting a sympathetic White female lead plaintiff, questioning the legal status of the Powell opinion in *Bakke*, equating the admissions process to racial quotas, and appealing to the conservative Fifth Circuit, CIR and Smith achieved a significant victory in their quest to eliminate affirmative action.

GRATZ V. BOLLINGER AND GRUTTER V. BOLLINGER:
LIMITING THE MEANS TO CONSIDER DIVERSITY

Shortly after the Fifth Circuit decision in *Hopwood*, CIR initiated two lawsuits opposing the use of affirmative action at the University of Michigan (UM). A neoconservative professor of philosophy, Dr. Carl Cohen, obtained UM's admissions grids through a Freedom of Information Act request and wrote a report deriding the use of affirmative action. After presenting his findings to Michigan's House and Senate, a number of Republican legislators responded to his concerns and contacted CIR regarding a potential lawsuit. CIR and Representative Deborah Whyman, who represented White suburban areas of the Detroit metropolitan area, then went on a media campaign to speak out against UM's admissions policies and solicit plaintiffs for their case.[56] CIR hoped that a second victory would ensure a federal rejection of affirmative action.

Representative Whyman sent CIR a list of two hundred potential plaintiffs, including Jennifer Gratz and Barbara Grutter, both White women. Gratz, a rejected undergraduate applicant to the College of Literature, Science, and the Arts (LSA), contacted Whyman after reading a newspaper article about a growing movement against affirmative action at UM.[57] Gratz was a high school senior with a 3.8 GPA who lived in suburban Detroit when she applied to UM.[58] Grutter, a forty-three-year-old mother of two, desired a career change and applied to the UM Law School but was also rejected.[59] CIR also included Patrick Hamacher, a White state-ranked baseball player from Flint, who had also been rejected by LSA.[60] In late 1997, CIR filed suit for Gratz (and Hamacher) in *Gratz v. Bollinger* and for Grutter in *Grutter v. Bollinger* in federal district court. At the time of these lawsuits, Lee Bollinger was the president of UM.

Again, CIR argued that affirmative action racially discriminated against Whites, violating Gratz's, Hamacher's, and Grutter's rights (and the "class they represent").[61] In order to make this argument, CIR claimed that diversity was not a compelling state interest, that there were different standards of achievement for Black and Brown students than for White students, and that race was a predominant factor in admissions decisions. This argument was easier to make for LSA, which used a grid system, and then a point system, but harder to determine in the case of the law school, which utilized individualized review of applicants. The point and grid systems represented a more mechanical approach to determining admissions decisions. They combined rankings of test scores, GPA, residency, extracurricular activities, race, and other factors, which resulted in an automatic acceptance or rejection, rather than providing a holistic consideration of each application, as was done in the law school.

In *Gratz v. Bollinger*, U.S. District Court Judge Patrick Duggan, a Reagan appointee, determined that U.S. Supreme Court precedent established that diversity was, in fact, a compelling state interest and that UM had provided evidence for this fact, utilizing the research presented by Dr. Patricia Gurin, a professor of psychology and women's studies.[62] The amicus briefs filed in support of UM's policy, including those from the Association of American Law Schools, Committee on Institutional Cooperation, and National Association of State Universities and Land-Grant Colleges, were further supportive of this point. Judge Duggan judged the grid system that UM had used from 1995 to 1997 to be an impermissible quota system but upheld the point system that UM subsequently adopted because it represented the consideration of race only as a "plus factor," among many measures, consistent with the Powell opinion in *Bakke*.

In *Grutter v. Bollinger*, Judge Bernard Friedman, also a Reagan appointee, determined that the law school placed a "heavy" emphasis on race in admissions. He was particularly influenced by the evidence provided by the plaintiffs showing that the odds of acceptance among Black, Latino, and Native American applicants were many times greater than among those of White applicants. Judge Friedman interpreted *Bakke* as *Hopwood* established: race should be considered as a remedy only for specific past discrimination.[64] Thus, in the district court, *Grutter v. Bollinger* struck down UM Law School's affirmative action plan. As this decision resulted in a victory and a defeat for both parties, both CIR and Michigan filed an appeal to the U.S. Court of Appeals for the Sixth Circuit.[63]

At the district court level, two Reagan-appointed judges came to opposite conclusions about the implementation of affirmative action policies—further pointing to what many argue is the unclear nature of the *Bakke* decision. UM immediately appealed the decision to the Sixth Circuit, which now had both *Gratz v. Bollinger* and *Grutter v. Bollinger* to consider. Barbara Perry argues that the Sixth Circuit was one of the most "ideologically contentious" among the federal appellate courts at the time because it was closely divided between liberals and conservatives; thus, appointments and nominations were often major issues of conflict.[65] CIR requested and was granted en banc hearings for both cases; this procedure, used for important cases, meant that *Gratz* and *Grutter* were heard by the full bench of judges (eleven at the time), rather than the three that typically heard most cases. In a 5–4 decision, the appellate tribunal upheld the law school's policy, thus reversing the district court decision. Whereas Judge Friedman had dismissed the law school's claim that a critical mass of minorities was not a set number, the appellate court accepted this claim and determined that it was in line with the *Bakke* decision.[66] The Sixth Circuit also allowed the intervention of Black and Latino students, represented by the NAACP LDF, with support from the Mexican American Legal Defense and Education Fund (MALDEF) and ACLU, in *Gratz* and of the Coalition to Defend Affirmative Action, Integration, and Immigrant Rights, and Fight for Equality By Any Means Necessary (known as BAMN) in *Grutter*.[67]

CIR vowed to take *Grutter* to the Supreme Court and petitioned the Court for a writ of certiorari so it could review the case. The inconsistency in decisions across the federal circuit courts (with the Sixth and Ninth Circuits supporting affirmative action and the Fifth Circuit rejecting it) encouraged the Supreme Court to grant the writ in order to provide "uniformity in the law."[68] By 2002, the Sixth Circuit had still not rendered a decision in *Gratz*, so CIR lawyers petitioned the Supreme Court for a writ of certiorari before judgment. This would allow the Supreme Court to consider both cases together. In 2002, the Supreme Court granted these writs.

CIR lawyers representing Gratz and Grutter targeted the Court's swing voter, Sandra Day O'Connor, whom everyone predicted would determine the decision in the case. They again argued that race was a predominant factor in admissions and violated their plaintiffs' right to equal protection under the law; they also asserted that (as the Reagan administration established) narrowly tailored affirmative action could be adopted only to remedy identified discrimination by the institution. Finally, they argued that both the point system used in the undergraduate college and the "critical mass" goal of the law school represented quotas, which were determined to be illegal in *Bakke*. In defense, UM lawyers argued that diversity enhanced the learning environment and thus served as a compelling state interest, that quotas were not utilized in either admissions procedures, and that these programs were specifically tailored in compliance with the Powell opinion in *Bakke*. They also argued that a decision rejecting UM's position on affirmative action would essentially overturn the *Bakke* precedent, with the potential for de facto resegregation of selective colleges and universities.[69]

Three-quarters of the one hundred amicus briefs filed in these cases were in support of UM's affirmative action plans and included briefs filed by well-known military generals, admirals, and superintendents from the U.S. Military Academy; corporations such as General Motors, DuPont, and IBM; organized labor (AFL-CIO); and other public and private universities across the country. The remaining amicus briefs supported Gratz and Grutter and were filed by conservative public interest organizations and think tanks such as the National Association of Scholars, Center for Individual Freedom, Center for the Advancement of Capitalism, and American Civil Rights Institute, an organization established by Ward Connerly and dedicated to ending affirmative action across the country. Importantly, George W. Bush's administration filed an amicus brief in support of Gratz and Grutter, making clear its position on affirmative action.[70]

In June 2003, Justice Sandra Day O'Connor rendered the 5–4 decision in *Grutter v. Bollinger*: the law school's policy was narrowly tailored and thus constitutional. Though she emphasized her hope that racial preferences would not be necessary in twenty-five years (legally interpreted by many as an expiration date), she upheld the law school's admissions policies. This decision reversed the *Hopwood v. Texas* decision.

Chief Justice William Rehnquist delivered the 6–3 decision in *Gratz v. Bollinger*: the admissions policy in the undergraduate program was not narrowly tailored to meet diversity interests because it did not require individual assessment of each applicant and, in fact, functioned as a quota. Again, these decisions resulted in both a victory and a defeat for the proponents and opponents of affirmative action. Rhetorically, the decisions affirmed diversity as a compelling state interest but required universities to narrowly tailor their policies in order not to discriminate against Whites. Justice Powell required narrow tailoring, a necessary element of the most rigorous standard of judicial review (strict scrutiny), in the *Bakke* case. The *Gratz* and *Gutter* decisions further defined how the standard of strict scrutiny must shape affirmative action policies: there must be proof of the need for diversity, the affirmative action policy must be both "least intrusive and most efficient" to meet the stated goals, the policy must be non-mechanical and adaptable, and, overall, there must be an expiration date for affirmative action.[71]

Universities across the country hurried to restructure their admissions procedures, spending millions of dollars in order to remain in compliance. Just the threat of lawsuits forced many universities to eliminate scholarships specifically earmarked for racial minorities and women, special recruitment trips targeting students of color, and summer programs aimed at recruiting minority students, while at least seventy universities opened them up to White students.[72] As CIR lawyers sought a federal elimination of affirmative action, they were unhappy with both decisions. CIR insisted that these decisions did not clarify the legality of racial preferences. Gratz and Grutter, also disappointed, began to pursue a ballot strategy like that which conservative elites and politicians had used to eliminate affirmative action in the California state constitution (see chapter 3).

The following chapter details the anti–affirmative action ballot contest in Michigan, but I note here that a challenge to the passage of this ballot proposition led to another Supreme Court case, *Schuette v. Coalition to Defend Affirmative Action (BAMN)* (2013), which ultimately decided that the electorate could legally enact state bans. In this case, BAMN, a coalition that also intervened in the *Grutter* case, sued the state of Michigan over the enforcement of the affirmative action ban, claiming that the ban violated the equal protection clause and reordered the political process in the state. The Sixth Circuit ruled that the affirmative action ban did violate the equal protection clause, but the Supreme Court upheld the anti–affirmative action ballot measure. In her dissent, Justice Sonia Sotomayor emphasized that the affirmative action ban "changed the basic rules of the political process in Michigan in a manner that uniquely disadvantaged racial minorities."[73] Continuing in her dissent, Justice Sotomayor wrote:

> While our Constitution does not guarantee minority groups victory in the political process, it does guarantee them meaningful and equal access to that process. It guarantees that the majority may not win by stacking the political process against minority groups permanently, forcing the minority alone to surmount unique obstacles in pursuit of its goals—here, educational diversity that cannot reasonably be accomplished through race-neutral measures. Today, by permitting a majority of the voters in Michigan to do what our Constitution forbids, the Court ends the debate over race-sensitive admissions policies in Michigan in a manner that contravenes constitutional protections long recognized in our precedents.[74]

White conservative elites had now reframed the equal protection clause to protect Whites from "discrimination," and BAMN's attempts to reclaim its intent failed in the Supreme Court.

The Michigan affirmative action cases were an important turning point in the legal history of affirmative action. On one hand, the decisions reinforced the determination that diversity is a governmental interest, clarifying the status of the Powell opinion in *Bakke*. Yet the decisions also reasserted the rigid legal standard of strict scrutiny, emphasizing that universities are required to consider race-neutral means of ensuring diversity before including race in the admissions process. The decisions also introduced the idea of an end date for affirmative action.

FISHER I AND *FISHER II*: STRENGTHENING STRICT SCRUTINY

After *Hopwood* dismantled affirmative action in Texas in 1996, Democratic legislators of color developed a policy that guaranteed university admission to the top 10 percent of graduating seniors in the state. I discuss this policy in detail in chapter 5, but it is also relevant here because this process admitted the top 10 percent of high school graduates in the state to any public university in the state, including the flagship campuses of Texas A&M University and UT Austin. Through this Ten Percent Plan, high-achieving high school graduates from inner-city, underresourced Black and Latino high schools could now gain access to these flagship campuses. At UT Austin, automatic admissions soon accounted for 92 percent of incoming freshman, though legislative challenges reduced this to 75 percent of incoming freshman. This policy made the competition for non–automatic admissions seats greater than that at Harvard University.[75]

After the Supreme Court decision in *Grutter v. Bollinger*, UT Austin conducted two studies to determine if it had a critical mass of underrepresented students in its student body. *Critical mass*, a term debated in *Hopwood*, *Gratz*, and *Grutter* (and often argued by conservatives to be a racial quota), is an unfixed number of underrepresented students meant to maintain an environment where students feel comfortable interacting and participating in university life. A lack of critical mass leads to racial isolation and tokenization of underrepresented students.[76]

The first study, which researched racial representation in undergraduate classes of five to twenty-four students in 2002, found that 65 percent of classes had no African American students and 90 percent had one or no African American students; 18 percent of classes had no Latinos and 43 percent had one or no Latino students; and 23 percent of classes had no Asian American students and 46 percent had one or no Asian American students. The second study, which surveyed the attitudes of students on diversity at UT Austin, reported that racially underrepresented students experienced isolation and that the majority of all students thought there was insufficient diversity on campus.[77] Administrators concluded that UT Austin had not reached critical mass, particularly when compared to the racial makeup of the state population, and proposed to introduce the consideration of race in the non–automatic admissions seats.

UT Austin admissions officials utilized a three-tiered system, which prioritized Texas residents. The first pool contained Texas residents, the second pool contained American residents of other states, and the third pool contained international applicants; each applicant competed with people in their pool for admissions seats. This admissions process allotted 90 percent of the seats to Texas residents, filled first with the automatic admissions students and then with the non-automatic admissions students. UT Austin filled the non-automatic admissions seats according to a combination of its Academic and Personal Achievement Indexes. Grades and test scores composed the Academic Index (AI), while the Personal Achievement Index (PAI) comprised three scores, two based on the application essays and the third drawing on multiple elements in the applicant's full file, including leadership roles, extracurricular activities, socioeconomic status, and home environment. After the *Grutter* decision, UT Austin added race as one of the many elements included in the PAI.[78] The majority of students were admitted to UT Austin through automatic admissions and the AI; however, after 2004, the inclusion of race in the PAI provided the opportunity for a challenge to UT Austin's admissions policy by conservative elites.

Enter Edward Blum, a former stocks trader and UT-Austin alum, working as a fellow for the conservative American Enterprise Institute. He began his political career suing districts that were drawn in ways to maximize voting power in majority-minority areas.[79] Later he became the Director of Legal Affairs for the American Civil Rights Institute, an organization founded to lead statewide campaigns to dismantle affirmative action in California and Michigan (covered in chapter 3). However, soon Blum turned his attention to challenging affirmative action at the federal level.[80]

After spending $4 million on the UM cases, CIR was ready to move on from affirmative action and focus on other libertarian causes.[81] However, Blum saw an opportunity presented by the outcomes of the UM cases, the retirement of Justice O'Connor and Chief Justice Rehnquist, and the cap placed on the UT Austin automatic admissions pool. He took up CIR's mantle and challenged the consideration of race in filling the non-automatic admission seats at UT Austin.[82]

In 2005, Blum founded the Project on Fair Representation (POFR), a one-man nonprofit cum legal defense fund, to challenge affirmative action. POFR was financially supported through a tax-exempt charitable organization called DonorsTrust, which raised money from anonymous wealthy donors and directed it to conservative causes.

According to federal law, donations to legal defense funds are taxable; however, funds routed through DonorsTrust to POFR became tax-deductible donations. Through DonorsTrust, POFR attracted such conservative donors as the Lynde and Harry Bradley Foundation and Searle Freedom Trust.[83] Commenting on the clandestine list of donors, *Mother Jones* magazine called DonorsTrust the "dark money ATM of the conservative movement."[84]

As lawyer Stephen Smith and CIR had done, Blum sought to find White students who had been rejected by UT Austin. He gave speeches at Young Conservatives of America meetings, petitioned all of his political contacts, and established the website UTnotfair.org, which solicited the stories of White rejected applicants. In 2008, his friend Richard Fisher, also an alum of UT Austin and a resident of the affluent Houston suburb Sugar Land, contacted Blum about his daughter Abigail, whose application for admission had recently been rejected by UT Austin.[85] Fisher obtained support from Wily Rein, a well-known Washington, DC, firm (one of whose partners had left to serve as President George W. Bush's counsel), and filed a lawsuit in the U.S. District Court in Austin. The suit claimed that either UT Austin's use of race in admissions did not fall into the constitutional restrictions of *Grutter* or that, if it did, *Grutter* needed to be overturned.[86] As Texas had already implemented the Top Ten Percent Law, Fisher argued that the consideration of race at UT Austin was unnecessary. Soon, another White female, Rachel Michalewicz, joined *Fisher v. University of Texas* as a plaintiff, though she withdrew before the case reached the Supreme Court.

UT Austin insisted that Fisher was not a good candidate: even if she had been given points for race, extracurricular activities, and leadership (she was given very few points in the latter categories), she would have still been rejected that year. Though the university did offer admission to students with lower test scores and grades than Fisher, forty-two were White, and only five were Black or Latino.[87] UT Austin also argued that the lawsuit was a challenge to *Grutter*, which was already decided law. The district court agreed. In 2009, Judge Sam Sparks (who ruled in favor of UT Austin's consideration of race in *Hopwood* at the district court level) upheld UT Austin's consideration of race in *Fisher* because it aligned with the *Grutter* decision.[88]

Following this defeat, Fisher's attorneys requested an en banc hearing, which they were denied. They then petitioned for a writ of certiorari from the Supreme Court, and in February 2012, the Supreme Court agreed to hear the case. The most junior Supreme Court justice, liberal Elena Kagan, recused herself from the case due to a conflict of interest: she was solicitor general when Fisher filed in district court and submitted an amicus brief in support of UT Austin's admissions policies.

Political strategists thought that the decision would come down to one vote—that of Justice Anthony Kennedy, who had never voted in support of an affirmative action plan but who supported the principle of diversity in education.[89] In the context of UT Austin's admissions standards and Fisher's index score, Justices Sotomayor and Ruth Bader Ginsburg, both liberals, asked whether the case was moot. Justice Ginsburg suggested that the Texas plan was more moderate than the UM plan upheld in the *Grutter* decision, and Justice Sotomayor accused the plaintiffs of trying to "gut" the *Grutter* decision.[90] Justice Stephen Breyer suggested that he felt no desire to reverse *Grutter*, which was supposed to stand at least twenty-five years (according to Justice O'Connor's decision) and not just nine.[91] On the other hand, Chief Justice John Roberts and Justices Antonin Scalia and Samuel Alito raised objections to UT Austin's admissions policy, indicating they were skeptical of the university's claims that a critical mass (and not quotas) was achieved through its individual review of applicants.[92] Justice Clarence Thomas, who typically remains silent during oral arguments, did not initiate a line of questioning; however, due to his record, he was expected to agree with the other conservatives (Roberts, Scalia, and Alito). Retired Justice O'Connor, the author of the *Grutter* decision, attended the court proceedings.

On June 24, 2013, the Supreme Court decided 7 to 1 to vacate the Fifth Circuit's ruling and to remand the case—that is, to send the case back to the Fifth Circuit for further review. Instead of making the final decision on whether UT Austin's use of race in admissions was constitutional, the Supreme Court concluded that the Fifth Circuit was too deferential to the university because it did not utilize strict scrutiny in assessing the affirmative action policy.[93] Although the Supreme Court reaffirmed diversity as a compelling state inter-est, the justices were not convinced that UT Austin's policies were narrowly tailored or utilized the least restrictive means. *Gratz* and *Grutter* established that universities had to institute race-neutral methods of achieving diversity, to the point of exhaustion, before considering race in admissions, and the Supreme Court decided that the Fifth Circuit had not properly examined UT Austin's actions in this regard.[94] Importantly, the Supreme Court's decision to vacate the ruling and remand the case underscored that the federal courts could no longer defer to universities in determining whether the con-sideration of race was necessary to ensure a diverse student body.

In the majority decision, written by Justice Kennedy, the Court emphasized that it is the university's burden to prove first that its admissions program is "narrowly tailored to obtain the educational benefits of diversity."[95] Once a university proves that a race-neutral plan is unworkable, then it can consider race as one of many fac-tors (and not the determinative factor) in university admissions. In the lone dissenting opinion, Justice Ginsburg stated that she did not find a need to revisit affirmative action, that race conscious-ness (rather than colorblindness) was the only way to address racial inequality, and that UT Austin's plan was appropriate because race was only "a factor of a factor of a factor of a factor" in its admis-sions policy.[96]

The Fifth Circuit's reconsideration of the case resulted in a 2–1 decision holding that UT Austin's use of race in filling the non–automatic admissions spots was constitutional. The judges concluded that UT Austin's admissions policy included a "holistic review" of each application and was "nearly indistinguishable" from that of the UM Law School (which *Grutter* upheld).[97] Fisher peti-tioned for a writ of certiorari from the Supreme Court, arguing that the Fifth Circuit did not apply strict scrutiny to the consideration of race. Interestingly, Fisher's team also argued that the inclusion of race in the non–automatic admissions process asserted stereo-types by assuming that the minorities admitted through automatic admissions were not dynamic enough; ultimately, they claimed that UT Austin's "qualitative" diversity rationale (derived from *Bakke* and *Grutter*) was based on racial stereotypes.[98] The Supreme Court decided to hear the case, designated *Fisher II*, to determine if the Fifth Circuit had correctly applied strict scrutiny. Justice Kagan again recused herself from the case.

In a 4–3 decision, the Supreme Court determined that UT Austin's consideration of race in admissions was constitutional. A surprise to legal commentators, Justice Kennedy's majority opinion upheld UT Austin's policy while emphasizing that the university (and others, by extension) would have to regularly review its policy and abide by strict scrutiny.[99] Undeterred, Blum sought to organize new cases that would challenge affirmative action at the University of North Carolina and Harvard University. Decisions in these cases are pending at the district court level. Abandoning the recruitment of White women as plaintiffs, Blum has now made Asian American students the face of Students for Fair Admissions (an organization that grew out of POFR) and anti-affirmative action litigation.

Overall, these legal cases have not eliminated affirmative action. However, they have significantly restricted the means by which it can be implemented. The federal courts no longer defer to universities' determination that the consideration of race is needed to ensure diversity. Universities now have to prove that diversity is necessary and attempt race-neutral methods before including race as a factor in admissions. Once universities prove that race-neutral plans are unworkable, any plan that considers race through measures beyond holistic, individualized review equates to the unconstitutional use of racial quotas. Universities have to exercise caution when articulating critical mass goals, as these can also be framed as quotas. In addition to setting an end date for the use of affirmative action, universities have to review their policies regularly. And, overall, universities need to apply the most rigorous legal standard of review, strict scrutiny, to their affirmative action plans. Affirmative action has surprisingly persisted through many challenges, but with the legal environment growing more hostile to affirmative action, the Supreme Court slanting even more rightward, and universities fearing costly lawsuits, the policy is on unsteady ground. The methodical chipping away at affirmative action, as the efforts of civil rights legal activists in unraveling de jure racial segregation, may ultimately lead to its elimination.

WHITE VICTIMHOOD STRATEGY IN THE FEDERAL COURTS

Conservative elites deployed a racial political strategy of White victimhood in the federal courts, appropriating civil rights legal tactics and rearticulating White subjectivity as being victimized (table 2.2). Although this strategy has yet to produce a federal elimination of

TABLE 2.2 Use of White victimhood strategy in the federal courts

Discourse (legal argument)	☐ Affirmative action violates equal protection under the law
	☐ Affirmative action allows different standards of achievement
	☐ Diversity is not a state interest
	☐ Specific racial discrimination is not identified
	☐ Separate committees, grid systems, point systems, and "critical mass" are all quotas
	☐ Narrow tailoring/strict scrutiny is not utilized
	☐ Race-neutral methods work
Target	☐ The state (via federal courts)
Tactics	☐ Class action lawsuits
	☐ White female lead plaintiffs
Outcomes (final decisions)	☐ Diversity is not a state interest *(Hopwood v. Texas)*
	☐ Race is to be considered only to remedy identified specific racial discrimination *(Hopwood v. Texas)*
	☐ Affirmative action can violate Whites' equal protection under the law
	☐ Diversity is a state interest
	☐ Affirmative action policies require narrow tailoring and strict scrutiny
	☐ Affirmative action has an expiration date
	☐ Courts should not defer to universities in exercising strict scrutiny
Rearticulation	☐ Affirmative action victimizes Whites

affirmative action, conservative legal strategists have used it to successfully chisel away at the means to implement the policy and have legally elevated colorblind methods to achieve diversity. The White victimhood strategy drives political struggle over affirmative action through the legal recognition of White victimization and the curtailed implementation of the policy. The persistent legal struggle over affirmative action also shapes the shifting boundaries of diversity and colorblindness.

In these cases, White conservative elite men appropriated racial and gendered vulnerability in the quest to construct a new White subjectivity. Conservatives' use of NAACP civil rights legal tactics represents a significant appropriation of Black oppositional strategy as a means of asserting White victimhood and consolidating colorblindness. In this way, conservative legal strategists claimed a fabricated moral descent from desegregation efforts and aimed to shift legal precedent and legal "sense" in favor of colorblindness. While legal strategists constructed a White victimized subjectivity in different ways throughout the cases, their use of White female plaintiffs communicated ideas about White women as sympathetic victims harmed by affirmative action. This gendered vulnerability, connecting the quite disparate life experiences of Cheryl Hopwood and Abigail Fisher, played a central role in rearticulating Whiteness as victimized and vulnerable. Additionally, the use of legal tactics in political struggle over affirmative action reflects the collective identity of White male institutional insiders with the resources and expertise available to mount multiple legal challenges.

Conservative legal strategists also mobilized racialized ideas about meritocracy and achievement to argue that White students' right to equal protection under the law had been violated. The reputation of elite public universities relies heavily on high achievement; thus, by framing their plaintiffs as high achieving and the underrepresented admits as mediocre, conservative legal strategists constructed affirmative action as harmful and unjust. Merit, a social construction of deservingness, shifts according to university priorities. Selective universities consider many factors in their admissions policies, including a high GPA, rigorous coursework, elevated test scores, and other personal qualities and engagements. Yet many still believe that certain kinds of students (often class-privileged White and Asian students with high test scores) are entitled to admission to selective universities. Thus, it is unsurprising that conservative legal strategists do not question admissions policies that privilege the children of alumni or wealthy benefactors and instead focus on students who have been historically excluded from admission. Equating multiple affirmative action programs to racial quotas leveraged the restrictions enforced by *Bakke*, and the emphasis of strict scrutiny also whittled down the means to ensure moderate diversity at selective universities. This is one way to ensure that universities will soon have few alternatives to race-neutral or colorblind policies.

The legal confusion regarding *Bakke*'s split decision provided ample opportunity for conservatives to challenge affirmative action and for the federal courts to take on anti–affirmative action cases. Though many liberals interpret the culmination of these affirmative action legal decisions positively because the policy still persists, these decisions contribute to the narrowing of affirmative action. The federal courts' emphasis on strict scrutiny and consistent review, and their rulings against multiple affirmative action plans legitimized the claim of White victimization by the policy. This legitimation of White victimhood redraws boundaries around state-recognized racial discrimination and elevates colorblindness in the law, redefining post–civil rights racial hegemony.

Court decisions clarified that diversity is indeed a state interest but that universities have to justify this interest on campus. These cases illustrate the persistence of the diversity logic, not only in universities but also in State agencies and the corporate sector, as evidenced by the numerous amicus curiae briefs submitted in support of affirmative action. Diversity has been a key racial logic in post–civil rights racial politics. It has endured as a defense of affirmative action, yet the suggestion of an expiration date indicates that diversity's persistence as a state interest may change over time. Affirmative action's legal justification has shifted from racial redress for past racial discrimination, to the benefits of diverse classes for campus culture. However, the more universities are forced to adopt race-neutral methods to ensure campus diversity, the greater the likelihood that the legal justification of diversity will disappear in efforts to prioritize colorblindness.

3

BOARD VOTES AND BALLOT INITIATIVES

Racial Political Strategy in Trustee Decision-Making and State Elections

You start out in 1954 by saying, "Nigger, nigger, nigger." By 1968 you can't say "nigger"—that hurts you, it backfires. So you say stuff like, forced busing, states' rights, and all that stuff, and you're getting so abstract. Now, you're talking about cutting taxes, and all these things you're talking about are totally economic things and the byproduct of them is blacks get hurt worse than whites. And, subconsciously, maybe that is part of it. . . . I'm saying that if it is getting that abstract and that coded then we're doing away with the racial problem one way or the other, you follow me? "We want to cut this," is much more abstract than even the busing thing . . . and a hell of a lot more abstract than "Nigger, nigger." So any way you look at it, race is coming on the back burner.

—Lee Atwater, Reagan advisor and campaign consultant and former chairman of the Republican National Committee, 1981

THIS OFT-QUOTED passage from an interview conducted by political scientist Alexander Lamis explicitly conveys how racial discourse has functioned as a key element of mid- to late twentieth-century Republican political strategy. Atwater's quote not only traces the evolution of racial discourse in Republican political strategy but also provides an example of the ways that a colorblind racial logic codes, but does not eliminate, racial attitudes and policies that disadvantage Black people in particular. Atwater claims that the role of racial meaning in this political strategy is "on the back burner." However, its active role in mobilizing the White electorate suggests discourse adaption to the post–civil rights racial hegemony, in which explicit articulation of racism is frowned on but coded racism flourishes. Racial political strategies are key to American conservative mobilization and policy platforms across space and time.

Rather than focusing solely on challenging affirmative action in the federal courts, conservatives' tactical repertoire also included the targeting of universities' internal decision-making through boards of trustees and developing anti–affirmative action ballot initiatives. Their efforts aimed to dismantle open admissions as well as affirmative action, targeting race- and class-access policies at elite and working-class institutions. In these political struggles, conservatives deployed two racial political strategies: (1) an inferior-race and -class strategy, in which they blamed institutional decline at the City University of New York (CUNY) on its working-class students of color, and (2) a racial preferences strategy, in which they framed underrepresented students as racially preferred in the states of California and Michigan. Both strategies provided conservatives with the justification for policy elimination.

In this chapter, I explore how conservatives influenced trustee decision-making in order to dismantle open admissions and affirmative action in the CUNY and University of California (UC) systems, and developed statewide affirmative action bans through ballot initiatives that voters approved in California and Michigan. Then I examine cases of failed ballot propositions in Colorado and Missouri, highlighting the factors that contributed to conservative defeat. Finally, I reflect on how racial political strategies shaped conservative mobilization in these cases.

UNDERMINING INSTITUTIONAL AUTONOMY: RACIAL POLITICAL STRATEGIES AND BOARDS OF TRUSTEES

Boards of trustees, also called boards of regents and boards of governors, supervise the activities of universities and guard institutional autonomy. As defined in *Sweezy v. New Hampshire* (1957), a Supreme Court case that upheld academic freedom in the face of McCarthyism, a university's institutional autonomy consists of the right "to determine for itself on academic grounds who may teach, what may be taught, how it shall be taught, and who may be admitted to study."[1] While the public widely understands faculty academic freedom as part of this institutional autonomy, court cases have clarified that academic freedom rests with the institution and not the faculty, granting trustees and administrators further authority.[2] The trustees of a university are responsible for preserving its institutional autonomy, reviewing its educational mission and programs, authorizing its long-term plans, safeguarding its financial solvency, enhancing its public image, and appointing (and firing) its president. Trustee boards at public institutions have, at times, functioned as a barrier between the university and the politicians and legislatures that try to influence it; however, because trustees are largely appointed by governors, state assemblies, and sometimes mayors, they can become the primary conduit through which political causes and controversies erupt at universities. With the expansion of mass higher education after World War II, boards of trustees were tasked with institutional maintenance, largely through fund-raising, and thus businesspeople, political hopefuls, and other elites were most often appointed to these positions.[3] In the CUNY and UC systems, these political hopefuls propelled the successful retrenchment of race- and class-inclusive admissions policies.

In their efforts to restrict and eliminate race- and class-inclusive policies, conservative elites targeted the decision-making of university boards of trustees, the primary governing bodies of American public universities. Conservative think tanks and elected officials formally and informally influenced the political agendas of trustee members, and Black and Latino trustees served as minority spokespersons for policy retrenchment. These tactics relied on the malleability of politically appointed trustees and focused on an internal dismantling of affirmative action and open admissions by the trustees, even in the face of opposition from faculty, students, and community members.

In this section, I examine conservative mobilization in political struggle over open admissions in the CUNY system and affirmative action in the UC system. In the CUNY system, conservative elites successfully utilized an inferior-race and -class strategy, which discursively framed Black and Latino working-class students as academically deficient and projected a vision of meritocracy and institutional efficiency. In the UC system, conservative elites mobilized a racial preferences strategy, framing underrepresented students as unfairly racially preferred and arguing that affirmative action violated the meritocracy of the prominent UC system. Conservative elites also utilized the racial preferences strategy in promoting anti–affirmative action ballot propositions in California and Michigan.

CITY UNIVERSITY OF NEW YORK: REMAKING THE MISSION OF A WORKING-CLASS INSTITUTION

In New York, affirmative action was not the center of political struggle; instead, challenges to open admissions threatened to redefine the mission of the CUNY system. The CUNY situation is significant for illustrating that a less selective institution and a class-based admissions policy won by Black and Brown students—open admissions— would also be targets of conservatives. While the policies are different, affirmative action and open admissions both emerged as a means of creating educational access for Black and Brown students, and both policies underwent challenges by conservative think tanks, politicians, and foundations in the 1990s.

Many scholars cite New York as the first target for neoliberal political and economic restructuring in the United States, beginning with investment bankers' "financial coup" over the city during the fiscal crisis of the 1970s.[4] The sacrifice of public services by city and state officials immediately had a direct impact on CUNY, which charged tuition for the first time in 1976.[5] Neoconservatives had complained about open admissions since its development, arguing that the policy promoted minimal educational standards and diverged from the history of the well-respected meritocratic city colleges.[6] Public primary and secondary schools in Black and Brown communities continued to decline as a result of a shrinking tax base and dwindling public funds, and the need for remediation grew as entering students, despite their high grade averages, were found to have significant remedial needs.[7] Remediation was the cornerstone of open admissions, and with almost 75 percent of incoming students in the senior (four-year) colleges needing at least one remedial class, it cost CUNY millions of dollars a year—an amount that was more than some trustees and think tank affiliates thought was appropriate.[8]

In 1994, the state of New York, politically divided by the liberal New York City metropolitan area and the more conservative upstate population, elected a new Republican governor, George Pataki. Pataki narrowly beat the Democratic three-term incumbent, Mario Cuomo, and was elected by upstate voters, capturing only a quarter of New York City votes—the city's lowest vote for a New York governor in the twentieth century.[9] Pataki promoted strong mayoral decision-making in the affairs of education. The Republican mayor of New York City, Rudolph Giuliani, known for his aggressive stance on crime and punishment, rapid transformation of seedy Times Square into a tourist destination, and privatization of failing public primary and secondary schools, was ready to make changes to the city's higher education system.[10] Political alignment among state and city officials created advantageous political conditions for a successful challenge to open admissions from inside the political bureaucracy.

Trustees appointed by Giuliani and Pataki ended open admissions in CUNY's senior colleges. Of the sixteen voting trustees, Giuliani appointed five, Pataki appointed six, four (including three liberals) had been chosen by the previous governor, and one represented the student senate. Additionally, one nonvoting member represented the faculty senate. Giuliani also placed three of his five appointees on additional committees across the city, signifying their loyalty to his political agenda. To chair the Board of Trustees, Pataki chose Anne Paolucci, a former English professor who was the wife of a leader of the New York State Conservative Party (the architect of Pataki's election campaign).[11] Additionally, he selected Kenneth E. Cook, a failed Conservative Party candidate for the state legislature, and attorney John Calandra Jr., the son of a prominent conservative senator who had publicly opposed open admissions.[12] At the time, the board presided over eleven senior colleges, six community colleges, and two graduate and professional schools.

Think tanks such as the Manhattan Institute for Policy Research, Empire Foundation (founded by the antitax lobbying group Change NY), and Olin Foundation campaigned and fund-raised for Pataki's

election campaign.[13] The Manhattan Institute, Empire Foundation, and American Council of Trustees and Alumni (a conservative
alumni lobby founded and led by Lynne Cheney, two years away from
serving as "second lady" of the United States) had all issued formal
reports and publications regarding what they called the "minimal
standards" at CUNY, the need to center the core curriculum around
Western civilization, and the demand to end open admissions.[14]

Heather Mac Donald, a fellow and writer for *City Journal*, the Manhattan Institute's magazine, reflected much of the Right's discursive
framing of CUNY. She claimed that CUNY students did not have the
"drive to work hard" and that the students participating in Search for
Education, Elevation and Knowledge, or SEEK (an academic support
program historically established for Black and Latino students) were
"academically deficient." She advocated that SEEK and its community college counterpart, College Discovery, be shut down and their
funds reallocated to the Honors College, a new CUNY experiment in
attracting more prestigious students.[15] Mac Donald wrote with nostalgia about a CUNY that was once majority-White and "elite" but
now was a "backwater of remediation and race politics."[16] This discursive framing of CUNY as a deficient, backward, and failed system
was essential to the mobilization against open admissions. For the
most part, this discourse did not refer to students of color explicitly; however, open admissions had made the already working-class
CUNY system majority-minority, and the characterization of this system and these students as deficient functioned as a racial code: these
"backward" and undeserving pupils were working-class students of
color. This characterization legitimized a larger vision that would
remake the system into a place more desirable to middle-class students. By characterizing the system as backward and deficient, without referencing decades of decreased state and city funding (policies
driven by conservatives), conservative elites worked to justify policy
retrenchment in the public sphere.

Conservative spokespersons of color, who signify the absence of
racial inequality and chastise the social and economic performance
of Black and Latinos, are important actors in racial political struggle
and serve as a significant element in the post–civil rights conservative tactical repertoire. Board Vice Chair Herman Badillo played an

important role as a Latino conservative spokesperson who opposed not only open admissions but also bilingual education (which he had championed earlier in his career as the first Puerto Rican congressman representing the Bronx).[17]

Badillo, appointed to the CUNY Board of Trustees in 1990 by Democratic Governor Mario Cuomo, had a respected political career, serving as a congressman, Bronx borough president, and deputy mayor under Mayor Ed Koch in the 1970s, and had built a loyal Puerto Rican constituency in New York City.[18] However, his reversal on bilingual education and rejection of remediation at CUNY, along with his disparaging comments about Latinos—including claims that Latinos had a "lax work ethic" and that Mexican and Dominican students from "the hills" did not come from a tradition of education and thus were inadequate students—turned many in the Latino community against him.[19] But by this point, the loss of support from Latino communities did not matter to Badillo; he had retained political relevance by serving as Giuliani's personal education advisor. Pataki promoted Badillo to vice chair of the Board of Trustees, and Giuliani appointed him cochair of the CUNY Advisory Task Force, an external committee organized by the mayor to research and develop an administrative agenda for CUNY.[20] This strategic appointment to vice chair of the Board of Trustees operated as expected: with the ear of Pataki, Giuliani, and the Manhattan Institute (which later appointed him as a senior fellow), Badillo led the charge against open admissions on the Board of Trustees and on the CUNY Advisory Task Force.

The CUNY Advisory Task Force's main function was to challenge the institutional autonomy of CUNY. The mayor tasked this group, also called the Schmidt Commission, as it was led by Benno C. Schmidt Jr., with researching and developing an administrative agenda for CUNY, an expected charge of trustee boards.[21] Giuliani stacked this task force with conservatives, including Heather Mac Donald, the Manhattan Institute fellow and writer who had already called for the end of open admissions, and Schmidt, president of the Edison Project, a for-profit educational management organization that worked to "charter-ize" elementary and secondary schooling.[22] Other members included the vice president of the Edison Project,[23] an investment banker,[24] the president of a private welfare-to-work city contractor,[25] and a liberal former state senate leader who had been indicted for mismanaging public funds.[26] New York City Council Speaker Peter F. Vallone said of this group, "The Task Force was not set up to do what's best for the educational system but to expedite privatization."[27]

The CUNY Advisory Task Force released its own report on the status of CUNY and directed board members (at the behest of Vice Chair Badillo) to prioritize a trustee vote on ending remediation. That report, titled *The City University of New York: An Institution Adrift*, called for a total restructuring of the university, including the designation of select campuses as flagship institutions, the implementation of stricter quantitative performance standards, and the elimination of remediation in the senior colleges.[28] Remedial education was central to the open admissions policy; with the end of remediation in the senior colleges and the adoption of more rigorous standardized testing, open admissions would be destroyed.

The Board of Trustees accepted the directives of the CUNY Advisory Task Force and prioritized a vote on ending remediation. As the vote approached and as political strategists, news reporters, and city council members debated the potential outcome, Pataki sought to speed up the approval of a new trustee who would take the seat of pro–open admissions trustee Susan M. Mouner, a liberal appointee of Cuomo. Liberal city politicians and board members claimed the governor and mayor were being too "heavy-handed" in influencing the politics of CUNY by rushing to appoint a trustee who would vote in their favor. Although the state senate did not approve Pataki's appointee before the vote, even Mouner's vote could not save the policy. On May 26, 1998, the board voted to end remediation, and thus open admissions, in the CUNY senior colleges by a 9–6 vote. Board Chair Paolucci commented to reporters after the vote: "We have had a period of 30 years of neglect. We are cleaning out the four-year colleges and putting remediation where it belongs."[29]

Students and faculty sued the Board of Trustees, claiming that the university violated the state's open meeting law by throwing out protestors and all public attendees during the vote on open admissions, and a judge granted them a preliminary injunction that halted the implementation of the vote.[30] The trustees responded by simply holding another vote in a larger auditorium during the winter break. While hundreds of students in attendance protested, the board again voted 10–5 to end remediation and open admissions.[31] The Faculty University Senate released its own report in response, *CUNY: An Institution Affirmed*,[32] and held hearings, speaking out against the proposed changes. Students protested inside and outside board meetings and at graduation ceremonies, and both faculty and students were arrested at these protests. The State Board of Regents subsequently approved a compromise plan, brokered by a coalition of former CUNY administrators and faculty (Friends of CUNY), that delayed elimination of remediation at the most impacted campuses and ended open admissions in CUNY's senior colleges.[33] In these three votes, much of what student activists accomplished as a result of their takeover of City College in 1969 had been eradicated. It soon became clear that the end of open admissions in the senior colleges was one part of a larger strategic plan to remake CUNY into an institution more attractive to middle-class students (as explored in chapter 5).

UNIVERSITY OF CALIFORNIA: THE EMERGENCE OF A POLITICAL WEDGE ISSUE

Conservatives eliminated affirmative action through a two-part process in California. The Board of Regents voted to end affirmative action in hiring and university admissions in the UC system on July 20, 1995, and a year later the California electorate voted to adopt a ballot proposition that ended affirmative action in university admissions, hiring, and state contracting. While I cover the ballot tactic separately in the next section, the events in both California and Michigan exhibit the use of multiple tactics to dismantle affirmative action and shape public opinion about race politics.

California has a liberal political reputation, though by the 1990s it largely leaned Republican in gubernatorial elections (with notable exceptions being father and son Pat and Jerry Brown). However, the electorate voted for Democratic candidates for many federal, state, and local offices, reflecting the large, diverse progressive populations in the San Francisco Bay and Los Angeles metropolitan area. In contrast, wealthier suburban and poorer White inland areas voted for Republicans. In the early 1990s, an economic downturn in the state, evidenced by massive job losses for the educated white-collar middle class, stagnating wages, and declining home prices ruptured the American Dream for many middle- and working-class families: more than 90 percent of Californians polled in 1992 and 1993 felt that they were living in bad economic times.[34] Republican Governor Pete Wilson was reelected in 1995, in the midst of an economic recovery and after the passage of the controversial Proposition 187 (which denied social services to undocumented immigrants and their children), launching him into the national political spotlight at this precise moment.[35]

At that time, the Republicans desperately wanted to reclaim the presidency in 1996. Many wondered if Governor Wilson, a moderate Republican, would become the Republican nominee for President.[36] Although Wilson had supported affirmative action earlier in his career and had signed twenty-four bills that included this policy, Republicans searched for an issue that could split the White male vote from the Democratic Party and could garner California's electoral college votes (which had gone to Bill Clinton in the previous election).[37] The California electorate did not rank affirmative action as a priority in any polling conducted in the state. However, the Republican Party saw affirmative action as a political wedge issue that could capture the electorate and gain the party more power statewide and on a national scale.[38]

By the mid-1990s, challenges to race-inclusive policies in the UC system were not new. The landmark Supreme Court split decision in *Regents of the University of California v, Bakke* (1978) eliminated racial quotas in UC Davis's Medical School admissions process and broadly reinterpreted affirmative action policies, so that race could be a factor in determining university admissions but could not be the defining factor. This decision forced educational institutions to abandon proactive, assertive affirmative action policies in favor of less legally vulnerable practices, which emphasized diversity alongside meritocratic values but facilitated a diminishing commitment to campus race and class diversity.

As early as 1988, the U.S. Department of Education's Office for Civil Rights began an investigation of admissions procedures at

UC Berkeley and UCLA after receiving complaints that these campuses were capping Asian student enrollment.[39] Asian students, who applied to and enrolled in UC schools in large numbers, had the highest grades and academic qualifications, and thus admission based solely on grades and test scores would have essentially rendered certain campuses (particularly the first-choice universities, UC Berkeley and UCLA) majority-Asian. While seventy-five graduate departments of UCLA were cleared of wrongdoing, the investigation concluded that the Mathematics Department had discriminated against Asians in 1987 and 1988. In addition, UC Berkeley's School of Law (Boalt Hall) was forced to change its admissions procedures, under which applicants of color competed against each other for spots.[40]

While the investigation concluded that UC Berkeley and UCLA had generally followed the appropriate procedures regarding admissions, the UC Berkeley chancellor apologized for the drop in Asian admittance in the late 1980s, although he denied that policies were in place to restrict Asian enrollment.[41] In the fall of 1990, for the first time, Asians outnumbered Whites in UC Berkeley's freshman class; this trend would continue, with UC Berkeley's 2017 undergraduate population composed of 42.4 percent Asian students and 24.5 percent White students.[42] Students of Chinese descent made up the majority of these Asian students at 18.6 percent, with "South Asians" following behind at 10.4 percent.[43] Overall, these investigations into enrollment caps and race-sensitive admissions policies in the UC system, at a time when elite public universities were becoming more competitive, provide an important context for the elimination of affirmative action policies in the mid-1990s.

The UC Board of Regents is a twenty-six-member body that governs the UC system (nine campuses in the mid-1990s); eighteen are appointees of the governor (for twelve-year terms), one is a student regent (for a one-year term), and the rest serve in state political positions (such as the speaker of the state assembly) or university roles (such as the president of the UC system and the president of the alumni association). Regents are popularly understood to receive appointments as a reward for generous donations to the political campaign of the governor.[44] In 1995, only one regent, conservative economist W. Glenn Campbell, had any previous relationship to academia: he had established the Hoover Institution, the nationally renowned conservative think tank at Stanford University. In the 1980s, twenty-six Hoover scholars were on leave working for the Reagan administration.[45] Governor Wilson's appointees included Meredith Khachigian, the wife of his campaign manager; Tirso Del Junco, the former chair of the state's Republican Party; and assorted business owners and attorneys.[46]

The public face of resistance to affirmative action was Regent Ward Connerly, a Black Republican businessman and close friend of Pete Wilson. Connerly fulfilled a role similar to that of Herman Badillo at CUNY: racial-minority spokesperson who champions conservative causes while claiming that his own success proves that racism has been overcome. Governor Wilson appointed Connerly to the Board of Regents in 1993.[47] Prior to his appointment, Connerly had made public statements against affirmative action in state contracting since at least 1991, though his own business had registered as a minority firm in order to benefit from the policy.[48]

In 1994, Jerry and Ellen Cook, White university educators from the affluent community of La Jolla in San Diego, contacted Regent Connerly and other regents with their own statistical reports about affirmative action in the UC system.[49] Though Ivy League and other elite universities had accepted their son James into doctoral and medical programs, the UC San Diego Medical School had rejected him. The Cooks determined that Chicano and Black students were many more times likely to gain admission to the UC San Diego Medical School than were White and Asian students.[50] Their personal campaign against affirmative action provided an opportunity for Connerly to justify elimination of affirmative action policies in the UC system. In the summer of 1994, Connerly urged regents board chair Clair Burgener, a former Republican state senator, to contact the UC Office of the President about this affirmative action problem. The Office of the President added a discussion about affirmative action to the October 1994 board meeting agenda.[51] At the same time, an initiative proposing to ban affirmative action throughout the state gained Connerly's attention and support. Connerly called for a formal review of affirmative action throughout the UC system, asking each campus to submit its affirmative action policies. Over the next few months, the regents would deliberate over affirmative action with the UC president, UC General Counsel, and campus specific leadership.

In February 1995, Governor Wilson spoke out against affirmative action at the California Republican convention. That spring, after receiving write-ups about his anti–affirmative action crusade in publications across the country, Connerly began to write publicly about the need to end affirmative action, penning "UC Must End Affirmative Action" in the *San Francisco Chronicle*.[52] Regents meetings were suddenly packed with press and protestors. At the June 1995 meeting, Connerly announced that he would present his proposals to end affirmative action at the July regents meeting.[53] He presented the following proposals to the board: Special Policy 1, the elimination of affirmative action in hiring and promotion, and Special Policy 2, the elimination of affirmative action in university admissions. Arnold L. Leiman, chair of the UC-wide Academic Council, complained that this short window of time (less than a month) did not give administrators, faculty, and regents enough time to discuss and consider the proposals, saying "These measures were presented to administration and faculty as legislative enactment that needed to be implemented, rather than proceed through the political course of analysis, compromise, and agreement."[54] The UC regents and administrators had generally discussed the merits and pitfalls of the multitude of affirmative action admissions plans utilized across the nine campuses in the previous year, but they had less than a month to respond to proposals to eliminate affirmative action at every level in the UC system.[55]

Connerly went on a public campaign in which he spoke out against affirmative action; wrote articles arguing for the end of the policy in *Policy Review*, a publication of the Hoover Institution, and other publications; and spoke to local and national news media.[56] In a piece that was published after the elimination of affirmative action in California but that reflected a larger campaign to end the policy in multiple states, Connerly said:

> Although their ancestors successfully struggled to overcome tremendous obstacles, many young blacks seem to be lacking in the area that matters most in a modern, global economy: a competitive desire and self-confidence in one's ability to compete in academic

pursuits. . . . The major obstacle facing the average black person in America is not race; it is the attitude and approach of black people toward their role in American society. If we have any hope of moving America forward in its attitudes toward race, we must get black people to acknowledge and act on their role in resolving this issue.[57]

In his comments here and elsewhere, Connerly projected a color-blind orientation by denying the persistence of the structural obstacles that African Americans face in the contemporary period and thus holding them responsible for racial inequality. Rather than acknowledge inherited disadvantage or admit that his own business and networks benefited from affirmative action policies (and propelled him into a position on the Board of Regents), Connerly portrayed himself throughout the article as a self-made man and argued that Black people are demeaned not by being subjected to institutional racism but by benefiting from affirmative action programs in education and employment. Similar to the political actors involved in ending CUNY's open admissions policy, he described Black people as deficient in confidence, aspiration, and ultimately academic skill. By framing Black and Latino students as lacking the motivation to succeed, though seeking admission to and enrolling in institutions of higher education is clearly a marker of ambition, Connerly reified stereotypes of Black and Latino inferiority. Conservative minority spokespersons mobilize these stereotypes by invoking community membership as a license to reprimand poor behavior.

Governor Wilson, who politically strategized with Connerly, sought to make affirmative action a political wedge issue as a means of gaining wide support for a possible presidential run. Affirmative action was an attractive issue, as it would provoke a largely White, but also Asian constituency across political parties.[58] Connerly, aligned with Wilson, pursued this battle to gain notoriety in the conservative world. It would not be hard to convince the other regents to abandon affirmative action; in fact, at least thirteen regents had contributed money to Governor Wilson's campaigns and would likely vote against policies he opposed.[59]

On July 20, 1995, during a twelve-hour meeting at the UC San Francisco campus—with hundreds of protestors, media, and even the

Reverend Jesse Jackson in attendance—the regents ended affirmative action in admissions and hiring in the UC system. The open meeting, broadcast live by local radio and television stations, quickly turned into a closed meeting; the regents decided to move to a contingency room when attendees began to sing protest songs and someone reportedly called in a bomb threat after the first vote on hiring and promotion.[60] Though Governor Wilson had not attended a Board of Regents meeting since 1992, he took control of this convening, telling the regents "We cannot tolerate university policies or practices that violate fundamental fairness, trampling individual rights to create and give preference to group rights. . . . The people who work hard to pay those taxes and who play by the rules deserve a guarantee that their children will get an equal opportunity to compete for admission to university—regardless of race or gender."[61] Many news publications later commented on his political grandstanding at the event.[62] Wilson's discourse framed affirmative action as antimeritocratic and mobilized principles of fairness and individual rights—hallmarks of colorblind ideology.

Jack Peltason, the president of the UC system, began his remarks at the meeting by proposing that the campuses institute a more comprehensive review of admissions and hiring practices without ending affirmative action. He noted:

> Our affirmative action and other diversity programs have been a powerful tool in helping us prepare California for its future. The chancellors, the provost, the vice-presidents, the academic student leadership are united in urging the Regents to reaffirm our 30-year commitment to the twin goals of diversity and excellence. So let me reassure you that whatever the board decides, we will faithfully carry out your policies.[63]

On the first vote, the regents ended affirmative action in hiring and promotion (15–10). On the second vote, they ended affirmative action in university admissions (14–10, with one abstention).

Notably, the president, provost, chancellors, academic senates, and student governments of every UC campus opposed an end to affirmative action in hiring, promotion, and admissions and made this clear at the regents meeting.[64] Additionally, delegates of the system's major staff organizations, representatives of the alumni associations, and faculty representatives on the Board of Regents disagreed with the elimination of affirmative action.[65] When asked by a reporter why no chancellor was able to persuade the board to vote differently, one regent said, "Who knows what a chancellor is? We were appointed by the governor and everyone knows what a governor is."[66] Governor Wilson held his largest fund-raiser soon after this vote.[67]

Wilson dropped out of the presidential race that fall, but Connerly went on to utilize his board influence and public visibility to champion the California Civil Rights Initiative, later Proposition 209 on the ballot (covered in the next section), which amended the California Constitution to outlaw affirmative action throughout the state. He also established his own conservative organization, the American Civil Rights Institute (ACRI), which aimed to eliminate affirmative action in states across the country. Subsequently, Connerly became a key leader in successful campaigns to end affirmative action in Michigan, Washington, Nebraska, and Arizona.

While conservatives utilized the same trustee tactic to dismantle race- and class-inclusive admissions policies, they mobilized different racial political strategies in the CUNY and UC systems as a result of the different institutional contexts and expectations. Connerly argued that affirmative action unfairly preferred Black and Brown students in a competitive admissions environment. As UC had garnered an elite reputation, anti–affirmative action crusaders' aim was not to transform the institutional mission or the system's elevated standing but instead to maintain the academically competitive environment. By framing underrepresented students as unfairly racially preferred, anti–affirmative action supporters questioned the ability of UC to maintain educational quality with ostensibly unqualified students on elite, competitive campuses.

On the other hand, the elimination of open admissions, with the goal of transforming CUNY into a more attractive system for middle-class students, communicated an explicit break with the reputation of the university system. CUNY leadership aimed to elevate the profile of the university and did this, in part, by disparaging working-class students of color, framing these students as academically deficient and as a reflection of the dysfunction of the CUNY system. The open admissions policy did not communicate race, yet it transformed CUNY into a majority-minority system; thus, racial coding accompanied class implications in anti–open admissions discourse. Conservatives utilized the racial preferences strategy as a means of preserving UC's elite status and the inferior-race and -class strategy as a means of elevating the CUNY system, in which they rejected its working-class educational mission and embraced a new strategic plan.

STATE CONSTITUTIONAL AMENDMENTS: RACIAL PREFERENCES STRATEGY AND BALLOT PROPOSITIONS

In the United States, direct vote processes in which petitions signed by citizens can place measures on the ballot to amend state constitutions or to repeal acts of the legislature exist in eighteen and twenty-five states, respectively. The following states have passed affirmative action bans by ballot proposition: California (1996), Washington (1998), Michigan (2006), Nebraska (2008), Arizona (2010), and Oklahoma (2012). I draw specific attention to ballot contests in California and Michigan because in both states the ballot propositions emerged as the second tactical assault on affirmative action. In California, the UC regents had already eliminated affirmative action in the UC system when the ballot campaign surfaced; in Michigan, after what conservatives determined to be defeats in *Gratz* and *Grutter*, the ballot campaign aimed to finish what the court cases could not.

These ballot contests relied on the racial preferences strategy, which appropriated and manipulated civil rights rhetoric and symbolism, and erased the term *affirmative action* from ballot language. Insidiously, the ballot language of these propositions broadly communicated "anti-discrimination" (historically referencing discrimination against African Americans and other racial minorities) to voters not invested in the political race. Yet in discourse about these propositions, conservatives framed Blacks and Latinos as not only unqualified but racially preferred in relation to the wronged, but deserving, White, and sometimes Asian, candidates. Key to this racial preferences strategy was the support of conservative think tanks, conservative racial-minority spokespersons (such as Ward Connerly and his cross-country anti–affirmative action campaign), White female spokespersons, and the illicit backing of state bodies that were supposed to guard electoral impartiality.

The inclusion of these anti–affirmative action measures on ballots marks the first time that major sectors of the U.S. population voted on civil rights legislation. Civil rights policies had always been enacted federally and through the representative system.[68] It is likely that civil rights policies would never have been implemented if the electorate had been responsible for directly passing legislation. When the federal government passed civil rights legislation, many local municipalities passed laws explicitly aimed at maintaining a White-supremacist racial order while others successfully aimed to resist enforcement of seemingly race-neutral policies, such as fair housing laws, that disproportionately impacted people of color.[69] Research illustrates that, when electorates are asked to vote on anti–civil rights initiatives (in areas as broad as desegregation, AIDS testing, and language accessibility), majorities are most likely to vote in favor of initiatives that deprive minority groups of access to resources and opportunities at the local and state levels.[70] Conservative elites presented their anti–affirmative action ballot measures in the form of the deceptively titled California Civil Rights Initiative (Proposition 209) and Michigan Civil Rights Initiative (Proposal 2). Affirmative action, a policy created and implemented as a result of the Civil Rights Act of 1964, was successfully eliminated by conservatives who appropriated civil rights language and symbols. After a brief discussion of the national sociopolitical context of the mid-1990s, I examine conservatives' successful use of the ballot tactic in California and Michigan, as well as unsuccessful ballot proposition efforts in Missouri and Colorado.

THE ANGRY WHITE MEN OF 1995

Ballot challenges to affirmative action emerged in the national sociopolitical context of the early to mid-1990s. Nationally, Republican

Party control over the U.S. Congress and increasing elite college competition contributed to the emergence of a movement against race- and class-inclusive admissions. In 1995, the Republican Party gained control over both houses of Congress for the first time in forty years. Wasting no time, the Republican Party set about enacting the "Contract with America," a one-hundred-day legislative agenda, co-authored by Republican House Speaker Newt Gingrich, but whose ideas originated from The Heritage Foundation and heavily borrowed from Ronald Reagan's 1985 State of the Union Address.[71]

Republicans successfully implemented a number of elements in this legislative agenda—notably, the Taking Back Our Streets Act (which expanded prison construction and defunded crime prevention programs) and the Personal Responsibility Act (which decimated welfare programs). Gingrich declared that ending affirmative action would be a priority after completion of the one hundred days, and, subsequently, many representatives from both parties came out against affirmative action.[72]

In February 1995, the House of Representatives voted to end an affirmative action program targeted at minority ownership of radio and television stations.[73] Republicans sought to harness their new power in preparation for winning back the presidency from Bill Clinton, whom they had effectively placed in a politically defensive position.[74] In response to the significant Republican political victories and the public's rejection of affirmative action, the media dubbed 1995 the year of "angry white men."[75]

The Clinton administration did not significantly change government attitudes toward affirmative action. Although President Clinton did not reverse the Reagan administration's civil rights retrenchment, he did little to preserve civil rights policies. Clinton, politically straddled between maintaining his party's platform and staying in office, even stated that it was a "psychologically difficult time for White males" during his address to the California Democratic Party convention in 1995, responding to the loss of entitlement felt among White men in the post–civil rights era.[76]

Ultimately, both the Democrats and the Republicans pandered to this constituency, resulting in a fertile environment for attacks on affirmative action policies. Clinton, provoked by Republican congressional control, initiated an investigation into the "fairness" of federal affirmative action policies; while he publicly claimed support for affirmative action, he suggested that it needed reform ("mend it, don't end it"), and the Democratic Party did little to intervene in prominent affirmative action and open admissions cases, particularly in California and New York.[77] Democrats determined that the political cost of defending affirmative action, a policy that did not poll well among Whites, was too high and consequently did not mount effective campaigns to defend it or avoided the issue entirely.

CALIFORNIA

In California, politicians spun affirmative action into a statewide issue, with much media coverage and political theater placing it at the forefront of voter consciousness. However, the California Civil Rights Initiative (titled Proposition 209 on the ballot) was the brainchild of two PhDs: Glynn Custred, a California State University professor, and Thomas Wood, an academic who had never secured a tenure-track position.[78] Custred watched his majority-White working-class classrooms become more racially diverse over the years, reflecting the changing state population. No longer identifying with his students, he was also displeased by the growing presence of faculty who advocated a multicultural curriculum rather than one rooted in Western civilization.[79] When the newly established Center for the Study of Intercultural Relations at his university organized a conference on multicultural perspectives in higher education, Custred was encouraged to attend by a university dean. Dismayed by the presentations of the speakers, Custred said, "I was there listening to some of the most god-awful things you can imagine. . . . I just found it terribly misguided."[80] He soon founded the California chapter of the National Association of Scholars, a conservative organization that opposes multicultural education and affirmative action and is funded by conservative bodies such as the Olin Foundation.

Wood blamed "reverse discrimination" for his inability to secure a tenure-track position. He had an inconsistent record of academic work from the time he received his PhD in the 1970s until the late 1980s. However, after he interviewed for a tenure-track position at

San Francisco State University, he believed he was not hired because he was a White male, saying "Count me among those angry men. . . . I know the sting of affirmative action. I was once passed over for a teaching job because, I was told privately, I was white and male. The worm has turned."[81] Though he admitted that the interview went terribly, he still held onto what his colleague in the department told him—namely, that they were looking for a "diversity hire." There is no evidence from the hiring committee (including tape-recorded interviews of serious job candidates and discussions involving former search committee members) that Wood was a serious candidate, but he continued to blame affirmative action for his poor employment options and used this rejection as motivation to act.[82] He soon joined the National Association of Scholars, where he met Custred.

Both Custred and Wood had spent considerable time independently researching the Civil Rights Act of 1964 and the decision in *Regents of the University of California v. Bakke* (1978). Now they joined forces to turn their research into a ballot measure that would dismantle affirmative action throughout the state. Because Wood's research on polling demonstrated that voters tended to support affirmative action but reject quotas, they were careful to frame affirmative action as "race preferences" and "preferential treatment," without reference to the term *affirmative action* in the ballot summary.[83] This discursive decision, which worked to racially code *and* confuse the objective of the proposition, proved to be influential in anti–affirmative action mobilization across the country. Conservative elites began to refer almost exclusively to affirmative action as programs of "preferential treatment" in ballot, court, and trustee challenges.

Custred and Wood began developing the California Civil Rights Initiative in 1991 and tried unsuccessfully to place it on the ballot in 1993. Though California allows ordinary citizens to organize signature campaigns for the purpose of placing measures on the state ballot, in the early 1990s it cost about a million dollars to obtain signatures and garner the appropriate political support, in effect placing the California referendum process under the control of special interest groups with massive financial resources.[84] Though Custred and Wood represented the views of many Californians, they simply did not, at that time, have the resources to place this initiative on the ballot.

Scholars in the field of law and economics, a conservative strong-hold in academia, helped Custred and Wood tighten the language of the ballot proposition.[85] Then, after connecting with UC Regent Ward Connerly, who had already begun to speak publicly against affirmative action, the two began to gain the attention of Republican state leaders and political strategists looking for the right wedge issue to increase the influence of the party and prepare Governor Wilson for a presidential run.[86] This attention resulted in the political support Wood and Custred needed to effectively launch the initiative. After the passage of Proposition 187, which banned the provision of state services to undocumented immigrants, media attention grew around a potential affirmative action ban.[87]

Wood, Custred, and their campaign team filed the California Civil Rights Initiative (CCRI) with the California attorney general in August 1995, one month after the UC regents had eliminated affirmative action in university admissions, hiring, and promotion. By fall 1995, Governor Wilson had announced his run for the Republican presidential nomination, but his campaign was short-lived, lasting only a few weeks. He was over a million dollars in debt and polling behind Republican Senate Majority Leader Bob Dole when he concluded his campaign.[88] However, both Wilson and the state Republican Party continued to support CCRI. By this time, Wood and Custred factored little into the leadership of the effort to pass CCRI. The campaign was now being run by a new team with more political savvy; it was led by Larry Arnn, president of the Claremont Institute, a conservative think tank, and included Arnold Steinberg, a Republican pollster, and Joe Gelman, a Los Angeles Board of Civil Service commissioner, described by journalist Linda Chávez as a "Republican Party activist."[89] The campaign team later recruited Connerly to head the initiative, knowing that they needed someone with public recognition. With the selection of Connerly as the director of the campaign in December 1995,[90] conservative elites had successfully selected their Black spokesperson to deliver the civil rights rhetoric of the campaign.

The CCRI team easily made its signature deadline, turning in over a million signatures by February 1996. But by July, it had run into a slight problem: a coalition of civil rights and women's organizations had filed suit against California Attorney General Dan Lungren due to the misleading ballot title and summary released about CCRI (now called Proposition 209).[91] Not only did the ballot summary omit the term *affirmative action*, but also public speeches, advertisements, and debates excluded it. In fact, this omission, along with the use of *racial preferences* as a misleading substitute, was key to the proposition's eventual success. Polling showed that 78 percent of California voters (including women, liberals, Blacks, Latinos, feminists, and affirmative action supporters) supported CCRI, but when they were told the initiative would ban affirmative action across the state, support decreased to 31 percent.[92] The title of the proposition—California Civil Rights Initiative—led people to believe that the ballot measure increased access to education and employment and protected racial minorities from discrimination; thus, it manipulated the common understandings of the public, rearticulated White subjectivity as being victimized, and presented Black and Latinos as unfairly favored.

Though state rules explicitly stated that members of the state attorney general's office were barred from meeting with proposition proponents in order to remain impartial, members of the CCRI campaign team met with Attorney General Lungren at the Republican state convention and received his support for the initiative. Additionally, Gelman, a member of the CCRI campaign team, privately met with Chief Deputy Attorney General David Stirling to specifically discuss the omission of "affirmative action" in the summary.[93] Sacramento County Superior Court Judge James T. Ford found that the materials were misleading and directed the attorney general to rewrite them, but the attorney general appealed and won. The Superior Court's opinion, written by Presiding Judge Robert K. Puglia, stated: "Even if we assume that . . . most or all of the impact of the prohibition will be borne by programs commonly associated with the term 'affirmative action' we cannot fault the Attorney General for refraining from the use of such an amorphous, value-laden term from the ballot title and ballot label."[94] Here, a Reagan-appointed judge worked to validate the illegal influence of the CCRI team on the ballot process. This decision strengthened the CCRI campaign.

The campaign also ran misleading commercial spots, such as one featuring a White single mother, widowed by the death of her

Mexican husband, who was rejected from a community college course due to affirmative action (when, in fact, she had not taken a prerequisite course).[95] This kind of advertisement capitalized on the "reverse discrimination" rhetoric and focused on the White female vote, though some of the largest opposition groups were led by White women, as the proposition also aimed to end affirmative action programs for women. Many advertisements appropriated language from Martin Luther King Jr.'s "I Have a Dream" speech, saying "We should be judged on merit, not by gender or the color of our skin."[96] However, King's family forced the Republican Party to pull these advertisements, objecting to the anti–affirmative action measure.[97] Another radio spot featured Connerly, who spoke about the death of a close friend who was White and highlighted that skin color had never come up as a topic of conversation between the two of them over decades of friendship.[98] The colorblind rhetoric clearly operated in all facets of the campaign, but the rampant manipulation of voters through the development of misleading campaign materials and media was a primary factor in CCRI's victory.

Much to the disgust of opposition campaign leaders, the California Democratic Party did not campaign against CCRI because members feared they would lose the support of White middle-aged voters. While student- and community-based organizations worked to resist the proposition largely through political education and efforts to get voters to the polls, larger political coalitions struggled to have an impact, raising little money without California Democratic leaders who were willing to serve as sponsors.[99] A statewide coalition of Northern and Southern California organizations, led by civil rights and women's groups, emerged to oppose CCRI, but the coalition fractured across tactical lines. Organizations in Southern California wanted to oppose CCRI outright, while Northern California organizations proposed to defeat CCRI by offering an alternative initiative that preserved diversity but rejected quotas. Though affirmative action programs did not include quotas in 1995, conservatives had successfully equated affirmative action with the use of quotas, and polling results showed that California voters believed that quotas were still being used.[100]

Ultimately, 54.6 percent of the electorate—including 66 percent of White men and 58 percent of White women—voted to enact

Proposition 209. However, it failed as a wedge issue, as California supported Bill Clinton again, helping him win a second term.[101] Though the UC regents reversed their decision to eliminate affirmative action in 2001, due to the plummeting enrollment of underrepresented students and a growing reputation for poor racial climates at their flagship campuses, this reversal was merely symbolic. Proposition 209 had altered the state constitution and forced the UC system to act in compliance.[102] As the first state to enact an electorate-endorsed affirmative action ban, California was an important test case for conservatives.

MICHIGAN

Michigan, a majority-White state known for its strong labor history and unionism, as well as its contentious race history, is an important site at which to examine hostile responses to efforts aimed at making public education more accessible and diverse. Some of the most well-known busing lawsuits occurred in Michigan, including the Supreme Court case *Milliken v. Bradley* (1974), in which the Court determined that the Detroit School Board engaged in de jure segregation and ordered one of the largest cross-district busing plans in the nation. White suburbanites greatly resisted this ruling, and antibusing protests were so widespread that many Detroit area residents and politicians feared violent uprising.[103] Michigan was one of the few states outside of the South where Alabama segregationist George Wallace won the Democratic primary in his 1972 presidential bid; it was also a key location where White Democrats defected to the Republican Party during the 1980s—and were dubbed "Reagan Democrats" by political strategists.[104] The state, rife with racial tension and economic depression, is home to the University of Michigan (UM), one of the most prestigious public research universities in the country. This site is important for understanding the emergence of anti–affirmative action Supreme Court cases *and* ballot contests.

In 2003, following what the Center for Individual Rights determined to be a defeat in the UM Supreme Court cases, lead plaintiff Jennifer Gratz joined with Ward Connerly to cofound a campaign to end affirmative action in Michigan using the California referendum tactic.

By this time, Connerly had already founded ACRI, an organization dedicated to ending racial preferences nationwide, and had also led a successful ballot campaign to end affirmative action in the state of Washington.

The Michigan Civil Rights Initiative (MCRI), essentially the same measure as proposed in California and Washington, aimed to end affirmative action in state contracting, state employment, and public university admissions. Twenty-one Michigan Republican legislators signed on as members of the MCRI steering committee. In January 2004, the MCRI team announced a petition drive to get it on to the November 2004 ballot and aimed to collect 400,000 signatures by July. The first signature came from Carl Cohen, the professor who had solicited conservative interest in UM's affirmative action policy, followed by those of former plaintiffs Jennifer Gratz and Barbara Grutter.[105] A coalition of progressive politicians, organizations, and activists formed a group to resist the initiative, Citizens for a United Michigan, and the organization By Any Means Necessary (BAMN) was particularly active in disrupting MCRI press conferences and public events.[106]

Grutter joined with Professor William Allen, an African American professor of political science at Michigan State University, to form the organization Towards a Fair Michigan (TAFM), an ideological project intended to "educate" the electorate about affirmative action through staged debates at various universities, churches, organizations, and public venues. Though TAFM claimed to be a nonpartisan organization not affiliated with MCRI and provided pro–affirmative action debaters at its events, every board and staff member supported MCRI.[107] The organization's purpose was to create a "fair dialogue" by emphasizing "education over indoctrination, reason over rhetoric, and civil debate over protest."[108] However, it arguably functioned as the ideological arm of the initiative effort and gained access to spaces that would not have welcomed people explicitly affiliated with MCRI. In fact, once they discovered TAFM's hidden relationships, many universities and organizations canceled programs scheduled at their institutions.[109]

As in California, the opposition confronted the campaign team's attempt to get MCRI on the ballot by legally challenging the misleading civil rights language of the initiative and questioning the validity of the collected signatures. In December 2003, Republican Representative Leon Drolet presented the proposed ballot language to the Board of State Canvassers, and it was accepted. BAMN immediately filed suit, arguing that the use of the term *civil rights* was misleading to voters. In March 2004, District Court Judge Paula J. Manderfield ordered the Board of State Canvassers to withdraw its approval. The MCRI team appealed the decision, and the appeals court reversed Judge Manderfield's decision.[110] Although this was a victory for MCRI supporters, they would have to wait until the 2006 election season to again file their initiative.

The majority of Michigan's White voters did not support affirmative action, but Black legislators and the Democratic Party established a united front in opposing MCRI, in contrast to the situation in California.[111] Both groups were involved in every legal challenge and played an important role in bringing allegations of petition fraud. In April 2005, BAMN and One United Michigan, a coalition of organizations including the National Association for the Advancement of Colored People (NAACP) and American Civil Liberties Union (ACLU), filed complaints with the Board of State Canvassers, claiming that MCRI volunteers collecting signatures had told people that the initiative would support affirmative action.[112] BAMN filed affidavits from over eighty initiative signers and five signature gatherers who said they had all been deceived. In July 2005, the secretary of state's office finished its review of MCRI petition signatures, concluding that 455,373 signatures were valid (more than required). As for BAMN's challenge of 325 signatures, the secretary of state's office rejected 88 and accepted 42 (for routine reasons such as incorrect address), leaving 195 unsettled signatures. The secretary of state accepted BAMN's documentation explaining the unsettled signatures but did not conclude that the signatures were invalid. At a public seven-hour hearing in July 2005, the Board of State Canvassers voted to reject the initiative, and MCRI supporters filed suit in the Michigan Court of Appeals. In December 2005, the appeals court ordered the secretary of state to put MCRI back on the ballot.[113]

The Michigan Civil Rights Commission, a state body that directs the Michigan Department of Civil Rights, organized hearings to investigate the allegations of voter fraud (the MCRI campaign team refused to participate) and concluded that there was a "disturbing picture of deception and misrepresentation" in the case of MCRI.[114] The commission submitted an amicus curiae brief in support of a request made by BAMN to the Michigan Supreme Court to prevent the proposition from going onto the 2006 ballot in *Operation King's Dream v. Connerly* (2007).[115] The U.S. District Court determined that the MCRI campaign was involved in "well-documented acts of fraud and deception" but that this fraud did not violate the Voting Rights Act because the campaign deceptively targeted all Michigan voters without regard to race.[116] Operation King's Dream, a coalition led by BAMN that included liberal Michigan politicians and state employee unions, appealed. However, legal wrangling prevented the rendering of a decision on the appeal until after the election had already taken place, and the U.S. Court of Appeals declared the case moot.[117]

Just as the California case, MCRI media framing drew on civil rights symbolism and iconography. Once MCRI appeared on the ballot as Proposal 2, print and television campaign advertisements featured images such as segregated water fountains and Black and White children sharing an ice cream cone.[118] The Black and White children evoked Martin Luther King Jr.'s "I Have a Dream" speech, which Proposal 2 was meant to symbolize, while the water fountains, displayed in the background as Connerly and Gratz spoke soberly into the camera, represented the racist past, a past to which society was returning because of "racial preferences." The racial preferences strategy communicated colorblindness by appropriating civil rights symbols while expressing the harm done to Whites by affirmative action.

In November 2006, Proposal 2 passed with 58 percent of the vote.[119] Around 66 percent of White Michiganders voted for MCRI. This proposition, now part of the Michigan Constitution, superseded the Supreme Court decisions in *Grutter* and *Bakke*, banning the use of affirmative action in public universities in the state. Various opposition groups sued the state of Michigan, arguing that this vote was invalid because Proposal 2 violated the equal protection clause and reordered the political process in Michigan. However, the Supreme Court upheld the decision of Michigan voters to end affirmative action in *Schuette v. Coalition to Defend Affirmative Action (BAMN)* (2013).

The ballot initiative tactic and the court challenge tactic represented challenges to the government, but the decision to directly engage the electorate resulted in more favorable decisions for conservatives. In both California and Michigan, actors promoting anti–affirmative action efforts through trustee decision-making and federal lawsuits decided to use the proposition tactic. Connerly's desire to end affirmative action and become a national conservative spokesperson on the issue meant that he and his organization would be involved in eight additional ballot initiative challenges across the country. Gratz continued to work against affirmative action, first with Connerly at ACRI (before accusing him of stealing donations and eventually resigning)[120] and then as the CEO of the XIV Foundation, an organization dedicated to conducting teaching and trainings against affirmative action.[121] Both received the benefits of public visibility and financial compensation from their work in challenging these policies.

In successful ballot contests, conservatives utilized a racial preferences strategy that reframed underrepresented students as racially preferred. This racial political strategy was dependent on conservative think tanks, the presence of conservative racial-minority and White female spokespersons, discourse that both appropriated civil rights rhetoric and symbolism and manipulated the popular understandings of the public, and the (legally prohibited) support of state bodies that were supposed to guard electoral impartiality.

THE CHALLENGE OF REARTICULATION: FAILED BALLOT CAMPAIGNS

Although ballot initiative campaigns have been largely successful, eliminating affirmative action in six states (California, Washington, Michigan, Arizona, Nebraska, and Oklahoma), this tactic failed in two states (Colorado and Missouri) and did not produce enough votes in the Utah House of Representatives to place the initiative on the ballot.[122] The failure of these initiatives, which were largely indistinguishable from those adopted in California and Michigan, is important, as the same tactic and racial political strategy were utilized across cases. However, the failure of *rearticulation*, or conservatives' ability to control the discourse on affirmative action and redefine White subjectivity as being victimized and Black and Latino students as racially preferred, had an impact on their defeat. Shifting political opportunity, as a result of organized resistance, the 2008 national election, and a lack of conservative consensus building in the local context, also contributed to the defeat of these ballot initiatives.

In fall 2007, ACRI, led by Connerly and Gratz (who served as the director of state and local initiatives), launched "Super Tuesday for Equal Rights," a campaign organized to place anti–affirmative action initiatives on the ballots in Arizona, Colorado, Missouri, Nebraska, and Oklahoma.[123] Working with local organizations such as think tanks and with state representatives, these conservative elites attempted to take advantage of direct vote processes on a grand scale, potentially impacting millions of people through hundreds of university admissions and employment plans.

After the successful elimination of affirmative action policies, orchestrated by Connerly and ACRI, in 1996 (California), 1998 (Washington), and 2006 (Michigan), local progressive organizations had the benefit of time and awareness in organizing opposition to ballot initiative campaigns in 2008. Additionally, organizations in Missouri and Colorado mounted stronger resistance to these proposed initiatives. In Missouri, WE-CAN (Working to Empower Community Action Now!), a coalition of community organizations, religious groups, students, labor, and businesspeople, formed to target the ACRI signature collection process.[124] The coalition informed the public through media and public education that the Missouri Civil Rights Initiative would ban affirmative action. WE-CAN also organized a voter education campaign, which included "Decline to Sign" and "Think Before You Ink!" directives.[125] Because the secretary of state's ballot summary accurately specified that the initiative would "ban affirmative action programs," ACRI challenged this clarified language in the Missouri Supreme Court, hoping to hide the true impact of the proposition.[126] In January 2008, the court changed the summary to include both the language of "racial preferences" and "affirmative action ban."[127]

Even though this outcome was less favorable to both sides of the issue, WE-CAN succeeded in influencing the public discourse about the affirmative action ban, which arguably played a role in the secretary of state's inclusion of an accurate description of the initiative in the summary. "Racial preferences" would be included in the ballot summary, but the phrase "affirmative action ban" did more than clarify the intent of the ballot; it resisted conservatives' attempts to appropriate civil rights rhetoric and adopt a victimized identity. Additionally, the ballot summary issue forced ACRI to spend more time in court, rather than on political organizing; now it was left with only four months to collect the majority of signatures.[128] Ultimately, ACRI was unable to collect the required number of signatures in time. Thus, the Missouri Civil Rights Initiative failed to make it on the ballot.[129]

In Colorado, Jessica Peck Corry, a research analyst for the libertarian think tank Independence Institute, chaired the Colorado Civil Rights Initiative (CoCRI), which encountered similar local grassroots resistance. Three Coloradan coalitions fought CoCRI's and ACRI's attempts to eliminate affirmative action: Colorado Unity, an already established coalition of civil rights organizations; Coloradans for Equal Opportunity (CEO); and Vote No on 46. The Colorado Title Board reproduced ACRI's ballot language, and the opposition challenged this language but failed in the Colorado Supreme Court; however, the publicity garnered from this challenge influenced public opinion.[130] Colorado Unity organized "decline to sign" campaigns and set up a hotline for people to call if they observed or experienced fraudulent actions by the signature gatherers.[131] Numerous people filed complaints with the secretary of state, declaring that circulators had told them the initiative would not dismantle affirmative action; these charges of signature fraud were covered in national media.[132]

After ACRI submitted 128,000 signatures in March 2008, Vote No on 46 filed a legal challenge, claiming that 69,000 signatures were invalid because some of the petition circulators were not Colorado residents and did not live at the addresses listed, that several of the notaries public who certified petitions were unlicensed, that many signatures did not match up with current voter files, and that 5,000 people signed the petitions twice.[133] Though Vote No on 46 did not win this court battle, these challenges were widely covered in local media, framing Amendment 46 proponents as potentially fraudulent and duplicitous.

CEO proposed an alternative initiative, Amendment 82, which sought to preserve affirmative action. However, Connerly and ACRI challenged the ballot title and summary in court, delaying the initiative for so long that CEO was unable to collect enough signatures.[134] CEO submitted more than 117,000 signatures, but the secretary of state disqualified a number of them; thus, Amendment 82 never made it to the ballot.[135] Still, the publicity around each of these attempts to stop Amendment 46 influenced voters. Additionally, the opposition to Amendment 46 received endorsements from the governor of Colorado, the mayor of Denver, administrators and coaches at local universities, and a variety of newspapers and media outlets.[136]

Ultimately, 50.8 percent voted against the anti–affirmative action ballot measure, making it the first anti–affirmative action ban to be defeated, though narrowly, at the ballot box.[137] Overall, "Super Tuesday" was a failure: on that day, only the anti–affirmative action ballot initiative in Nebraska passed. Initiatives did not make it onto the ballot in Arizona, Missouri, and Oklahoma in 2008, though conservative efforts did succeed later on, with affirmative action bans later being approved in Arizona (2010) and Oklahoma (2012). Grassroots resistance proved to be an important factor in the failure of effective conservative mobilization in 2008, but the failure of conservatives to control the discourse over affirmative action also impacted their defeat.

In the states where ballot propositions failed, conservatives had not effectively evaluated the political landscape. When Connerly announced his "Super Tuesday for Equal Rights" campaign for the 2008 election season, he was aware that an African American man, Barack Obama, was a front-runner for president. In fact, he believed that Obama's ascendance was proof that institutional racism no longer existed, justifying this national campaign to end affirmative action.[138] However, in evaluating the political moment, ACRI and CoCRI failed to consider two factors that would increase voter turnout in Colorado: the presidential election, in which great numbers of progressives were mobilized to vote, and the large ballot, which included fourteen statewide amendments and ballot proposals and countless other county-specific issues.[139] High voter turnout—

particularly among liberals, young people, and minorities, the groups more likely to support affirmative action—would not be favorable to the success of Amendment 46. Thus, high voter turnout impacted the ability of conservatives to control the narrative about affirmative action in Colorado. The political opportunities for success had shifted from previous ballot contests.

Connerly's growing national visibility and outsider status also played a role in grassroots resistance to proposed affirmative action bans. The opposition in Missouri and Colorado singled out Connerly in their advertisements against the proposed constitutional amendments, with local media repeatedly calling him a "carpetbagger."[140] Activists knew that Connerly was well resourced and had successfully orchestrated affirmative action bans in other states. Media coverage of these successful bans extended beyond regional media markets to nationwide audiences. The discourse of local activists highlighted these proposed affirmative action bans as not only unjust but also not organic to the local political environment. Activists had successfully shifted the political opportunity in their favor.

After the "Super Tuesday" failures in 2008, Connerly began to realize the consequences of his public visibility for the unsuccessful outcomes of these ballot contests. Thus, when the New Hampshire legislature discussed banning affirmative action in 2011, Connerly said, "We decided to keep a low profile, because the moment I surface it seems to draw out all of the national crowd."[141] New Hampshire's affirmative action ban took effect in January 2012 with little public debate, outcry, or resistance. Directly targeting state legislatures in an effort to ban affirmative action, without public engagement and national political figureheads, may prove to be a consistent tactic used on the Right in political struggle over affirmative action.

Relationships between ACRI, local state officials, and conservative leaders appeared to be weaker in cases of failed mobilization. While ACRI may have expected the approval of their ballot title and language, as in California, Michigan, and Washington, the Missouri secretary of state's inclusion of "affirmative action ban" in the ballot summary worked to clarify the intent of the ballot measure, benefiting the opposition. And even though pro–affirmative action organizers' fight to clarify language in Colorado failed, the publicity garnered by this legal fight and by the opposition's pro–affirmative action ballot measure worked to undermine Amendment 46. Importantly, while opposition in Colorado and Missouri included prominent community organizations, faith groups (including the Missouri Episcopal Diocese), and Democratic elected officials, the ballot initiatives *lacked* significant endorsements from local conservative leaders. In a year when large numbers of young people, racial minorities, and progressives were expected to vote, local conservatives likely avoided public endorsements of the initiatives in order to retain their contested political positions and ensure the success of higher-priority initiatives.

This lack of consensus building by ACRI in the local context extended to Utah, a majority-White and -Republican state, where ACRI organizers assumed that they would find another success. In 2010, ACRI paid lobbyists to petition Utah legislators who were considering amending the state constitution to ban affirmative action. Fifty votes were required for the proposed amendment to make it out of the Utah House of Representatives, but the initiative did not garner enough votes and failed to make it onto the ballot. Though ACRI gained the support of a few Republican state legislators— especially Asian American Representative Curtis Oda—many refused to vote for the measure. Some shared the sentiments of Republican Representative Sheryl Allen when she said, "I'm not against the idea itself, but I am against this rush job."[142] Some conservatives rejected changes to the constitution while others doubted that affirmative action posed a real problem in a state that claimed a 90 percent White population.[143] Ultimately, the lack of relationships between ACRI and local conservative leaders and the resulting absence of important endorsements undermined proposed affirmative action bans. United resistance on the Left and a lack of conservative consensus building, in addition to factors such as high voter turnout, contributed to a failure of conservative rearticulation and thus the failure of these anti–affirmative action ballot propositions. Changing political opportunities for conservatives meant that the racial political strategies that had produced prior ballot successes would not work in these subsequent cases.

RACIAL POLITICAL STRATEGIES IN TRUSTEE
DECISION-MAKING AND BALLOT CONTESTS

In political struggle over affirmative action, White conservative elites utilized a racial preferences strategy to influence trustee decision-making and amend state constitutions through ballot propositions (table 3.1). Conservatives shared tactics across affirmative action challenges, but instead of deploying a racial preferences strategy to dismantle open admissions, political actors used an inferior-race and -class strategy, which was more specific to the open admissions policy and institutional context of CUNY (table 3.1). Conservatives mobilized racial meaning in the political struggle over both policies, but these meanings were tied to the status of the institutions and the extent of policy reform.

In trustee decision-making and ballot contests concerning affirmative action, conservative actors rearticulated Black and Latino people as unfairly racially advantaged, which violated the supposed post–civil rights colorblind meritocratic social contract. In the context of university admissions, they argued that this racial advantage undermined the academically rigorous, elite reputation of the UC system, and especially the status of its flagships, UC Berkeley and UCLA. In contrast, conservative actors rearticulated CUNY, a system that served working-class students of color, as inferior. By framing the system as inferior, and open admissions as the cause of this inferiority, conservatives aimed to reform the system through the adoption of higher student performance standards; more investment in science, technology, engineering, and mathematics fields; and the establishment of an honors college to serve as a testing ground for the cultivation of a more elite environment. The elimination of open admissions was but one prong in a plan to remake the CUNY system.

As institutional reform framed conservative discourse about open admissions, conservatives blamed the policy for CUNY's institutional failure (table 3.1). Open admissions opened educational access to working-class students of color, many of whom were nontraditional students who worked full-time, had children, supported family members, and took more than four years to graduate. Elected officials, trustees, and think tank fellows framed students' needs for remedial

TABLE 3.1 Racial political strategies in trustee decision-making and ballot contests

	Inferior-Race and -Class Strategy	Racial Preferences Strategy
Location	CUNY	UC California, UM
Discourse	☐ Working-class students (of color) make our system inferior	☐ Blacks and Latinos are unfairly racially preferred
	☐ The money spent on remediation is better spent on recruiting middle-class students	☐ Racial preferences violate meritocracy and colorblindness
		☐ Racial preferences are anti–civil rights
Target	Board of Trustees	Board of Trustees; the electorate
Tactics	☐ Appoint and promote trustees that support the end of the policy	☐ Appoint and promote trustees that support the end of the policy
	☐ Employ spokespersons of color	☐ Eliminate the term *affirmative action* from ballot language and political discourse
	☐ Create and/or promote the influence of external bodies on Board of Trustees	☐ Employ spokespersons of color and White female spokespersons
		☐ Mobilize civil rights symbols and discourse
		☐ Retain support from impartial state agencies (ballot contest)
		☐ Marshal resources and signatures to place initiative on ballot (ballot contest)
Outcomes	The end of open admissions in CUNY senior colleges	UC affirmative action ban; state affirmative action bans in university admissions, hiring, and state contracting
Rearticulation	A system that prioritizes working-class students of color is inferior	Black and Brown people are racially advantaged

courses and for a longer period to complete a degree as evidence of a too permissive, degrading educational system. Though the open admissions policy was colorblind, conservatives' nostalgia for the past reputation of the city colleges—based on what they framed as meritocratic educational practices—served as a coded racial appeal to the "good ol' days" of institutional segregation. Thus, conservatives implicitly suggested that the disappearance of White students in the CUNY system signaled institutional failure, framed as the decline of meritocracy and educational quality. However, these were coded racial appeals, as open admissions had always been a colorblind policy aimed at providing wide educational access for working-class students.

Conservatives' elimination of open admissions was not simply a means of elevating CUNY's reputation; it also reflected trends in neoliberal policy reform. While the trustees eliminated remediation in the senior colleges, emphasizing the high cost, CUNY would increasingly rely on the services of private testing companies, such as Kaplan, to manage remedial test preparation.[144] As discussed in chapter 5 of this book, efforts to remake CUNY would instead focus on middle-class students, a population from which the CUNY system could extract more tuition dollars.

In their tactical assault on open admissions, politicians elevated and appointed trustees who would vote against the policy (table 3.1). Politicians also increased the influence of conservative think tanks, such as the Manhattan Institute for Policy Research, through their representation on the CUNY Advisory Task Force, an external body intended to steer the Board of Trustees. Herman Badillo, as a spokesperson of color, was central in deploying the racial discursive framing of CUNY students (oftentimes more blatant than and not as coded as the discourse of think tanks and politicians) and driving decision-making within Board of Trustees.

Mobilization against affirmative action also included a spokesperson of color, Ward Connerly, who influenced the internal decision-making of the UC Board of Regents and extended his leadership role to anti–affirmative action ballot propositions across the country. In Michigan, this kind of role also translated to White conservative female spokespersons, such as Jennifer Gratz and Barbara Grutter.

However, conservative discourse here raised "racial preferences" and eliminated reference to "affirmative action," communicating that Black and Latino students were racially advantaged (and thus White and Asian students were racially disadvantaged) (table 3.1). While conservatives and liberals alike suggest that affirmative action is unfair because it benefits wealthy and middle-class African Americans, this logic largely ignores the ways that middle-class Blacks are disadvantaged compared to middle-class Whites.

When this racial preferences discourse appeared in the ballot proposition summaries in California and Michigan, the language manipulated the electorate into believing that the amendment strengthened race-access policies. Not stopping there, conservatives appropriated the language and symbols of the civil rights movement in support of their cause, making a moral argument for colorblindness through a manipulation of the words and sentiments of civil rights activists (table 3.1). As the UC system maintained an elite reputation, conservatives emphasized that affirmative action threatened that system's educational quality. They also relied on external bodies—state agencies that were intended to guarantee impartial, fair elections—to get their propositions (and discursive framing) on the ballot. These efforts brought affirmative action to an end in California and Michigan and rearticulated Black and Brown people as racially advantaged. By rearticulating racially disadvantaged groups as advantaged, conservatives effectively justified the need for a legal rejection of race-conscious policy and an embrace of colorblind ideology. Where anti–affirmative action ballot initiatives did not succeed, factors including the failure of rearticulation and shifting political opportunities contributed to their defeat.

Overall, an examination of conservatives' racial political strategies highlights important points of comparison and divergence in their deployment of racial discourse and tactical approaches and ultimately in their attempts to rearticulate racial meaning in the post–civil rights period. However, it is also important to consider what is not present in conservatives' racial political strategies. Asians have been largely absent from the racial discourse, though they make up a signfificant portion of the student bodies at both CUNY and UC. In CUNY's colorblind, but coded, racial discourse, conservatives did not make significant allusions to the Asian population, as CUNY's pre–open admissions past did not include high numbers of Asians either. In Michigan, where Asians are less than 4 percent of the state population, they were virtually absent from the discourse. And in California, when conservatives referenced Asians, they were framed as model minorities across ethnic and class backgrounds. Those that oppose affirmative action often pit Asian academic statistics against Black and Latino admissions rates, though research suggests that, even with disproportionately higher test scores and grades, Asians are admitted at rates lower than those of Whites.[145] Even still, many of the Asians that are able to gain admittance to elite universities are class advantaged—the individual holistic review of applications, which affirmative action requires, from poor and disadvantaged Asians would likley benefit these groups.[146] But it appears now that conservatives' lack of inclusion of Asians in racial discourse and retrenchment politics is shifting: since 2015, Edward Blum's legal challenges to affirmative action have featured Asian, rather than White female, plaintiffs. Framing his front organization, Students for Fair Admissions, as representing the voices of Asian American students, Blum seeks to dismantle affirmative action by mobilizing strategically undisclosed, anonymous Asian victims. This strategy may prove to be succesful.

The events in California and Michigan suggest that civil rights rhetoric was still hegemonic over racial politics during this period. Thus, White appropriation of this rhetoric as a means to claim racial victimization marks a significant shift in the racial political landscape. Resistance to race-access policies is not new, as White southerners enacted anti–civil rights ordinances in the wake of federal civil rights legislation, claiming violation of southern tradition and states' rights. However, the retrenchment of civil rights policy at the ballot box by significant segments of the U.S. population is a more recent phenomenon. Though civil rights rhetoric, that refers to the resistance of African Americans, is dominant in how we understand the past, it may be less important in understanding racism in the post–civil rights period.

The social status of universities and their specific race- and class-access policies in practice necessarily shape conservative mobilization, but the challenges to affirmative action and open admissions discussed here illustrate how conservatives aim to disadvantage Black and Latino students across economic classes and across elite and working-class institutions. Blatant and coded racial discourse is key to how conservatives produce and exploit this disadvanatge. This is true whether they are attempting to overturn a colorblind policy (open admissions) or a policy that targets race (affirmative action).

Finally, organized resistance to conservative retrenchment is important. Failed ballot initiatives suggest that organized resistance can shift the political opportunities available to conservatives. And even though resistance does not always succeed, it has the potential to impact future political opportunities by cultivating activist networks and challenging the dominant discourse. Successful mobilization on the Left provides hope for the power of organized resistance against the heavily resourced conservative network. However, those who wish to sustain race- and class-access policies must stay attuned to shifting conservative tactical repertoires and racial political strategies. Additionally, the Left must develop its own assault on conservative platforms that is not merely defensive but also offensive.

4

A FORCE OF NATURE

Student Resistance to Policy Elimination

*The Campanile Tower is a symbol representing the University,
and the Ivory Tower of elitism and exclusionism. Our occupation
defies the passage of Proposition 209. Our occupation is an act of
resistance and reclamation. . . . Representation of people of color
on the UC campuses will decline by 50 to 70 percent as a result of
Proposition 209 being implemented (figures from the UC Office
of the President). If the University decides to comply with 209
they will essentially be locking us out. This occupation
represents us taking back our right to education.*

—Excerpt from "Message from the Tower," statement and list of demands written
by a coalition of protesting UC Berkeley students, 1996

STUDENT PROTESTORS resisted attacks on race- and class-inclusive admissions with their voices and bodies, jumping on the tables at board of trustees meetings, occupying campus spaces, and banding together with nonstudents in the streets. Critiquing and rejecting the university discourse on diversity, meritocracy, and reform, multiracial coalitions of students demanded the right of higher education for students marginalized by race and class, drawing inspiration from student movements of the 1960s in their own efforts to defend open admissions and affirmative action. Students are the population most impacted by policy retrenchment.

In this chapter, I illustrate how they operated as engaged political actors in struggles over the end of race- and class-inclusive admissions on their campuses. Student mobilization, though unsuccessful in saving these policies, served as an exercise in building counter-hegemonic racial projects, reclaiming public education as a tool to fight social injustice on campus and beyond.

In the 1990s, student activists connected attacks on affirmative action and open admissions to the persistence of the structural inequalities that shaped the social world. Political struggle over race- and class-inclusive admissions served as a training ground for activists. Mobilization led to the formation of social justice organizations; participation in citywide, regional, and national campaigns that challenged globalization, mass incarceration, and the wars in Iraq and Afghanistan; and the development of lifelong activism. In this way, student activists articulated a vision that went beyond open admissions and affirmative action to freedom from oppression and exploitation.

I first examine student organizing led by a group called Student Liberation Action Movement (SLAM!), which challenged trustee-led open admissions retrenchment at the City University of New York (CUNY); then I consider student mobilization led by a cluster of organizations at the University of California, Berkeley (UC Berkeley) that protested the elimination of affirmative action by the Board of Regents and the electorate. In this discussion, I highlight action at Hunter College in New York and UC Berkeley in California, where student organizations developed cross-national relationships with each other and were embedded in larger grassroots Left networks. University administrators utilized diversity as a defense of moderate racial inclusion and as an institutional commodity, whereas students' racial production challenged both diversity and colorblind racial logics through their analysis of power and their practice of civil disobedience.

The national organization BAMN (Coalition to Defend Affirmative Action, Integration, and Immigration Rights, and Fight for Equality By Any Means Necessary) organized protests against the federal court cases in Michigan and Texas, along with legal intervention in *Grutter* and *Schuette* (see chapter 2). However, I do not consider its Michigan and Texas demonstrations here because BAMN was not a student-led organization. Although high school students and adults protested at its events, radical lawyers organized BAMN's platform. In this chapter, I explain how student protestors in California, and elsewhere, experienced BAMN as a dangerous, divisive organization that attempted to hijack the pro-affirmative action movement and destroy student organizations for its own purposes.

CITY UNIVERSITY OF NEW YORK: A LEGACY OF RADICAL STUDENT ACTIVISM

CUNY's history of radical student activism much precedes the 1990s. During the 1930s and 1940s, socialist and communist CUNY students organized openly during a period of great political repression. These activists were mostly Jewish immigrant students from eastern and southern Europe, though civil rights leader Bayard Rustin was also an organizer with the Young Communist League while a student at City College during this period.[1] In the 1960s, chapters of Friends of SNCC and Students for a Democratic Society emerged at campuses such as City College, Brooklyn College, and Queens College.[2] The most widely known mobilization among student activists led to the implementation of open admissions policies in 1969, as discussed in chapter 1.

Attempts to save open admissions were always tied to larger efforts to resist neoliberal retrenchment—which took the form of budget cuts, increased tuition, the elimination of remediation, and the abandonment of the university's commitment to poor and working-class New Yorkers. In 1989 and 1991, students occupied buildings in response to tuition hikes and budget cuts proposed by Governor Mario Cuomo.[3] These student strikes delayed, but did not eliminate, budget cuts; however, they became part of the recent institutional memory of CUNY, linking student activism of the 1990s to the open admissions strikes of 1969 and asserting a radicalism that would take different forms from 1995 until 2004.

ANTECEDENTS TO THE STUDENT LIBERATION
ACTION MOVEMENT

In January 1995, newly elected Governor George Pataki announced several changes affecting CUNY in the state budget proposal: the elimination of the Search for Education, Elevation, and Knowledge (SEEK) and College Discovery[4] programs (both of which were key to opening educational access at CUNY), a reduction in the Tuition Assistance Program awards, a $1,000 increase in tuition, and $158 million in cuts to CUNY's budget.[5] The mainly working-class population of students—many of whom worked full-time, supported families, and received public assistance—felt unfairly attacked by this budget proposal. Many feared they would be unable to continue school with reductions in financial aid and increases in tuition; additionally, many felt that the elimination of SEEK and College Discovery was an insult to the legacy of open admissions at CUNY, a victory secured by SEEK student activists of the 1960s.

The CUNY student movement abandoned the occupation of campus buildings as a tactic, as students understood that the administration was now more punitive and would arrest occupiers;[6] now they focused on planning large mobilizations. New organizations and coalitions formed during the planning and in the aftermath of a massive protest on March 23, 1995. The organization SLAM! emerged after this protest and was key in mobilizing students to support open admissions; however, it had two important antecedents: the Student Power Movement (SPM) and the CUNY Coalition Against the Cuts (CUNY Coalition). Both groups developed around the same time, though there is disagreement around whether SPM played a role in the creation of the CUNY Coalition or whether the two emerged independently of each other.

SPM began as a grassroots organization of largely Black and Latino students at Baruch College, though it later spread to other CUNY campuses.[7] Students with varying political orientations established SPM; however, many of these students had had experience in leftist political organizations or had been mentored by veteran activists from the Black Panther Party, Republic of New Afrika, and Puerto

Rican Independence Movement.[8] All the early members of SPM were students of color, representing Black, Latino, Asian, and Arab leadership. SPM articulated student issues in terms of the historical oppression experienced in poor communities of color. As expressed in one of its pamphlets:

> We should never separate ourselves from our communities. Our entry into higher education is but a means to address the funda- mental problems affecting our peoples. All people of color suffer from racism, police brutality, run-down housing, lack of social ser- vices, mis-education and disproportionate unemployment. We have no other option but relentless struggle to bring about change.[9]

SPM explicitly framed the responsibility of students: to use education to challenge and eliminate oppression and exploitation. This fram- ing is rooted in an understanding that structural oppression shapes and disadvantages communities of color and that urgency is needed to transform these social, political, and economic conditions. This analytical position also influenced the development of SLAM! and its approach to agenda setting and programming.

In response to the proposed budget cuts, students and commu- nity members began to gather at various CUNY campuses such as the Graduate Center to discuss what collective actions they could take. The group that resulted, the CUNY Coalition Against the Cuts, hosted large, open meetings of over a hundred people in order to make deci- sions regarding collective action.[10] Many of the participants were also politically experienced, having been members of Left organizations such as the Progressive Labor Party, Love and Rage Anarchist Federa- tion, Revolutionary Communist Youth Brigade, and Young Commu- nist League. Boisterous energy, sectarian debates, audience members shouting down speakers, and chaotic decision-making character- ized CUNY Coalition meetings; White men dominated the speaking roles.[11] CUNY Coalition ad hoc committees were open to all; on some campuses, CUNY Coalition participation was tied to student gov- ernment and major student organizations while on other campuses students without affiliation participated. Members of SPM began to attend these meetings, nominally diversifying the sizable, largely

White group of participants. The CUNY Coalition decided to plan a mass mobilization at City Hall. Protest slogans such as "The cuts are not a force of nature" and "Shut the city down" became mantras for the planned protest.[12] Organizers decided not to apply for a permit for a march down Wall Street, framing that decision as a means of resistance against municipal and state authority, linking budget cuts to this symbol of financialization and economic greed.[13]

As students organized to plan the mass mobilization on March 23, some members of radical leftist political organizations enrolled in CUNY for the purpose of participating in the political work, not to attain an academic degree.[14] Student activists also built relationships with unions and other community organizations, so that the large mobilization also included community members without student affiliation.[15] During this period, CUNY was a hub of political activity in the city.

On March 23, 1995, between twenty and twenty-five thousand college and high school students, professors, workers, and other community members rallied in City Hall Plaza against budget cuts.[16] When the crowd attempted to march, police officers in riot gear spewed pepper spray and fought protestors trying to leave the barricaded area. When police attempted to arrest protestors, surrounding protestors would pull their comrades back into the crowd. This battle between students and police lasted a few hours; police arrested over sixty people, and eleven police officers were sent to the hospital with minor injuries.[17] The legislature minimally scaled back the proposed cuts and tuition hikes after the demonstration: CUNY's budget was reduced by $100 million (instead of $158 million), tuition was increased by $750 (instead of $1,000), SEEK and College Discovery were reduced by 25 percent (instead of being completely eliminated), and the Tuition Assistance Program was reduced by 10 percent.[18] Yet the remaining cuts still had an incredible impact on CUNY: 617 faculty took early retirement incentives that ruled out hiring replacements (as opposed to being dismissed), 168 instructional staff positions were eliminated, and New York Mayor Giuliani refused to allow ten thousand enrolled students on welfare fulfill new workfare requirements at CUNY.[19]

Many consider the 1995 march to be the height of the CUNY student movement after 1969. However, the CUNY Coalition began to decline as a result of continued disagreement over goals, aims, and political ideologies and dissolved by the end of the 1995 spring semester. However, during the winter of 1995, students reconvened with a new structure to ensure that those who participated in decision-making actually represented their bases on various campuses. This new structure required each CUNY campus (and participating public high schools) to designate four members (representing four votes) to participate in CUNY-wide meetings and limited off-campus participation to invited groups.[20] Private colleges and high schools were given two votes. Rules required that delegations be composed of at least half women and half people of color.[21] This structure encouraged a higher level of organization and addressed some of the White male dominance in meetings.

City College activist David Suker, a White working-class student from Long Island, suggested that this new version of the CUNY Coalition be called the Student Liberation Action Movement (SLAM!) after an activist youth of color organization he participated in while a student in Washington, DC.[22] Hunter College students took the lead in organizing this new group, though versions of SLAM! continued to exist on the City College campus after the winter of 1995 and included an established chapter after 2003.[23] Kamau Franklin, a Black CUNY student and SPM organizer, said about the emergence of SLAM! after the March 23 protest:

> It was a lot of those [March 23 protest] organizers and activists who later on helped create SLAM! or kept SLAM! going. . . . It definitely started what was sort of a pinnacle, in some ways, a resurgence of student organizing, radical student organizing—really sort of Left-field folks with the ability to make strong demands, a capacity to do civil disobedience or direct action, and people with various ideological belief systems who were very out about it."[24]

Though SLAM! emerged in the period after the March 23 protest, this "resurgence of . . . radical student organizing" linked the student mobilizations of the 1990s to a historical legacy of CUNY activism. Hunter College activists, understanding that a major obstacle for the CUNY Coalition was its lack of resources, decided to run a full

SLAM! slate for student government, which would assure resources for university- and community-based activism. SLAM! won control of the student government during the 1996 spring semester, putting in motion almost a decade of student activist control over student government at Hunter College. While many critiqued SLAM! for pursuing elected office, its occupation of student government allowed the organization long-term management of campus resources, influence over campus decision-making, and the ability to shape student life.

1996–2004: SLAM! SUSTAINING MOVEMENTS THROUGH STUDENT GOVERNMENT

SLAM! simultaneously functioned as a leftist campus organization, a community organization, and the student government at Hunter College. Though rooted in radical left politics, the organization was surprisingly nonsectarian and was able to maintain political unity despite Marxist-Leninist, communist, anarchist, Black liberationist, feminist, and Third World revolutionary tendencies all being represented. Core leadership took all of these tendencies seriously and was able to develop organizational unity through a variety of study groups, campus events, sustained programs, and participation in citywide coalitions. After students elected a full slate of SLAM! members to Hunter student government, those members occupied student offices and made bureaucratic decisions.[25] SLAM! also remained a student club, in which collective decision-making occurred; in this organizational space, members generated ideas, planned direct actions, and made programming decisions.[26] Many SLAM! members and friends (often called SLAM! Fam) noted that there was a core cadre of SLAM! leaders, many of whom had prior leftist political experience in other organizations or came from socialist, New Left, and Third World revolutionary families; this core played a significant role in establishing the vision and strategic agenda of the organization.[27]

Taking a page from the Dodge Revolutionary Union Movement's 1968 takeover of the Wayne State University newspaper, the *South End*, SLAM! activists took over the Hunter College newspaper, *The Envoy*, as well as the alternative paper, *The Spheric*, filling various editorial and writing positions. From about 1996 to 2004, SLAM! used student publications to shape the narrative of the student movement, critique CUNY policies, and spread information regarding social movement activity occurring in New York, as well as places as far as away as Chiapas, Mexico, and Palestine.[28] Control of both student government and student publications ensured that SLAM! had a voice in decision-making, resource allocation, and framing the narrative of the student movement on the Hunter campus and throughout CUNY. These were the tools that SLAM! would use as the CUNY Board of Trustees became increasingly more aggressive in its attempts to end open admissions.

SLAM! AND THE ATTACK ON OPEN ADMISSIONS

As early as 1992, Black media, such as the *New York Amsterdam News* newspaper, questioned whether the CUNY trustees and administration intended to maintain open admissions.[29] After the 1995 budget cuts, university trustees voted for a plan to streamline CUNY programs, subjecting academic programs to yearly efficiency reviews. Many feared these changes would lead to the closure of politically and economically vulnerable programs in ethnic studies and liberal arts.[30] By the 1995 spring semester, CUNY trustees had barred students who were judged to be unable to complete all remedial courses in their freshman year from enrollment in the CUNY senior colleges.[31] On March 21, 1996, the newly formed SLAM! organized a mobilization in which one thousand students marched from Times Square to Madison Square Park to protest another round of budget cuts proposed by Governor Pataki, including a $100 million reduction in the Tuition Assistance Program statewide, which impacted the poorest students in the state.[32] CUNY college presidents concluded that the cuts would result in a $97 million shortfall and a 10 to 18 percent reduction in full-time faculty and staff.[33] Although this march was significantly smaller than previous CUNY Coalition protests, as the first mobilization of SLAM! it signified a smaller but more organized resistance against attacks on CUNY.

From the election of the first SLAM! slate at Hunter College in spring 1996 through the approval of the end of remediation in CUNY's four-year colleges in January 1998, SLAM! activists continued sustained protest against the growing attack on open admissions. At their various mobilizations at the CUNY central administration offices and elsewhere, they called for Chancellor W. Ann Reynolds and Herman Badillo, vice chair of the Board of Trustees, to step down. They protested inside and outside of trustee meetings and public hearings and were dragged out by CUNY security officers and arrested for disturbing the peace. They teamed up with faculty from the Professional Staff Congress, a progressive faculty and staff union at CUNY, and organized Speak Out events on campus, where students could express their feelings and outrage regarding the proposed changes.[34] They employed theatrics during protesting: students and faculty often dressed up in graduation robes and staged Halloween-themed protests, utilizing fright masks and mock masks of trustees.[35] SLAM! also incorporated student artists into its protests: graphic artists designed signs, papier-mâché coffins, masks, and effigies, which students carried at protests, while spoken-word artists and musicians performed at mobilizations.[36] Hunter College's newspaper, *The Envoy*, engaged in investigative journalism to expose the troubling relationships between the conservative Manhattan Institute for Policy Research and CUNY trustees, affiliations of and financial contributions to members of the Schmidt Commission (formally called the CUNY Advisory Task Force), and plans to privatize remediation through companies connected to commission members.[37] Mainstream media covered trustee meetings and deliberations over open admissions regularly, but they often ignored or downplayed student protests. SLAM!-related media, including student newspapers, covered events meticulously and highlighted actions of the student movement.

On May 26, 1998, at the first vote of the Board of Trustees to eliminate remediation, SLAM! activists shouted down trustee members and protested outside of the meeting with outraged faculty members. Activists continued to shout and disrupt the meeting, knowing that the board would pass the plan to end remediation anyway. Trustees called the police, cleared the room, and had twenty-four people arrested.[38] After the board voted 9–6 to end remediation, students and faculty banded together and filed a lawsuit against the trustees for unlawfully clearing a public meeting and violating the state's open meeting law.[39] Although this tactic resulted in a temporary injunction preventing the implementation of the new admissions plan, trustees held a second vote in a larger auditorium during the winter break of 1998–1999. Again, SLAM! activists mobilized hundreds of students to attend this meeting, though it occurred over winter break, and they shouted down trustee members and disrupted the meeting. The trustees again voted to end open admissions 10–5.[40] Still, the State Board of Regents had to approve the Board of Trustees plan.

CUNY students and faculty had been writing to the state regents for months, encouraging them to maintain remediation in the CUNY senior colleges. These letter drives were partially organized by the Friends of CUNY, an ally collective of liberal faculty and former CUNY administrators who wanted to keep remediation in the senior colleges. However, unbeknownst to student activists, Friends of CUNY worked to broker a compromise with the state regents.[41]

Approved on November 22, 1999, this compromise ended remediation in the senior colleges but delayed its implementation for a year at Lehman College and City College, two of the senior colleges with the highest proportion of students who relied on remediation. Additionally, the compromise allowed up to two thousand admitted freshmen who had not passed one of the entrance exams to enroll under temporary waivers. With a research study to be completed on the effects of the end of remediation and with all compromise stipulations set to expire in 2002, this compromise was limited and temporary. The state regents were admittedly uncomfortable with voting to end remediation, but after being reassured by the Friends of CUNY, they voted 9–6 to approve the end of remediation more than a year after the trustees' initial vote.[42] With influence from Mayor Giuliani, Governor Pataki, the Manhattan Institute for Policy Research, and Trustee Badillo and with liberal consent from the Friends of CUNY, the CUNY Board of Trustees and the State Board of Regents eliminated remediation, effectively ending open admissions in the senior colleges.

SLAM! media and documents utilized a number of frames to make sense of the end of open admissions. They situated the end of open admissions within a historical context that considered the adoption of open admissions in 1969, the imposition of tuition in the CUNY system in 1976, and the immense cuts to CUNY from the late 1970s to the 1990s. In a flyer titled "Myths & Facts About CUNY," SLAM! contextualized the ability of students to stop the end of open admissions:

MYTH #3: There is nothing students can do to stop the attacks on CUNY! Students don't have any power. FACT: In the Spring of 1969 Black and Latino students united in mass resistance at City College to fight for the opening of CUNY doors for folks of color. At the time, CUNY was an overwhelmingly white university. Black and Latino students demanded access to the university as well as departments to reflect their history and culture. During the struggle for Open Admissions, the students chained the gates and burned down a part of the Finley Student Center at City College. As a result of this organized movement, many of us are here today.[43]

Here, SLAM! members position themselves as the product of this radical student legacy, their presence the outcome of student activists taking power in 1969. CUNY enrollment ballooned after adoption of the open admissions policy, illustrating the demand for an accessible (and free) college education. Referring to the 135-year history of free tuition at city colleges, SLAM! framed the imposition of tuition in the midst of the financial crisis in 1976 as a means to curtail widespread educational access to students of color.[44] Students of color were not admitted to CUNY institutions in high or even moderate numbers until after the adoption of open admissions, and, thus, most students of color experienced free tuition only from 1970 to 1975. This historical frame identified the end of open admissions as a conservative strategy utilized to return CUNY to a majority-White university system.

Media from the Manhattan Institute for Policy Research already demanded that CUNY return to its pre–open admissions academic policies, when the system enrolled few Black, Latino, or Asian students.[45] The city colleges were established as institutions for the city's immigrant, poor, and working-class communities; CUNY's institutional mission had not been fully realized until 1969, and students now argued that the retrenchment of open admissions undermined this commitment. This historical frame consciously mobilized educational access as an issue of race and class and the elimination of open admissions as an attack on Black, Brown, and poor people. Rather than using the discourse of diversity, students focused on the political struggles and victories of Black and Brown activists in democratizing higher education.

SLAM! activists also utilized a political-economic frame that connected open admissions retrenchment to larger processes of privatization and shrinkage of the public sector, evidence of political-economic shifts on a national and global scale. In campus newspaper articles, they illustrated how students on welfare were forced out of CUNY by new workfare policies that required them to take low-skilled jobs rather than complete their education.[46] They tracked how neoliberal policies of the International Monetary Fund and World Bank led to unstable political and economic conditions in Third World countries and, as a result, compelled many family members of SLAM! members and CUNY students to flee to the United States.[47] While they detailed the end of remediation in senior colleges and CUNY's promotion of tutoring services provided by new, private standardized testing companies, they also connected the end of open admissions to larger attacks on the public sector and public goods. Instead of making sense of retrenchment as an attack on "diversity," they understood it as the outcome of neoliberal restructuring and the reduction of the public sphere.

However, this political-economic frame was not divorced from a racial analysis. In a flyer encouraging students to join SLAM!—titled "Do You and Your Friends Want to Go to College?"—SLAM! listed the populations that Giuliani aimed to keep out of CUNY senior colleges: the students enrolled in remedial coursework, including "75 percent of AFDC recipients, 81 percent of Low income women, 82 percent of Single mothers," and "65 percent of Black freshmen, 66 percent of Asian freshmen, 68 percent of Latino freshmen, 45 percent of White freshmen." The flyer ends with the following statement: "With cops shooting people like Amadou Diallo down in the street, new prisons being built, and college doors being slammed in our faces, the time has come to do something to defend our future. . . . It's Not Too Late to Stand Up for Your Right to an Education!"[48] Here, SLAM! not only communicated the losses that all racial groups and low-income groups would experience with the end of remediation but also linked policy reform efforts to police violence and mass incarceration, both areas that were the target of massive resistance in the 1990s. By connecting the attack on open admissions to racial oppression in their everyday social world, SLAM! activists framed the sources of these injustices as interconnected while practicing social movement solidarity.

These frames were present throughout articles written by SLAM! activists in Hunter College's *The Envoy* and City College's *The Messenger*, in SLAM!'s pamphlets and political education materials, and in interviews with former student activists. Even after the end of open admissions, SLAM! newspaper staff continued to critique Pataki's persistent tuition hikes in commentary resembling missing-persons announcements. These "advertisements" featured the picture of a young person and a description of hair and eye color, followed by a short narrative such as the following: "He is a Creative Writing major who wants to teach English to non-native speakers. He will be lost as of fall 2003 due to Governor Pataki's Tuition Hikes for CUNY."[49] The reward is "An Educated New Yorker," and "if found" contact information lists the governor's office.

Though SLAM! was unable to save open admissions, its members soldiered on, organizing a variety of projects and mobilizations, participating in larger left coalitions, and making Hunter College a hub of youth organizing in New York City. Still, SLAM! activists describe the loss of open admissions as demoralizing. Many SLAM! members would later describe their eventual loss of student government in 2004 as a consequence of the post–open admissions changes in the race and class demographics of Hunter College.[50]

SLAM!'s focus on open admissions was but one part of its scope, and its control of student government, and thus its control of space and resources on campus, allowed its members to connect to various organizations and activists outside of Hunter's campus. They allowed various New York–based organizations, including DRUM (Desis Rising Up and Moving), FIERCE, and MXGM (Malcolm X Grassroots Movement), to utilize the resource center and computer lab to make flyers and photocopies and to conduct organizational business. SLAM! joined the citywide Coalition Against Police Brutality and its People's Justice 2000 campaign, organized in response to the 1999 murder of Guinean immigrant Amadou Diallo and brutal assault of Haitian immigrant Abner Louima. As part of this coalition, SLAM! participated in organizing significant mobilizations and community political education programming against police brutality in New York City.[51] SLAM! also joined national mobilizations advocating for political prisoners from the Black Liberation Movement, particularly activist-journalist Mumia Abu-Jamal.[52]

SLAM! activists, along with about four thousand other protestors, took to the streets in Philadelphia to protest the Republican National Convention (RNC) in 2000. SLAM! was key to the planning of RNC direct action, which included the creation of protest art and banners (including hundreds of puppets); the development of new, independent media networks; and massive direct action influenced by anarchist black bloc tactics.[53] Of the over four hundred protestors arrested at the convention, twenty-five were SLAM! members. While some SLAM! activists were detained as long as fifteen days and one faced $500,000 bail, they worked with "general population" detainees to publicize a list of demands, which included the prevention of beatings by jail staff, medical attention, and an end to waiting for two or more years to go to court.[54] SLAM! members were subjected to both physical and sexual assault, and the fate of an arrested undocumented member hung in the balance.[55]

SLAM! also developed the High School Organizing Program (HSOP), a program that trained high school students to become community organizers. In doing so, it utilized some of the curriculum from the School of Unity and Liberation (SOUL), a program developed by participants in the UC Berkeley student movement to save affirmative action. After the end of open admissions, SLAM! members saw this program as especially important for high school students who would not be able to benefit from open admissions. SLAM! hoped that by politicizing a new generation of students and giving them the skills to take on leadership roles in their communities, the program would spark activism at an earlier stage in the educational pipeline.

Though students could not save open admissions, SLAM! resisted the elimination of remediation and the effective end to open admissions and, more broadly, contested political-economic policymaking that devalued working-class communities of color. SLAM!'s organizing and discursive frames mobilized an entitlement to public education and, by extension, to the greater public sphere, rejecting efforts to restrict access to formerly public goods and promoting a redistribution of wealth and resources. Overall, these students' structural analyses and practices of race and class politics served as a counterhegemonic racial political project in the service of radical liberation.

UNIVERSITY OF CALIFORNIA BERKELEY: A SPLINTERED FIGHT FOR EDUCATIONAL ACCESS

UC Berkeley has a rich history of leftist student activism: many associate the campus with the free speech movement of the mid-1960s and key anti–Vietnam War mobilizations, including collective draft card burnings, sit-ins at Selective Service offices, and protests on campus.[56] The ethnic studies strike of 1969, led by the Third World Liberation Front, pressed for an education system accessible to racial minorities and for ethnic studies programs.[57] Additionally, large anti-apartheid protests and divestment campaigns emerged at UC Berkeley in the 1980s, as they did on campuses across the country. In the 1990s, students organized mobilizations around the Rodney King beating and efforts to save ethnic studies, which were consistently threatened with budget cuts.[58] Student organizing to save affirmative action at UC Berkeley differed from student organizing at CUNY in that it was fraught with more internal contention and thus became more fractured and less stable early on. Additionally, UC Berkeley affirmative action mobilization more clearly centered on the single issue of saving affirmative action. As UC Berkeley was the most exclusive public university in California, the class backgrounds of students there were more varied as well. While the student mobilization at UC Berkeley reflected a diversity logic that focused on promoting multiculturalism and preserving the population of students of color, disagreement over this framing contributed to movement fractures, as some students centered racism and power in their critique of diversity *and* affirmative action retrenchment.

1995: PROTESTING THE BOARD OF REGENTS VOTE

In California, the Board of Regents eliminated affirmative action in admissions and hiring in the UC system, and then a ballot proposition banned affirmative action in admissions, hiring, and contracting throughout the state. The regents' decision could be reversed (and, in fact, this happened in 2001), but the decision of the electorate amended the state constitution, rendering the ban permanent. Because the regents' decision occurred quickly, coming as a surprise to even UC campus chancellors, student mobilization mainly occurred in the spring of 1995 and during a period that began a few weeks before the regents' vote on July 20, 1995. Student mobilization continued from July 1995 through the ballot vote on November 5, 1996. While Regent Ward Connerly had initiated a review of campus affirmative action programs up to a year before he proposed its end in 1995, he did not submit a proposal to end the policies to administrators until less than a month before the board voted in July 1995.

During the summer break, students organized quickly across the state to protest at the regents' meeting.[59] Two thousand students protested inside and outside of the meeting, and public figures like Jesse Jackson and Mario Savio of the free speech movement testified, demanding that the board save the threatened policy. A number of students of different racial backgrounds and from different UC campuses testified in support of affirmative action during the meeting. Every UC chancellor supported the continuation of affirmative action policies.[60] Still, the board voted to end affirmative action in hiring (15–10) and in university admissions (14–10) throughout the UC system. In response, students flooded the streets in protest: reports claimed that two hundred to one thousand protestors (including Jesse Jackson) marched without a permit down San Francisco streets and blocked a busy intersection.[61] Not wanting to encourage more people to protest, Governor Pete Wilson ordered the San Francisco Police Department to refrain from arresting protestors.[62]

Over the next year and a half four of the nine UC chancellors resigned from their positions, although none referenced the regents' affirmative action decision as their reason for leaving. UC Berkeley

Chancellor Chang-Lin Tien was the most outspoken UC administrator in his support of affirmative action after the decision, and UCLA Chancellor Charles Young (who served for twenty-nine years) cited great frustration with the Board of Regents in the wake of its affirmative action ban.[63] However, the regents' affirmative action ban was just the beginning, as Regent Connerly became the spokesperson for a state ballot campaign that aimed to end affirmative action in state contracting, hiring, and university admissions across California.

SUMMER 1995–SPRING 1996: DEVELOPING ORGANIZATIONS AS A MOBILIZING FORCE

The experience of protest and disruption at the July 1995 regents' meeting politicized participating students.[64] At UC Berkeley, a multiracial organization called Diversity in Action (DiA) emerged out of the network that organized the July protest. It formed as a coalition organization whose members represented other organizations on campus, such as the Black Student Union, Movimiento Estudiantil Chicano de Aztlán or MEChA (a national Chicano student organization), and the Black and Latino Retention Centers, as well as White students.[65] As a coalition organization, DiA worked to mobilize student clubs and unorganized students to pressure the regents to reverse their decision. These students at UC Berkeley were not the only ones working to mobilize the public, pressure the regents, and convince the California electorate to save affirmative action.

The United States Student Association (USSA), the UCLA Affirmative Action Coalition, and other student organizations mobilized two thousand students at UCLA to protest against the regents' decision and to vote against Proposition 209.[66] At UC San Diego, No Retreat, a multiracial student direct action organization, organized letter-writing campaigns, protested at regents' meetings in Sacramento, and began holding town hall meetings on affirmative action (and other political education efforts).[67] Four Latino UC Irvine students began a hunger strike but were arrested two weeks into their protest after police officers declared their tent encampment, in front of the UC Irvine administration building, illegal.[68] Statewide, USSA connected campus-based student resistance efforts and developed a network of student activists against affirmative action retrenchment.[69] DiA participated in this statewide network and served as an important coordinator of statewide resistance efforts, including campaigns to get voters to the polls and disruptive direct actions. DiA organized with the awareness that Berkeley, as the most selective UC campus, would be most impacted by the end of affirmative action.

During the first week of the 1995 fall semester, DiA organized a rally and campus march, during which three hundred students protested the regents' decision.[70] It also began holding teach-ins and collaborated with Berkeley faculty and staff. However, tension emerged in the group early on. Although much of this internal conflict was a consequence of dealing with another protest group, BAMN, and its influence on the campus protest environment, disagreement also emerged over tactics and recruitment. Some students, newly influenced by socialism, wanted to utilize more radical tactics, which conflicted with the overall liberal and progressive ideology of the group. Many objected to the idea of "diversity," which they saw as depoliticized because it did not provide a compelling analysis of power and exploitation.[71]

DiA's efforts to organize students who were not members of campus organizations also became a point of contention. Student participants of color felt that this focus devalued their existing campus organizations. Though DiA was a multiracial organization, a significant number of Whites were members, and the lack of students of color in DiA leadership positions left Black and Brown students questioning the legitimacy of the organization. Black and Brown students in the coalition felt compelled to act as representatives of their communities on campus and felt tokenized in the organization. They also felt that White participants in DiA had abandoned the campus organizations of students of color and were taking up their issues without including them.[72] As a consequence of these issues, many of the students of color left to start a more militant organization called the No Name Collective.

The No Name Collective was smaller, committed to more militant methods of protest and disruption, and centered power and racism in its political analyses rather than "diversity," which did not recognize structural inequality. While DiA committed to mobilizing on campus, the No Name Collective desired deeper connections between campus and community. Many members were first-generation college students and wanted to prioritize the intersections between the political issues of their communities of origin and university concerns.[73] Frustrated by BAMN's efforts to take ownership of student-planned political actions and by public figures' attempts to act as spokespersons for the UC Berkeley student movement, these students felt it necessary to emphasize "no name" in the political work they organized.[74]

Still, on October 12, 1995 (Indigenous People's Day), DiA and the No Name Collective pulled together to organize a large mobilization on campus as part of events planned across the state for the National Day of Action for Affirmative Action, called by the statewide Students Civil Rights Network. Women within DiA and the No Name Collective took leadership in organizing this collective series of events.[75] For that day, the two groups organized a teach-in, a campus walkout, and a rally of about five thousand students on campus.[76] Some reported peak participation of up to ten thousand people at UC Berkeley in support of affirmative action that day.[77] After the rally, a crowd of one thousand marched through Berkeley and Oakland and unsuccessfully attempted to take over a local freeway.[78]

For the rest of the fall semester, student activists attended regents' meetings, where they testified and participated in planned disruption. The regents ordered that security guards frisk student activists before entrance to meetings, restricted civil disobedience actions, and physically removed students who testified for more than thirty seconds. Members of the No Name Collective also occupied campus administrative buildings and planned disruptive actions at regents' formal dinners in San Francisco hotels.[79] Still, this small group of students began to turn its attention to other areas: some members focused on political education and activist training, and others focused on campus recruitment of students of color (as a means to offset dwindling numbers). By the 1996 spring semester, both DiA and the No Name Collective had fallen apart. Although another organization, Students Against Proposition 209, emerged in their wake and focused expressly on opposing the state ballot measure, it is important to examine the challenging conditions that impacted student organizing at Berkeley.

BY ANY MEANS NECESSARY: DISRUPTING THE BERKELEY
STUDENT MOVEMENT

Early conflict in the student political landscape, only months after organizing had begun, contributed to the fragility of student organizations. Without significant involvement from politically experienced students, these organizations were likely to run into common obstacles. Specifically, they faced problems in building coalitions due to different engagements of race and gender, reconciling conflicting political ideologies and orientations, resolving disagreements over tactics, and prioritizing targets and campaigns. However, one of the biggest forces in the splintering of student organizations was the emergence of BAMN.

BAMN, a singular entity and not a coalition, was a front organization for the Revolutionary Workers League (RWL), a small Trotskyist organization from Detroit.[80] Though BAMN was a small and unknown organization in 1995, it was able to mainstream itself after the political struggle at UC Berkeley and achieve legitimacy in the federal courts (its national chair was a civil rights attorney). BAMN soon became a national name in political contention over affirmative action, organizing disruptive actions at press conferences and rallies in Michigan, coordinating the legal intervention in *Grutter v. Bollinger* in the lower courts, and serving as the plaintiff in the Supreme Court case *Schuette v. Coalition to Defend Affirmative Action (BAMN)* (2014), which upheld the Michigan electorate's vote to eliminate affirmative action.[81] However, BAMN truly got its start protesting the end of affirmative action at UC Berkeley and attempting to take over the student movement.

Trotskyist organizations in the United States have a reputation for sectarianism and disruption, leading to many internal splits in their organizations and coalitions; these organizations are also known to attack other leftist groups that they perceive as adopting the wrong political line.[82] Berkeley student activists' accounts of dealing with BAMN communicate great frustration: they cite divisive tactics, an unwillingness to listen or reflect at group meetings, and, most often, actions that placed student activists in physical danger.[83] They accused BAMN members of physically and verbally assaulting them at events, grabbing the microphone at rallies, pushing unprepared students into clashes with police officers, and provoking arguments and confrontations in meetings.[84] In addition to publishing "hit" pieces on the DiA leadership, BAMN claimed that it was at the forefront of a youth-led movement, though none of its leaders were young people.[85] BAMN members also engaged in minor actions that displeased the Berkeley community, including campus vandalism and frequent thefts of thousands of copies of the *Daily Californian*— the UC Berkeley student newspaper, which had published pieces critical of BAMN and had supported anti–affirmative action policies.[86] BAMN's presence in the Berkeley student movement created an environment of mistrust in the larger campus community and alienated the student body.[87]

Student activists also felt that BAMN decreased their productivity because, in addition to planning actions to resist affirmative action retrenchment, students had to prepare to deal with BAMN's disruptive tactics. Some students felt that they could not experiment with radical tactics because BAMN had completely shifted the environment in which to resist affirmative action with legitimacy.[88] Different organizing groups would even indicate at the bottom of posters that they were "Not BAMN affiliated," in hopes that students who supported affirmative action might actually participate if they knew BAMN was not involved.[89] The *Progressive Populist*, an independent progressive paper, described BAMN's presence at Berkeley as "thuggish" and "violent" and claimed that many student activists left organizing "traumatized . . . bitter and disillusioned" after dealing with BAMN.[90] In a letter to the editor of the *Daily Californian*, one student expressed their frustration:

> I believe I speak on behalf of many progressives on campus when I say: Thanks a lot, BAMN, for ruining it for everyone. Thanks a lot for making us lose all our credibility with your rantings and ravings. Thanks a lot for driving so many sensible students on this campus to support [Proposition] 209. You are the kiss of death and you ought to be ashamed of yourself.[91]

BAMN had also been asked to leave direct action at California State University, Northridge and the University of Michigan, where its members were accused of trying to take over the Black Student Union.[92] Before its reinvention as BAMN at UC Berkeley, its previous iteration, the RWL, had been asked to cease involvement in the University of Michigan's chapter of ACT-UP, an AIDS direct action organization. Students at the University of Michigan specifically attributed internal group conflict to the RWL's efforts to take over political agendas, disregard democratic meeting procedures, and assume control of the organization.[93] BAMN's hostile campus presence—reflected in acts that sowed seeds of distrust among student organizers, created fear over safety, and produced exhaustion from fighting internal and external battles—fueled the demise of DiA and the No Name Collective by the end of the 1996 spring semester.

SPRING 1996–FALL 1996: ANTI-PROPOSITION 209 CAMPAIGN

By spring 1996, student activists affiliated with DiA and the No Name Collective had begun working with a new statewide organization, Californians for Justice (CfJ). This organization aimed to build long-term power in low-income communities of color by encouraging voting and cultivating the leadership of young people. CfJ-affiliated students formed Students Against Proposition 209, a single-issue organization meant to get out the vote against Proposition 209.[94] That summer four women active in UC Berkeley campus organizing—Rona Fernandez, Harmony Goldberg, Tho Vinh Banh, and Amanda Enoch—founded the School of Unity and Liberation (SOUL), a summer training program for youth of color modeled after civil rights institutions such as SNCC's Freedom Summer Project and the Highlander Folk School in Tennessee.[95] SOUL, CfJ, and Students Against Proposition 209 organized efforts to get voters to the polls, coordinated with other statewide coalitions such as the Northern California Coalition to Defeat Affirmative Action, and worked diligently to prevent the success of Proposition 209. After David Duke, a Ku Klux Klan grand wizard and Louisiana politician, endorsed Proposition 209, Students Against Proposition 209 released a poster featuring a hooded KKK member, a burning cross, and a caption reading "The Klan Supports 209, Should You?"[96] While Students Against Proposition 209 collaborated with liberal statewide campaigns that highlighted the importance of diversity and the mistruths about affirmative action spread by the Proposition 209 campaign, it also used messaging tactics such as this poster to point out the outright racism that motivated the anti-affirmative action ballot measure. Many of these student activists anticipated a loss and began working on actions to protest the unfavorable results. On November 5, 1996, Proposition 209 passed with 54.6 percent of the vote, eliminating affirmative action statewide.

The following day UC Berkeley students organized two major actions. First, they coordinated a rally, attended by UC Berkeley students, high school students who had walked out of school, and other supporters of affirmative action.[97] One thousand student protestors marched down the four lanes of Telegraph Avenue, a major thoroughfare that borders the UC Berkeley campus and continues through Oakland.

In the second action, a smaller group of students from Students Against Proposition 209 and the campus chapter of MEChA occupied the Campanile, a campus clock tower, which they framed as a symbol of the "ivory tower."[98] Five Chicana students chained themselves to the tower, and others hung a banner declaring "Revolution" from the top. Two hundred students spent the night at the tower and drafted a statement and list of thirteen demands, called "Message from the Tower." The students demanded that the university not comply with Proposition 209, that it increase funding for education ("schools, not prisons"), and that it increase student representation on the Board of Regents; they also demanded live TV and radio interviews with student coalition members.[99] In anticipation of a police response, another five students chained themselves to the building, and fifteen students blocked the elevator. At five in the morning, the police came in with batons; they dragged students out of the tower, cut the chains off the protestors, and arrested twenty-five.[100] The following days were filled with more marches and teach-ins at UC Berkeley and across the state.

Notably, the Coalition for Economic Equity (represented by the ACLU) filed suit in federal district court to stop the implementation of Proposition 209, based on a legal precedent that had stopped the implementation of a Washington State antibusing ballot measure in *Coalition for Economic Equity v. Wilson*. The court granted a preliminary injunction that halted enforcement of the ban, and students continued to protest throughout the injunction period. However, during the 1997 spring semester, the Ninth Circuit Court of Appeals overturned the injunction, allowing enforcement of the affirmative action ban statewide. In response, Students Against Proposition 209 participated in an occupation of Sproul Hall. They secured the doors with rope and bike locks and stopped the building elevator, but they were quickly met with pepper spray and police in riot gear.[101]

Though they lost the battle against Proposition 209, student activists continued to engage in political activity. SOUL, the summer training program that anti–Proposition 209 campus activists founded, developed into a full-time organizing program for young people of color across the country, providing them with training in organizing skills (ranging from electoral campaigns to direct action tactics), technical assistance, and political education. Similar to SLAM!, SOUL became a hub for young organizers in the Bay Area.[102] SOUL and SLAM! began their relationship through mutual contacts and their meeting at a conference organized by the prison abolition organization Critical Resistance in 1998.[103] SLAM! invited SOUL members to New York multiple times, and SOUL ran activist trainings at CUNY, including a SOUL-SLAM! Summer School—an intensive eight-day training program for CUNY activists and allies in the skills and theoretical foundations of organizing for social change.[104] SOUL persists as a model on the Left for training activists and cultivating youth leadership in social justice organizations.

Though the statewide campaign to save affirmative action centered notions of diversity that championed multiculturalism, student activists also debated over structural analyses that focused on oppressive power relations, as well as liberal perspectives that concentrated primarily on racial representation. The political struggle in California highlights the ways that racial production is not static but dependent on structural conditions, political ideology, and campus context. The elite status of UC Berkeley, and the UC system as a whole, shaped the conditions under which student organizing emerged and, in particular, shaped the liberal frame of diversity in student mobilization. Yet those in the UC Berkeley student movement also included analyses of power and racism in political struggle.

CONCLUSION

Student movements at CUNY and UC Berkeley failed to save race- and class-inclusive policies. However, their efforts to resist in a field constrained by a lack of political opportunities still produced political practices and openings in the afterlife of retrenchment. Student mobilization served as counterhegemonic racial political projects, discursively challenging the racial logics and practices of those in power, including administrators, state actors, and conservative activists. Their production of race and class, through political study, organizing, and mobilization, centered the structural reorganization of resources to benefit those marginalized by race and class. Still, CUNY activists included a more critical engagement of class in political struggle due to the class location of their university and student body.

The race making of student activists through mobilization suggests that the institutional context and social movement landscape influenced their social movement frames and organizing. Activists at both campuses formed links to communities off campus, creating solidarity and producing long-lasting social movement relationships. CUNY's institutional context, as a working-class university with a recent history of radical student activism, shaped the emergence of SLAM!, along with the greater political activity of New York City in the mid- to late 1990s. SLAM!'s membership, which demographically reflected the working-class-of-color student body and working-class New York City, developed frames that linked race and class marginalization and contextualized attacks on open admissions within greater political-economic shifts. UC Berkeley student activists, from a variety of race and class backgrounds but enrolled in an elite public university, grappled with framing political struggle over affirmative action— that is, whether to uphold the logic of diversity or to center race and power analyses. Along with disagreement over targets and tactics, BAMN's presence contaminated the social movement landscape, causing distrust among activists and making it harder to attract unorganized students to the movement to save affirmative action.

Open admissions and affirmative action are different educational access policies, but the student struggles clearly illustrate linkages across educational institutions of different strata. Student activists recognized how retrenchment would bar access to race- and class-marginalized students, but they also extended their work to communities that could not access higher education. As these students were members of these communities, as well as university communities, their layered experiences allowed them to make connections between higher education retrenchment and race and class inequalities in the larger society. These experiences transformed many of them into lifelong activists.

When the Black Lives Matter movement emerged in 2013 and 2014, campus activism around affirmative action, diversity, and student inclusion resurfaced, with students making some of the same demands of their counterparts of the 1990s and 1960s. This persistence of resistance forces us to consider how administrators made decisions in the wake of policy elimination and how these decisions shaped the conditions for subsequent mobilization.

5

THE LIMITATIONS OF DIVERSITY

Defensive Innovation After the End of Affirmative Action and Open Admissions

---

The belief that diversity adds an essential ingredient to the educational process has long been a tenet of Harvard College admissions. Fifteen or twenty years ago, however, diversity meant students from California, New York, and Massachusetts; city dwellers and farm boys; violinists, painters and football players; biologists, historians and classicists; potential stockbrokers, academics and politicians. The result was that very few ethnic or racial minorities attended Harvard College. In recent years, Harvard College has expanded the concept of diversity to include students from disadvantaged economic, racial and ethnic groups. Harvard College now recruits not only Californians or Louisianans, but also blacks and Chicanos and other minority students. Contemporary conditions in the United States mean that, if Harvard College is to continue to offer a first-rate education to its students, minority representation in the undergraduate body cannot be ignored by the Committee on Admissions.

—Appendix to Opinion of Justice Powell, "Harvard College Admissions Program," *Regents of the University of California v. Bakke* (1978)

THE BAKKE decision has done more to define and legislate affirmative action than any statute or policy enacted before or since. That the boundaries of affirmative action have been defined in the courts, rather than among experts or policy makers, illustrates the piecemeal nature of policy development and its inherent vulnerability. The *Bakke* case, and the Powell opinion in particular, banned racial redress as a permissible purpose of affirmative action, defended campus diversity as a state interest, and elevated Harvard admissions practices as the model use of affirmative action in university admissions—all of which influenced university administrators as they developed their affirmative action programs.

As noted in Justice Powell's explication of Harvard's affirmative action program in the epigraph to this chapter, racial and ethnic identity is but one element—along with geographical residence, special talent or skill, academic interest, and intended occupation—comprised in "campus diversity." Here, racial and ethnic identity is held equal to these other kinds of factors so that racial-minority applicants do not obtain an advantage over White applicants. While diversity can include race and ethnicity, the Powell decision elucidates that diversity need not (and should not) refer solely to racial and ethnic categorization. In addition to region of residence, social and academic interests, and special talents, campuses have considered gender, sexual orientation, political beliefs, religious background, physical ability, and more in their understanding of diversity.

The Harvard admissions plan provides a framework for incorporating racial identity in university admissions and allows universities the autonomy to compose their student bodies in a way that reflects the mission and character of their campuses. The Supreme Court's split decision struck down racial quotas—a fixed number of seats set aside for racial-minority students or separate evaluation committees for racial-minority applicants—and thus redefined the discourse about minority inclusion in higher education. Desegregation and antidiscrimination were no longer the primary frames utilized to identify and structure these programs. Now, the discourse of diversity became standard and was replicated across the field of higher education. Diversity became a legally permissible defense of affirmative action, but it also became central to the ways that selective universities defined a high-quality liberal arts education.

Political scientist Daniel Lipson cites the isomorphism of the field of higher education—that is, the shared structures and programs across universities—as central to the institutionalization of the same kinds of affirmative action practices across selective campuses.[1] This isomorphism, drawing on the boundaries of diversity set by *Bakke*, also extends to the rhetoric of diversity as central to the public character of selective colleges. Diversity is a key frame mobilized at elite universities as a means of signaling a well-rounded education.[2] It is common for competitive public and private universities to have an office dedicated to diversity and inclusion, for this office to be referenced in university brochures and materials, and for racial and ethnic cultural events and initiatives sponsored by university offices and student groups to be featured as a consistent part of campus life. In speeches and at public appearances, university presidents regularly state how campus diversity is an asset and helps their institution meet its stated mission, and universities' visual branding features students of varying races, ethnicities, religions, and physical abilities as active members of the campus community. If one was to discover that a selective, elite university did not make these programmatic and symbolic commitments to diversity, one might conclude that the institution did not provide a sophisticated, high-quality education. In the age of competitive admissions, diversity is a commodity that universities utilize to appear progressive and desirable. Unlike racial redress as a justification for policy implementation, the principle of diversity is legally permissible—and unthreatening to White students and their tuition-paying parents.

Now that the diversity logic has been institutionalized, what happens when the primary means for achieving racial and ethnic diversity is stripped from the institution? How do administrators and legislators respond to these chnages discursively and through educational policy? How do these responses mobilize conceptions and practices of racial politics? In this chapter, I explore how administrators responded to the end of race- and class-inclusive admissions in practice and rhetoric. Specifically, I examine the *defensive innovation* of university administrators—that is, the new and revised practices developed to protect racial diversity at the campus level and the discursive frames university presidents and administrators adopted in response to these changing, legally prescribed practices. Public universities are uniquely caught in this tension between the diversity logic, which is hegemonic in the field of higher education, and the anti–affirmative action campaigns of conservative political actors who seek to make the principle of colorblindness hegemonic across civil society.

That administrators embrace the diversity logic, even when they are legally restricted in how they implement it on campus, does not suggest that the field of higher education is a counterhegemonic space. In fact, because diversity is a commodity that still supports the neoliberal project and does not offer new visions for more equitable power relations or a radical reenvisioning of higher education, it is also limited. And yet conservatives' successful challenges to affirmative action and open admissions constrain the racial landscape through which we understand university administrators' efforts and make their somewhat progressive attempts to defend diversity appear even radical. Administrators use defensive innovation to maintain diversity as hegemonic in higher education while conservatives challenging these policies seek a new kind of racial hegemony that centers colorblindness, eliminates diversity as a state interest and dominant logic, and reifies pre–civil rights racial logics. Yet, while affirmative action and open admissions bans prescribe policy retrenchment, they do not specify program revision. In the wake of retrenchment, administrators are tasked with developing new admissions frameworks.

In this chapter, I first examine policy adoption after the end of open admissions at the City University of New York and after the affirmative action bans at the University of Michigan, University of Texas at Austin, and University of California. With the adoption of a new strategic plan, the City University of New York implemented new admissions procedures that include stricter quantitative performance standards, but the emergence of the honors college, along with New York State's "free college for all" program, has raised questions regarding college access.

In the absence of affirmative action, universities have implemented holistic review of applicants, giving greater consideration to family background and opportunities available at students' high schools, and have expanded student recruitment to increase the admissions pool. Other universities have implemented percent plans, sometimes referred to as class-based affirmative action, which admit a fixed percentage of top students to the state university system. The Texas percent plan has been specifically praised for its ability to admit underrepresented minorities through a framework that targets interactions between race and class. These measures have enabled the university to consider the ways that location, school districts, and/or individual schools are racialized and informed by class. Percent plans have also expanded the attention that admissions offices give to class through consideration of these proxies, though percent plans are not foolproof. I then examine the discourse frames that accompanied policy reform at these institutions. Administrators have mobilized various frames, largely based on the ideals of pluralism and democratic inclusion, to defend their commitment to diversity. During this period of retrenchment, administrators have worked to innovate within new constraints. These new attempts to ensure diversity without the consideration of race have yet to meet significant challenges, suggesting that there may be opportunity to learn from policy development after affirmative action retrenchment.

NEW POLICIES AND RENEWED PRACTICES

University administrators and state legislators responded to the end of race- and class-inclusive admissions by expanding practices already utilized in tandem with affirmative action policies, such as targeted recruitment of underrepresented students before application submission and increased financial support offered to admitted students. Because these universities could no longer consider race in making admission decisions, some sought to widen the pool of minority applicants, hoping that this practice would increase the likelihood of enrolling a more diverse group of students.

Some public institutions developed percent plans, dependent on race and class segregation of their state's high schools, to admit diverse groups of students. These percent plans are viewed as the cornerstone of "class-based affirmative action"[3] because they are race neutral and target top-performing students from a variety of school districts, including those in urban, suburban, rural, underresourced, and wealthy areas. Although institutions have employed different forms of percent plans over the years, the admission of a fixed top percentage of students, largely without consideration of their standardized test scores, is a new practice.

REMAKING THE UNIVERSITY: THE CITY UNIVERSITY OF NEW YORK AFTER OPEN ADMISSIONS

While it is important to consider as a whole the new practices and resulting outcomes at the four universities highlighted in this book, separate attention to the City University of New York (CUNY) is warranted, as the end of open admissions challenged its very mission as a system based on widespread access to higher education. Black and Latino student activists pushed CUNY to live up to its educational mission in 1969, making the institution more accessible to all New Yorkers. The elevation of standardized testing, elimination of remediation, and development of an honors college as an institutional priority suggest larger institutional change. The elimination of open admissions cannot be understood separately from the remaking of the institutional mission.

Open admissions in the senior colleges ended in 1999, with the adoption of stricter standardized testing criteria and the elimination of remedial education. A new strategic plan for the CUNY system followed in 2000, and with these major changes, a tension emerged between the CUNY mission of educational access, established at the founding of City College as an institution for the poor, and the push to achieve "educational excellence"— or to raise the reputation of the system by making admissions more selective. This new emphasis was articulated in the 1999 CUNY Advisory Task Force report, *The City University of New York: An Institution Adrift*, which prioritized achieving national ranking for a number of CUNY senior colleges and recruiting more academically competitive students.[4] The CUNY Master Plan for 2000–2005 reflects this same vision by outlining plans to establish a university-wide honors college, create a "flagship environment," and funnel more resources into the science, technology, engineering, and mathematics fields in the senior colleges.

Some CUNY faculty critiqued this new plan. Sandi E. Cooper, a history professor at the College of Staten Island and former chairwoman of the CUNY Faculty Senate, said about the plan, "It's motivation is not rooted in respect for high standards, as its authors proclaim, but in a mix of business school management mantras married to the conviction that public higher education is primarily a gateway to corporate employment."[5] Comments like this illustrate that many faculty members anticipated large-scale change and were uncomfortable with the lack of transparency regarding trustee decision-making in crafting a new vision for the CUNY system. In response to concerns regarding the impact of institutional changes and the provision of broad access, the CUNY Advisory Task Force answered, " 'Access to what?' "—asserting that this new vision would reverse CUNY's "spiral of decline" and emphasize "access to excellence."[6]

When open admissions ended, the CUNY admissions process at the senior colleges changed from a one-part process that guaranteed admission to applicants with a high school diploma, with placement evaluated according to grades and campus-specific criteria, to a two-part process that inserted new criteria to evaluate admissions and eligibility. In this new process, applicants' grades, high school coursework, and skills in mathematics and English are first evaluated against minimum criteria. If applicants meet these minimum criteria, they are conditionally accepted to a campus. At the second stage, applicants are required to demonstrate proficiency through their scores on the Scholastic Assessment Test (SAT) or New York Regents Examination (the statewide standardized high school test). Applicants who meet this second criterion become eligible for enrollment. Applicants with low scores do not become eligible until they pass another round of standardized tests, called the CUNY Basic Skills Tests, which evaluate reading, writing, and mathematics. If applicants fail one or more of these tests, they are given the option to retake the test(s) after participating in a skills immersion workshop or to enroll in remedial courses in one of the system's community colleges. Applicants who fail one or more of the tests again are denied access to the senior colleges and are required to enroll in a community college to remain in the CUNY system.[7]

Data show that, rather than enroll in CUNY community colleges, many applicants either opt to enroll in other educational institutions, such as private or for-profit schools that offer remedial instruction in New York, or fail to enroll anywhere.[8] While these new admissions processes do not articulate race, the racial implications are clear. Significantly, much research has shown that Black and Latino students perform less well than White and Asian students on standardized tests; thus, elevating the role of standardized testing in university admissions can penalize Black and Latino students.[9] For this reason, an institution committed to providing widespread access to higher education might implement an admissions process that does not elevate the role of standardized testing. CUNY trustees instead emphasized that New York City high schools should better prepare their students for college.[10] They prioritized making CUNY into a more competitive, recognized, and respected institution by elevating academic standards and willingly restricting educational access.

The introduction of these policies significantly impacted CUNY's demographics. Research illustrates that only four years after the adoption of this new admissions process, more than half of White applicants (52.8 percent) were deemed eligible for enrollment (based on standardized test scores), while only 18.8 percent of Black applicants and 22.3 percent of Latino applicants were deemed eligible. As high school graduation rates in the city increased over this period (from 1999 to 2003) and CUNY increased the number of freshman seats, the number of first-time freshmen (FTF) in the CUNY system increased across the board. However, while White FTF increased by 29.1 percent, Black and Latino FTF increased by only 6.7 percent and 12.9 percent, respectively (table 5.1).[11]

TABLE 5.1 City University of New York changes in enrollment by race/ethnicity, 1999 and 2003

Racial/Ethnic Group	1999		2003		1999–2003	
	N	Percent	N	Percent	Change in N	Percent Change
Total	8,448	100.0	10,208	100.0	1,760	20.8
Black	1,957	23.2	2,089	20.5	132	6.7
Latino	2,233	26.4	2,520	24.7	287	12.9
White	2,741	32.4	3,538	32.7	597	29.1

Source: Parker and Richardson (2005)

Note: Percentages do not total 100 percent. In addition to rounding, the categories Asian and American Indian are not included.

Research also depicts a decline in Black and Brown enrollment in the senior colleges, as well as a clustering of Black and Brown students at "second-tier" senior colleges. Of the CUNY senior colleges, the top five most competitive institutions (Baruch, Hunter, Brooklyn, City, and Queens Colleges) constitute a first tier while the remaining senior colleges (York, Lehman, John Jay, City Tech, Medgar Evers Colleges, and College of Staten Island) constitute the second tier. Across all senior colleges, Black enrollment declined 4 percentage points among FTF, from 30 percent in 2001 to 26 percent in 2010. However, among top-tier colleges, Black enrollment declined 7 percentage points among FTF, from 17 percent in 2001 to 10 percent in 2010. Figure 5.1 illustrates that Black enrollment declined in each sector of CUNY, even if only moderately, since 2001. While 54 percent of Black FTF were enrolled in senior colleges in 2001, 56 percent of Black FTF were enrolled in community colleges by 2010, illustrating how the Black CUNY population shifted toward the community colleges. This is especially troubling considering that, between 2001 and 2008, CUNY senior colleges increased their enrollment by 37 percent.[12] This evidence indicates that CUNY had indeed raised academic standards and that students formerly eligible for the top-tier schools had dropped a tier and more.

As the CUNY system expanded 37 percent between 2001 and 2008, Latino enrollment rose from 29 percent to 33 percent. However, as figure 5.1 illustrates, Latino gains reversed in the senior colleges by 2010. While the Latino population in second-tier colleges decreased by 3 percentage points to 30 percent (2 percentage points higher than ten years earlier), gains made at top-tier colleges disappeared, returning Latino enrollment to 19 percent.

Black and Latino students had been concentrated at a variety of second-tier colleges since the adoption of open admissions in 1969; however, they also had maintained significant representation at top-tier colleges. Now, as Black and Latino enrollment in top-tier colleges declined, many students in these populations clustered at community colleges.

For example, during the last year of open admissions in 1998, Hunter College (one of the more selective colleges in the CUNY system, with a 30 percent acceptance rate) enrolled 20.2 percent Black,

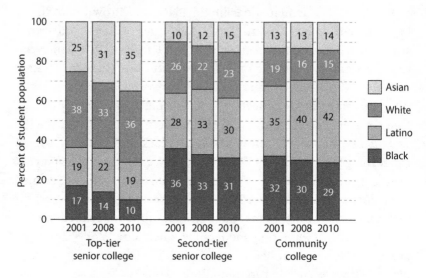

FIGURE 5.1 Racial/ethnic composition of each CUNY tier.

Source: Treschan and Mehrotra (2012).

22.3 percent Latino, 16.7 percent Asian, and 40.6 percent White students. However, by 2013, Hunter College enrolled 12.5 percent Black, 18 percent Latino, 23.5 percent Asian, and 45.8 percent White students. The Black and Latino enrollments declined by 38 and 19 percent, respectively, and the White and Asian enrollments increased by 12.8 and 40.7 percent, respectively (table 5.2). At Hunter College, the immense increase in Asian students and the drastic decrease in Black students are notable.

TABLE 5.2 Hunter College changes in enrollment by race/ethnicity (%)

	1998	2013	Percent Change
Black	20.2	12.5	−38.11
Latino	22.3	18.0	−19.2
Asian	16.7	23.5	+40.7
White	40.6	45.8	+12.8

Source: CUNY Office of Institutional Research (2014).

Note: Percentages do not total 100 percent. In addition to rounding, the category American Indian is not included.

Similar to Black student enrollment, Latino student enrollment at community colleges increased, suggesting that the adoption of higher academic standards increased competition for admission to senior colleges. However, Latino decreases appeared in relationship to the recession of 2008, suggesting that admissions competition at CUNY increased as college tuition across the country became less affordable during economic downturn.[13] Over the years, CUNY significantly raised tuition (and state budget cuts reduced education grants); however, its tuition, less than $7,000 a year in 2014, made it a bargain even among public institutions—and thus desirable for poor, working-class, and middle-class students. Importantly, CUNY still educated a significant portion of working-class and poor students: during the 2014–2015 academic year, 53.3 percent of CUNY students received federal need-based Pell Grants.[14]

On the surface, these demographic changes may seem moderate. However, with Black and Latino rates of decline, though the number of admission seats has increased, and with the small numbers of Black and Latino students in four-year colleges nationwide, these changes are significant. When CUNY adopted open admissions, it became the largest degree-granting institution for Black and Brown students across the United States.[15] These changing conditions continue to have very real implications for educational access in New York City, a city with high rates of income inequality.

These data indicate a few things. While CUNY may maintain racial and ethnic diversity, declines in Black enrollment suggest that Black students benefited the most from open admissions. Black students continue to enroll in the community colleges; however, the end of open admissions in the senior colleges meant that Black and Latino students, in particular, encountered more obstacles, including more tests, higher tuition, fewer services, and the cumbersome process of transferring from community college to senior college to obtain a bachelor's degree. A large percentage of CUNY students have been nontraditional students—working full-time, serving as caretakers of family members, and taking a considerably longer time to attain degrees compared to traditional students. In the long term, CUNY restructuring marks a transition to recruitment of more traditional, middle-class college students, who will be disproportionately White and Asian. CUNY is one of the most successful educational systems in the country for intergenerational mobility: six CUNY campuses rank in the top ten for social mobility (that is, the ability of students in the bottom economic quintile to reach the top fifth of income distribution).[16] That a significant portion of working-class Black and Brown students may not be able to access these opportunities now due to CUNY restructuring calls its educational mission into question.

New policies undermine educational access, especially for Black students, and force us to consider the limitations of diversity. If CUNY is able to maintain itself as a majority-minority system, or a system that educates large numbers of immigrants and racial minorities, but it prevents many poor and otherwise marginalized students from enrolling in the senior colleges, is it serving its educational mission? CUNY trustees argue that it is not the university's responsibility to serve unprepared students just because they are socially marginalized. However, in a period of increasing social inequality, CUNY's mission to educate the underserved is even more significant. The university's failure to address the consequences of institutional change may mean more barriers on the educational and occupational paths of those marginalized due to race and class.

CUNY has tried to widen its pool of applicants and has implemented summer immersion programs,[17] but many of these programs have already been abandoned, with no alternative policies to replace them.[18] However, the Search for Education, Elevation and Knowledge (SEEK) program remains an opportunity for poor students, who are overwhelmingly Black and Latino, to remain at CUNY. City College established SEEK prior to open admissions in the mid-1960s as a vehicle to recruit Black and Latino students who had intellectual promise (but who did not test well) into the CUNY system. The SEEK program serves both educationally and economically disadvantaged students; enrollees cannot make more than $21,978 if in a household of one or $44,955 if in a family of four.[19]

Students who are not admitted to CUNY under the standard educational guidelines can still be admitted if they are accepted by SEEK, though post–open admissions criteria strip SEEK of the power to keep students enrolled. SEEK's success was built on the availability of remedial education in the senior colleges; now all SEEK can offer students is a one-year window in which to pass standardized tests while enrolled, rather than having to pass all exams prior to enrollment, as required by the standard admissions procedures.[20] However, this means that students with remedial needs are being admitted to CUNY through the SEEK program without access to remedial courses. SEEK now conducts a longer and more intense summer immersion program, and students are encouraged to participate in supplemental instruction sessions to help them pass eligibility exams.[21]

Many CUNY senior colleges are dependent on SEEK for significant representation of Black and Brown students. In 2014, Black students represented about 21 percent of SEEK students system-wide, with Latinos representing 41 percent, Asians representing 29 percent, and Whites representing 8.4 percent.[22] Still, SEEK has seen more than a 20 percent reduction in funding since 1994, and multiple New York governors have threatened to eliminate the program entirely.[23] The persistence of the SEEK program is significant, considering the restructuring of CUNY, but professors and staff who work with SEEK students told me in interviews that they predict more budget cuts and retrenchment of the program.[24] SEEK is constantly under threat of elimination—just another example of how CUNY's priorities have shifted.

The vision to remake CUNY into a more selective public higher education system is also being realized through the Macaulay Honors College, established in 2001 by the Board of Trustees. The honors college targets high-performing students who, according to trustees and conservatives, "took flight" during open admissions.[25] Students who gain admission through the honors college are given free tuition, a $7,500 spending account, and a free laptop. Macaulay students also have access to smaller classes and special academic programs. A $30 million donation by William E. Macaulay to the college in 2006 (the largest donation ever made to CUNY) secured a building for the honors college on the Upper West Side of Manhattan.[26] While 38.1 percent of students in CUNY senior colleges are the first in their families to attend college,[27] 18 percent of Macaulay students are first-generation college students.[28]

The Hertog Scholars program, established at Macaulay by the Hertog Foundation, provides free course materials and books, academic mentoring, and an additional $2,000 stipend. It emphasizes a classical education based on the study of Western civilization, with philosophical questions stated throughout the brochure (and a picture of Karl Marx),[29] although Roger Hertog, the founder of the Hertog Foundation, is chair emeritus of the Manhattan Institute for Policy Research and trustee of another conservative think tank, the American Enterprise Institute. Macaulay Honors College is a significant site of institutional change in the CUNY system, and the resources funneled into the college (many of them from corporate sponsors) are evidence that trustees and administrators view this as a priority on the CUNY agenda. The high cost of remediation partially justified the end of open admissions; in contrast, by 2009, the honors college had received over $50 million in support and was projected to raise $100 million by 2015.[30]

Following the 2016 election cycle, during which college affordability became a prominent talking point among Democratic presidential contenders, New York Governor Andrew Cuomo proposed and passed a free college program for students enrolled in public postsecondary education in the state, including the State University of New York (SUNY) system and CUNY. This Excelsior Scholarship program, billed as the country's "first accessible college program," targets middle-class students through its funding structure, which is intended to keep public college graduates in New York State after graduation. Poor students in New York (including CUNY students) are already able to fund their tuition through a combination of federal Pell Grants and state Tuition Assistance Program grants. The Excelsior Scholarship, first available for students who enrolled for the 2017 fall semester, provides a tuition credit for the difference between tuition and these grant programs. For students who do not qualify for those need-based grants, the state will pay their full tuition, reimbursing SUNY and CUNY if they enroll.[31] In 2017, families that earned up to $100,000 (almost twice the state median income) benefited from this program; by 2019, this income level increased to $125,000.[32] New York public universities are some of the most affordable in the nation (tuition was less than $7,000 for CUNY and SUNY schools in 2017). Nevertheless, this program will eliminate some of the debt burden of middle-class students who might take out loans to fund their college education.

Eligible students have to be a resident of New York State, enrolled as a full-time student (taking thirty credits a year) at a CUNY or SUNY college, maintain a 3.0 grade point average (GPA), and graduate on time (in two years for a community college degree or four years for a bachelor's degree). Importantly, there is a postgraduation residency requirement: students have to remain in New York State for a period equivalent to the time in which they earned their degree (two or four years). If students take longer than the allotted time to graduate, their GPA drops, they fall to part-time status, or they leave the state after graduation, their free tuition can convert into a loan that requires repayment.[33] This program covers only tuition, not school fees, room and board, or the other expenses that often double the cost of college for students. On a campus level, if demand exceeds capacity for enrollment in the free college program, institutions may utilize a random lottery to grant the Excelsior Scholarship rather than offer it to all eligible students.[34] The program also contains a provision that allows colleges to raise tuition every year for the students who do not meet its eligibility requirements and have to pay tuition themselves—such as the students who take longer to graduate.

This tuition hike provision, along with the eligibility requirements, makes clear that the program is not about meeting the needs of the underserved; rather, it focuses on college affordability for middle-class students. Students who attend school part-time because they are working to pay school fees and support family members, and students with remedial needs, may be further burdened by this program, which seeks to support middle-class students, potentially on the backs of working-class students. At public institutions nationally, 22 percent of full-time students finish community college in three years, and 59 percent finish their bachelor's degree in six years,[35] meaning that a significant percentage of New York State students that enroll in the Excelsior Scholarship program are at risk that their free tuition will convert into an educational loan. Additionally, this program may give CUNY and SUNY an incentive to pursue out-of-state and international students, who pay more than twice the amount of tuition that New York State residents pay. An early report on the Excelsior Scholarship program from the Center for an Urban Future finds that only 2.3 percent of students enrolled in CUNY senior colleges received awards. The majority of applicants to the program (70 percent) were rejected, with the heavy credit requirement serving as the primary obstacle to most applicants.[36]

In the case of CUNY, trustees, Advisory Task Force members, and state legislators seek to place middle-class students at the center of their vision of college access. This redefinition of the model CUNY student aligns with the effort to transform CUNY into a more marketable educational system. Administrators, who have long dealt with budget cuts and limited capacity, largely did not object to this new direction for CUNY; they were likely swayed by new plans to increase revenue streams and reduce costs related to remediation. CUNY administrators capitulated to this new vision more readily than administrators dealing with a post–affirmative action landscape. Thus, CUNY administrators did not engage in defensive innovation to maintain access to the senior colleges for working-class and/or Black and Brown students. While faculty protested these changes, their considerations were largely ignored in the development of a new strategic plan for the CUNY system.

The outcomes of policy revision reify race and class inequality in the quest for a CUNY that is comparable to more selective educational institutions. CUNY illustrates how the economic conditions of a working-class, less-selective institution can make it vulnerable to policy retrenchment and how retrenchment can shift the focus to new kinds of students who are more class privileged and more often White or Asian. Because CUNY continues to be a majority-minority system, marketing diversity comes easily to the institution. However, now that CUNY leadership seeks to create demand among middle-class students, affordability and rising academic standards are the primary commodities marketed to the public. This new vision for CUNY simultaneously reifies the logic of colorblindness through its abandonment of open admissions and its pursuit of more advantaged students, and the logic of diversity, through its majority-minority status.

DIVERSITY RETENTION EFFORTS: EXPANDING THE POOL AND HOLISTIC REVIEW

During and after the use of race- and class-conscious admissions policies, the University of Michigan (UM), University of Texas at

Austin (UT Austin), and University of California Berkeley (UC Berkeley) made efforts to widen their recruitment pools, employing high school visits in minority-dense areas and utilizing faculty, students, and alumni of color to persuade students to apply to and attend their institution. These institutions focused on raising the yield rate, or the rate at which accepted students decided to attend the university. As top public and private universities often target the same pool of talented racial-minority students for enrollment, these universities offer additional scholarships and other incentives to encourage these students to enroll.

At UC Berkeley, Chancellor Chang-Lin Tien developed the Berkeley Pledge immediately after the end of affirmative action. This program, dedicated to recruiting underrepresented students and maintaining a diverse student body, expanded summer bridge programs in partnership with K–12 schools to expose disadvantaged students (defined by enrollment in underresourced or underrepresented schools and/or low family-income levels) to a college environment, increased scholarships for disadvantaged students, and employed letter-writing campaigns to high schools to identify high-performing students.[37] This program also sent UC Berkeley faculty and students into these K–12 pipeline schools to assist with curriculum development, tutoring, teacher training, and other kinds of in-class support.[38] The *Master Plan for Higher Education in California*, first issued in 1960 by the California State Department of Education, determined that the UC system would admit the top 12.5 percent of graduating seniors in the state. However, many underresourced schools did not offer the coursework needed for students to become UC eligible; thus, only 11 percent of California high school seniors were eligible for admission to a UC campus. The Berkeley Pledge focused on preparing students to become UC eligible. Yet, by 2001, administrators had reorganized the Berkeley Pledge program, renamed it the School/University Partnership program, and housed it in the newly created Center for Educational Partnerships.[39] The numbers of enrolled underrepresented students had not returned to affirmative action levels.

UCLA, whose 18 percent admit rate rivals UC Berkeley's 17.5 percent rate, instituted similar recruiting methods, which senior admissions staff identified as "intrusive recruiting," in which they offer tours, academic and financial advice, and other recruitment resources to high school freshmen. UCLA recruiters have expanded their reach beyond identified high schools to churches, community festivals, and popular coffee chains, working to make the idea of UCLA admission attainable to potential applicants and their families.[40] These efforts, along with an increase in the admissions recruitment budget from $1 million to $1.7 million, have made UCLA more successful at enrolling underrepresented minority students than UC Berkeley. In 2016, UCLA and UC Berkeley each admitted an additional 1,000 freshmen for the 2016 fall semester, increasing the number of students of all ethnicities. As a result of these additional seats, increased admission offers to Black and Latino applicants led to the largest boost in Black and Latino enrollment at each school since the passage of Proposition 209.[41] UCLA increased offers to Blacks by 37.7 percent and to Latinos by 20.6 percent, resulting in an undergraduate student body that was 4.8 percent Black and 20.9 percent Latino. UC Berkeley increased offers to Blacks by 17.3 percent and to Latinos by 8.10 percent, resulting in an undergraduate student body that was 3.2 percent Black and 14.2 percent Latino.[42] (See table 5.3.)

These campus compositions should be understood in the context of the 2016 state audit of the UC system, which accused administrators of prioritizing the admission of higher-tuition-paying

TABLE 5.3 University of California undergraduate enrollment demographics (%)

	UC Berkeley			UCLA		
	1999*	2006	2016	1999*	2006	2016
Black	4.7	3.4	3.2	4.7	2.9	4.8
Latino	10.3	10.9	14.2	14.6	15.0	20.9
Native American	0.8	0.5	0.6	0.6	0.4	0.5
Asian	39.4	41.3	38.4	37.0	38.4	32.1
White	30.3	31.5	25.9	33.7	34.2	26.27

Sources: UC Berkeley Office of Planning and Analysis (2017b); University of California Office of Institutional Research and Academic Planning (2018a)

Note: Percentages do not total 100 percent. In addition to rounding, the categories Unknown and International are not included.

* The UC system does not make pre-1999 undergraduate racial demographic data available to the public.

out-of-state and international students over that of California residents. Nonresidents pay over $20,000 more in tuition than California residents, and between 2010 and 2015, nonresident enrollment increased 82 percent across the UC system.[43] As a result of this audit, the UC system adopted 18 percent caps on nonresident enrollment at five UC campuses while instructing the most competitive campuses (which had the highest nonresident populations) to cap nonresident enrollment at their current percentages. In 2016, non-California residents made up 24.4 percent of UC Berkeley's student body and 22.8 percent of UCLA's student body.[44]

While UC Berkeley and UCLA enroll more Pell Grant recipients than UM or UT Austin (31 percent and 37 percent, respectively, as compared to UM's 16 percent and UT Austin's 25 percent), their high percentages of nonresident students are an indicator of the class status of enrolled students.[45] The growing costs of a university education, along with a national shift toward merit-based scholarships (in contrast to need-based financial aid), means that competitive universities continue to cater to more affluent students.

UM has had ups and downs in trying to maintain significant numbers of underrepresented students. Among the universities featured in this book, and even among highly selective public universities across the country, UM students had the highest median family income, at $154,000.[46] These class dynamics certainly shape the ability to attract and admit Black students. Though the administration established the Center for Educational Outreach and Academic Success to facilitate partnerships with K–12 schools, UM initially struggled to recover the level of Black students it had under affirmative action policies. Black FTF enrollment plunged to 3.7 percent in 2014, almost half that of fifteen years earlier (table 5.4). However, during this same period, the FTF enrollment of all other racial groups increased.

In 2014, UM hired Dr. Kedra Ishop as associate vice president of enrollment management.[47] Ishop had been the admissions director at UT Austin, which maintained significant numbers of Black and Latino students after an affirmative action ban, and she ushered in new initiatives to attract, admit, and maintain populations of underrepresented students at UM. In 2016, UM rolled out an $85 million

TABLE 5.4   University of Michigan first-time-freshman enrollment by race/ethnicity (%)

	1999	2007	2014	2016
Black	7.2	5.6	3.7	4.3
Latino	3.6	4.5	4.3	6.3
Asian	13.1	12.6	14.7	16.1
White	65.0	63.7	65.9	61.6

Source: University of Michigan Office of the Registrar (2017)

Note: Percentages do not total 100 percent. In addition to rounding, the categories American Indian and Unknown are not included.

five-year strategic plan for diversity, which aimed to ensure a diverse campus by developing an inclusive campus climate, creating diverse student and faculty bodies through recruitment and retention, and supporting the incorporation of diversity into curriculum development and the evaluation of faculty service commitments.[48]

A year after Ishop began her tenure at UM, the numbers of underrepresented freshman students increased for the first time since the affirmative action ban in 2006 (table 5.4). The university has now focused on increasing the yield rate, or the number of students who are offered admission and enroll, through aggressive outreach to admitted students. Once students are admitted, alumni, students, and faculty encourage them to enroll; admissions officers have also increased student aid offers to these students, repackaging them as "tuition scholarships" because they found families responded better to that phrasing than to a dollar amount. UM has also eliminated the waiting list, which favors higher-income White and Asian students who can make a deposit to reserve their space at a university while they wait on an admissions decision from another.[49] Another pilot initiative, the need-based High Achieving Involved Leader (HAIL) scholar program, walks low-income applicants through the admissions process, offers them vouchers to cover application fees, establishes personal connections between these students and the admissions office, and, if they are admitted, provides a full scholarship to cover tuition and fees.[50] UM has not regained affirmative action levels of Black students, but these combined efforts have resulted in a freshman class that is 4.9 percent Black (a 12.6 percent increase from 2010), 5.6 percent Latino (a 33.8 percent increase from 2010), 13.5 percent Asian (a less than 1 percent decrease from 2010), 0.14 percent Native American (a 12.5 percent decrease from 2010), and 61.42 percent White (an 11.5 percent decrease from 2010).[51] Before the implementation of these new admissions practices, Black FTF enrollment had declined by almost 50 percent (table 5.4).

Admissions offices worked to increase the impact of recruitment through larger budgets, expanded programs, cross-university collaboration, and additional admissions staff. UCLA, UC Berkeley, and UM were unable to attain affirmative action levels of African American students after their state bans, but they attained higher levels of Latino students, in addition to high populations of Asian and White students.

Administrators utilized defensive innovation to pursue campus diversity without the means to formally consider race in admissions decisions. The most common way that they pursued diversity without the consideration of race was through the practices that had already been utilized, such as a holistic review, or a balanced consideration of a student's academic performance (measured through grades and test scores), extracurricular activities, letters of recommendation, student essays, and educational context, including high school quality, region, and family background.[52] Though there is not always consensus among administrators about what constitutes holistic review, according to *Grutter v. Bollinger*, which upheld the consideration of race within the holistic review of applications at the UM Law School, it incorporates the individualized consideration of each application and does not employ automatic acceptance (or rejection). In practice, holistic admissions approaches vary from methods that simply evaluate each aspect of the application, to those that highlight the unique contributions of each student, to those that evaluate the applicant in light of educational opportunities, family background, and other environmental contexts.[53] Overall, students are evaluated according to what they can potentially contribute to the campus learning environment, which is often specific to the institutional mission or culture of each university. The continued use of holistic review, without the consideration of race, is a common approach universities use to develop and maintain diverse campuses without the ability to formally consider race.

A greater consideration of students' educational context is most clearly seen in percent plans, but admissions officers also focus on maximization, or the extent to which students enroll in the most rigorous courses available to them. In states where affirmative action has been banned, "maxing out" curricular offerings improves admissions chances for all students, yet research shows that low-income and Black and Brown students are least likely to maximize their high school curriculum as a result of de facto tracking.[54]

Diversity is a commodity important to university administrators; their institutions have spent millions of dollars trying to ensure diverse campuses after affirmative action bans. Diversity, hegemonic across the universities considered here, functioned as a valuable commodity even when the legal defense of racial diversity was not available to these campuses. Although colorblindness may have shaped the admissions processes legally, universities engaged in a variety of methods to pursue campus diversity. The most heralded of these approaches is the percent plan utilized in the state of Texas.

PERCENT PLANS: "CLASS-BASED AFFIRMATIVE ACTION"

Percent plans guarantee admission to a state college system for a top percentage of high school graduates. Because they admit a fixed percentage of top high school seniors within a state, these percent plans have the potential to benefit high-achieving students across class context, equalizing the status of underresourced, middle-class, and affluent high schools. For this reason, these programs are often referred to as class-based affirmative action, though the institutions themselves rarely characterize the plans in this way. Residential and educational segregation persists across the country, and the ability of these percent plans to admit racially underrepresented students into selective universities is dependent on these patterns of institutional inequality remaining unchanged. Percent plans with different objectives and methods have been implemented in Texas, California, and Florida.

While research conveys the limitations and failures of these percent plans in restoring even small populations of underrepresented students after affirmative action bans, they have been the most comprehensive policy response to the elimination of affirmative action. Thus, it is important to examine percent plans as an example of defensive innovation in Texas and California.

UNIVERSITY OF TEXAS TEN PERCENT PLAN

A few Texas legislators were unwilling for the *Hopwood v. Texas* affirmative action ban to be the last word on diversity in higher education, so they began to research possible responses. Irma Rangel, a Mexican American Texas state representative (and chair of Texas House Committee on Higher Education) initiated this process, forming research committees to assess and address methods to maintain Black and Latino representation in the state's higher education system.[55] First, a committee of lawyers, assembled by Mexican American Senator Gonzalo Barrientos focused on litigation strategies that would preserve affirmative action; they ultimately concluded, with the *Hopwood* decision prominently in their minds, that the Fifth Circuit's decision undermined their moral argument, rooted in diversity as a compelling state interest. Race neutrality was the law of the land.

Representative Rangel pushed the legislature to pass House Bill 2146, which required the Texas Higher Education Coordinating Board to research the impact of the elimination of affirmative action on Black and Latino admissions in undergraduate and graduate schools; the resulting report showed that, even with race-conscious admissions, minorities were being admitted in very low numbers at UT Austin, one of the state's two flagship campuses. For example, in 1975, UT Austin's student body was 2 percent Black and 5 percent Latino; in 1996 (the last year of affirmative action in Texas), its student body was only 3 percent Black and 15 percent Latino while the state population was 12 percent Black and 27 percent Latino.[56] The report also highlighted the need to understand minority admissions in the context of educational opportunities in Texas—a state whose primary and secondary schools reflected high levels of racial segregation. Throughout the state, test scores were highly determinative in the admissions process, and elites performed better on standardized testing across racial groups.[57]

As a result of this report, Representative Rangel and Senator Barrientos commissioned another study to explore the ways that diversity could be encouraged on university campuses without using affirmative action. Dr. Jerry Gaston, a sociologist from the Texas A&M University, chaired this study, which ultimately recommended that parents' education level, family income level, and the economic status of the school district be considered in admissions criteria. The study also suggested that standardized tests not be a major factor in admissions decisions or financial aid allocation.[58] In addition, the legislators assembled a task force of students, academics, and attorneys from the Mexican American Legal Defense and Education Fund (MALDEF) and the National Association for the Advancement of Colored People (NAACP) to explore legislation that would restore Black and Latino representation in Texas universities.[59] This group organized itself into smaller subcommittees in order to explore specific options.[60]

The research from these various groups led to a number of conclusions, including that Blacks and Latinos were not the only applicants performing poorly on high-stakes aptitude tests. In fact, poor and working-class White students had low scores and were not gaining entry to UT Austin either. Ultimately, the students from more rigorous, higher scoring, and well-resourced schools had the most access and the highest admissions rates: graduates from 10 percent of Texas high schools made up 75 percent of UT Austin's student body. And yet these research committees also discovered that both the SAT and the LSAT did little to predict academic success at UT Austin. A small working group headed by UT Austin sociologist and historian David Montejano proposed admitting a hard percentage of graduates from each Texas high school. This ultimately became the Texas Ten Percent Plan.[61]

The Texas Ten Percent Plan (House Bill 588 and its companion, Senate Bill 177) guaranteed admission to the public university of their choice to the top 10 percent of students in each high school graduating class. In Texas, high school graduates had the option of qualifying for one of three different types of diplomas: the Minimum High School Program (MHSP), the Recommended High School Program (RHSP), and the Advanced (Distinguished) High School Program. For students to be eligible for the Ten Percent Plan, they had to obtain at least an RHSP diploma and be ranked (by district or individual school) in the top 10 percent of high school graduates in their public or private school. While the SAT or ACT does not factor into admissions eligibility, students are required to submit scores from one with their application. Additionally, they must pass the state reading, writing, and mathematics examinations. Students who qualify are able to choose whichever state institution they prefer, including the state's two flagship institutions, UT Austin and Texas A&M. While most students admitted through this automatic process are able to pursue their major of choice at UT Austin, they are not guaranteed access to competitive majors such as architecture and engineering.[62]

The Ten Percent Plan was an innovation of previous admissions policies. Up until 1993, the UT system granted automatic admission to the top 10 percent of student applicants. That is, students in the top 10 percent of their graduating class were admitted to the Texas system, without a choice of campus. In 1994, decision makers altered the policy to include a more restrictive combination of high school class rank and SAT scores.[63] The new Ten Percent Plan distinguished itself by excluding standardized test scores and including access to the flagship institutions.

Even poor-performing, financially strapped public high schools, in both urban and rural areas, could now send the top 10 percent of their graduates to the flagship campuses. White conservative rural legislators, whose constituents' children had historically rarely gained admission to either of the flagship campuses, should have supported the plan, as it sought to make the university more economically and racially representative. Some counties in West Texas had never sent students to UT Austin. Yet, because the leadership for the measure was predominantly liberals of color, the rural conservative vote for the proposal was not guaranteed. The Ten Percent Plan passed by a single vote in the Texas House of Representatives, with votes cast largely along party lines. Notably, four Republicans who did not represent rural areas—Toby Goodman (Arlington), Tony Goolsby (Dallas), Pat Haggerty (El Paso), and Ted Kamel (Tyler)—voted in favor of the Ten Percent Plan.[64]

Governor George W. Bush was slow to support the plan. However, his strategists advised him to back the plan after it passed through the legislature because it would garner him Latino votes, and he signed the measure into law in May 1997. Bush even staged two signing ceremonies, one in Austin and one in the largely Latino city of Brownsville, within walking distance of the U.S.-Mexico border.[65] After the purported success of the Ten Percent Plan, Bush largely took credit.[66]

Yet there were challenges to the Ten Percent Plan from within and outside of UT Austin. In 2008, the automatic admission of students through the Ten Percent Plan accounted for 92 percent of incoming freshmen. Larry Faulkner and Bruce Walker, the president and admissions director at UT Austin, respectively, wanted to maintain the discretion of the admissions office. They were both wary of accepting so many students using one criterion and felt that the Ten Percent Plan overdetermined the students who were admitted.[67] It is likely that concern over the admission of legacy students and the role of alumni donations played a role in their rejection of the Ten Percent Plan. In 2008, the competition for the 841 non–automatic admission seats was greater than for the seats at Harvard.[68]

Many legislators proposed bills to restrict the top 10 percent to the top 5 percent of high school students (House Bill 656), to restrict 10 percent students from admittance to their first-choice campus (House Bill 37), and to eliminate the Ten Percent Plan entirely (House Bill 750 and Senate Bill 320). In 2009, the legislature revised the plan through Senate Bill 177, which capped the proportion of students admitted under the Ten Percent Plan at no more than 75 percent of the freshman class, beginning in 2011. As a result, the percentage used for automatic admission would shrink according to the applicant pool: in 2011, it was the top 9 percent, and in 2012, it was the top 8 percent.[69] Thus, more accurately, the Ten Percent Plan encompassed approximately the top 7 percent for fall 2017 applicants.[70]

A comparison of enrollments during the different admissions regimes at UT Austin is informative (table 5.5). In the first year of the affirmative action ban, but before implementation of the

TABLE 5.5 University of Texas at Austin first-time, full-time freshman enrollment by race/ethnicity (%)

	Affirmative Action	Affirmative Action Ban	10 Percent Plan, No Race			10 Percent Plan, Race		
	1995	1996	1997	2001	2003	2004	2013	2016
Black	3.3	2.9	2.5	3.8	4.1	4.5	4.7	4.4
Latino	14.1	14.0	12.1	13.1	16.3	16.9	22.9	23.8
Asian	14.5	14.7	16.2	14.8	14.0	14.2	20.1	22.2
White	66.0	66.1	67.1	55.8	56.9	53.9	45.6	39.3

Source: University of Texas at Austin Office of Institutional Reporting, Research, and Information Systems (2017)

Note: Percentages do not total 100 percent. In addition to rounding, the categories American Indian and Unknown are not included.

Ten Percent Plan (1997), Black freshman enrollment decreased by 0.4 percentage points, or about 13 percent, and Latino freshman enrollment decreased by 1.9 percentage points, or about 14 percent. After a few years of using the Ten Percent Plan, Black freshman enrollment reached 3.8 percent, while Latino enrollment still remained below affirmative action levels at 13.1 percent.

After the *Grutter v. Bollinger* decision, which asserted that race could be considered in university admissions through narrowly tailored means (and which superseded *Hopwood*), UT Austin reintroduced the consideration of race for the non–automatic admission seats, or 25 percent of the freshman seats. With the consideration of race *and* the use of the Ten Percent Plan, representation of racially marginalized groups increased (table 5.5). Under this new admissions regime, Black FTF enrollment increased 15 percent from numbers generated under the sole use of the Ten Percent Plan, though by 2016 it had gone back down to previous levels; Latino FTF enrollment increased over 45 percent.

The sole use of the Ten Percent Plan, without the consideration of race, also improved Black and Latino representation at UT Austin. During the first years of the Ten Percent Plan, Black and Latino enrollments did not return to affirmative action levels (table 5.5). However, by the last year of the sole use of the Ten Percent Plan, without the consideration of race, Black FTF enrollment increased by 41 percent over what it had been since the affirmative action ban and by 24 percent over affirmative action levels. Latino FTF enrollment increased by 70 percent over what it had been since the affirmative action ban and by 68 percent over affirmative action levels. Still, it is important to consider that, even with these significant increases, Black FTF enrollment remains under 5 percent and Latino enrollment remains under 25 percent (table 5.5). These numbers are significant in relationship to shifts in Texas's population demographics (table 5.6). Whites continue to be the largest racial group in the state while Latinos are the second-largest ethnic group, at 39.1 percent, though Latinos can be classified as White and non-White. Blacks continue to hover between 11 and 13 percent, and Asians are at less than 5 percent of the state population.

Under the Ten Percent Plan, the numbers of Black and Latino students returned to the levels of the affirmative action era. Combining the plan with the consideration of race for non--automatic admission seats has resulted in more representation of Blacks and Latinos at UT Austin. However, much research on the Ten Percent Plan, pioneered by sociologist Marta Tienda and her research teams, suggests that the policy is limited. One study illustrates that students in the top 10 percent had already gained admission to UT Austin prior to the Ten Percent Plan; the elimination of affirmative action most impacted second- and third-decile Black and Brown students.[71] The Texas plan has been called class-based affirmative action more than any other percent plan, but further research shows that the class composition of admissions pools at UT Austin and Texas A&M has not

TABLE 5.6 Texas population demographics by race/ethnicity (%)

	1990	2000	2016
Black	11.9	11.5	12.6
Latino	25.5	32.0	39.1
Asian	1.8	2.7	4.8
White	75.2	70.9	79.4

Source: U.S. Bureau of the Census (2018)

Note: Percentages do not total 100 percent. In addition to rounding, the categories American Indian and Native Hawaiian are not included.

significantly changed, pointing to an alarming "socioeconomic rigidity" of applicant pools. The application rate from poor high schools has not increased since the adoption of the Ten Percent Plan and, in fact, dropped after implementation of the plan, while private Texas colleges with higher tuition, such as Rice University, have received a larger share of low-income applicants.[72] Students at poor and under-resourced high schools are not informed about the Ten Percent Plan, or they decide not to apply because they are concerned (and often misinformed) about the cost of tuition, they are expected to live close to family, and school counselors guide them to apply elsewhere. Four years after the Ten Percent Plan went into effect, rank-eligible Latinos were 11 percentage points less likely to know about the policy than were their Black or White counterparts, probably because information about the plan circulated to parents was available only in English. Nearly one-fifth of Black and Latino rank-eligible seniors who do not know about the Ten Percent Plan do not enroll in college at all, though they would have been automatically admitted to the flagship institutions—pointing to a significant loss of minority talent in Texas.[73] The Ten Percent Plan is dependent on racial segregation to work, but concentrated poverty entangled with racial segregation shapes the ability of students to know about the plan and take advantage of it.[74] Nevertheless, the plan has been successful in increasing Texas geographic diversity within the student body at flagship campuses.[75]

The varying responses to limiting the Ten Percent Plan convey a number of interpretations of the plan at various stages. UT Austin admissions officials rejected the plan because it limited their autonomy in constituting the student body. Specifically, they articulated a rejection of the percent plan in favor of affirmative action, even when they were legally barred from utilizing race-conscious admissions. While their public support of affirmative action may have conveniently covered their concern over legacy admissions and alumni dollars, their stance points to the hegemony of diversity (and a specific means to achieve it) in the field of higher education. The Texas Ten Percent Plan, an innovative policy response to the end of affirmative action, serves as an example of defensive innovation in a field constrained by the legal limitations of colorblind racial politics.

UNIVERSITY OF CALIFORNIA TOP FOUR PERCENT PLAN

The ban on affirmative action in California prompted review of the UC system's general admissions practices and eligibility requirements for applicants. The *Master Plan for Higher Education in California*, first adopted in 1960 and revised multiple times since, mandated that the UC system admit the top 12.5 percent of high school graduates in the state.[76] However, research conducted by the California Postsecondary Education Commission showed that only 11 percent of California high school graduates were UC eligible—that is, they had taken the right courses and had reached the minimum GPA that made them eligible for admission to the UC system.[77] In California, a high school diploma was not enough to gain access to the UC system; it was simply a more competitive system than that in Texas.[78] Even for the top 11 percent of California high school seniors who were UC eligible, admission to the most competitive campuses of UC Berkeley and UCLA was not guaranteed.

Propelled by the research of the California Postsecondary Education Commission, the UC's Board of Admissions and Relations with Schools suggested a percent plan to fill this 1.5 percent gap. Many called this plan, championed by new Democratic Governor Gray Davis in his inaugural speech, the Four Percent Plan—though its official title is the Eligibility in the Local Context (ELC) program. The purpose of this plan is not to restore the UC population of African American and Latino students after the affirmative action ban; instead, it aims to fulfill the standards set by the *Master Plan for Higher Education in California* by making 12.5 percent of California high school seniors UC eligible. Thus, this plan greatly differs from that in Texas.

First, ELC guaranteed admission to the UC system to the top 4 percent of the graduating classes at comprehensive public and private high schools, though not necessarily to first-choice flagship campuses. In 2012, decision makers extended the criteria to the top 9 percent of graduating seniors and later increased the SAT score requirement by 130 points. ELC requires students to complete eleven units of UC-eligible courses by the end of their junior year. After high school administrators identify the top 10 percent of juniors, the UC system recalculates their GPA according to those eleven course units, for which students must have at least a 2.8 GPA. Then the UC system notifies students of their ELC status by the beginning of their senior year. Students submit college applications during the regular admissions cycle and attach their ELC identification number. During their senior year, students are expected to complete four additional units of UC-eligible coursework and take the SAT or ACT, as well as 3 SAT II subject tests. While test scores are not a barrier to general admission into the UC system, individual UC campuses use test scores in their admissions decisions; thus, tests scores still factor into eligibility at the more selective campuses. Ultimately, ELC does not suspend traditional admissions considerations for applicants.[79] The UC system also adopted measures not included in the ELC program that guarantee transfer from a California community college to a UC campus for students who fall within the top 4 to 12.5 percent.[80]

Overall, ELC is a colorblind attempt to respond to the end of affirmative action by focusing on increasing the eligibility of California students throughout the state. Yet, by focusing on increasing eligibility through a complicated, multistep process and by not significantly altering existing admissions practices, this policy more closely resembles efforts to widen admission pools rather than attempts to truly increase access to higher education for students marginalized due to race and class.

A comparison of UC-wide enrollments in the last year of affirmative action and under the ELC program provides a complicated picture that is very much related to fluctuations in state demographics. A new UC campus, UC Merced, began accepting students in 2005, adding an additional 1,600 freshman seats to the UC system and thus increasing opportunities for admission. Over this almost-twenty-year period, Latino freshman enrollment more than doubled while Black freshman enrollment stayed relatively steady, increasing 5 percent (table 5.8). The significant population increases in the state among Latinos and Asians may partially account for their significant share of UC seats. White freshman enrollment decreased by almost 49 percent, now representing 20 percent of the UC system's freshman population, while Asian freshman enrollment declined by 8 percent, representing a third of the UC system's freshman population.

TABLE 5.7 Race/ethnicity of first-time freshmen in the University of California system and California residents (%)

	UC System			California		
	1997	2016	Percent Change	1997	2016	Percent Change
Black	3.8	4.0	+5.3	7.6	7.2	−5.3
Latino	12.7	26.4	+107.8	30.6	38.9	+27.1
Asian	36.4	33.4	−8.2	11.8	16.3	+38.1
White	40.2	20.6	−48.8	50.5	39.0	−22.7

Source: University of California Office of Institutional Research and Academic Planning (2018b); U.S. Bureau of the Census (2018)

Note: Percentages do not total 100 percent. In addition to rounding, the following categories are not included: American Indian, International, and Unknown.

Enrollment at the state's flagship schools provides more insight into the shifting demographics (table 5.8). At UC Berkeley, Black freshman enrollment decreased by a staggering 61 percent while Latino freshman enrollment stayed relatively steady, increasing by less than 2 percent. Asian freshman enrollment increased by less than 5 percent, while White freshman enrollment decreased by 12 percent. In the 2016 UC Berkeley freshman class, Asians made up a significant minority, at 43 percent, and Whites followed behind, at 25 percent.

TABLE 5.8 Fall freshman enrollment by race/ethnicity at UC Berkeley, UCLA, and UC Merced (%)

	UC Berkeley			UCLA			UC Merced
	1997	2016	Percent Change	1997	2016	Percent Change	2016
Black	7.2	2.8	−61.1	5.6	5.9	+5.3	7.6
Latino	13.3	13.5	+1.5	14.9	22.4	+50.3	60.4
Asian	41.4	43.2	+4.4	38.7	32.2	−16.7	20.4
White	29.1	25.6	−12.0	33.0	24.2	−26.6	9.2

Source: University of California Office of Institutional Research and Academic Planning (2018c)

Note: Percentages do not total 100 percent. In addition to rounding, the following categories are not included: American Indian, International, and Unknown.

At UCLA, Black freshman enrollment remained relatively steady, increasing by 5 percent while Latino freshman enrollment increased by 50 percent. Meanwhile, Asian freshman enrollment declined by about 17 percent while White freshman enrollment declined by 26 percent. Asians made up a significant minority of UCLA's 2016 freshman class, at 32 percent, but Latinos and Whites were not far behind, at 22.4 percent and 24.2 percent, respectively. The contrast between Berkeley's and UCLA's demographics likely reflects the increased commitment UCLA admissions made to recruitment, rather than the adoption of the ELC program.

Some might argue that, with the end of affirmative action, racially marginalized students would not disappear from the system but instead would be more highly represented at less competitive UC campuses. UC Merced, the newest UC institution, is the least selective in the system, with a 73.7 percent acceptance rate, and Black and Latino students are more highly represented there. In UC Merced's freshman class of 2016, Black enrollment, at 7.6 percent, was more than twice that of UC Berkeley and more than 125 percent that of UCLA. Additionally, Latino enrollment, at 60 percent, made up over half of the freshmen class. Although Black representation across the UC system has slightly increased (it has always been small), the end of affirmative action in the competitive UC system meant that Black students have become more highly concentrated at the less competitive campuses while their representation dwindles at the most competitive campuses. The ELC program has made little difference in Black representation in the UC system. Latino representation has increased in the UC system, with a notable increase at highly selective UCLA, but it is difficult to say if these increases are the result of ELC successes or the result of a growing Latino population in California.

Research by the Civil Rights Project suggests that 60 to 65 percent of students in ELC already met UC eligibility criteria without participation in the program and would have received admission to the system regardless.[81] Taken with Tienda's evidence regarding the admission of Texas students in the top 10 percent of their class (without the percent plan), this research suggests that the positive implications attributed to these percent plans have been somewhat overstated.

The California ELC program has been largely ineffective in returning the numbers of Black and Latino students at flagship institutions to affirmative action levels because it was not created for this function. The percent plan does not shift or suspend previous admissions considerations. Students who attend schools where less rigorous coursework is available remain penalized because they cannot become UC eligible. Standardized test scores and course rigor are still utilized. Regional race and class dynamics were not considered in the development of this new policy. Without the consideration of regional race and class dynamics or the expansion of the top 4 percent of students to a more significant number (such as 10 percent), this percent plan cannot restore Black representation at the UC flagship institutions. However, various attempts to widen the admissions pool and recruit talented underrepresented students, as evidenced at UCLA, may prove to have more impact on the admission and enrollment of these students.

It is inaccurate to label percent plans as class-based affirmative action, because the plans do not give special consideration to class-disadvantaged students; rather, in the best-case scenario, these plans uniformly apply eligibility criteria in an attempt to not penalize students who attend resource-poor high schools. Sociologist Sigal Alon suggests that the best route for producing broad diversity on college campuses requires a "race within class model," in which class-disadvantaged students receive an admissions edge, and then race is also considered.[82] Percent plans do not solve the problem of ensuring diversity at selective institutions.

University administrators produced and upheld conceptions of race in their responses to the end of affirmative action. Administrators who engaged in defensive innovation, actively working to address the racial and ethnic composition of student bodies after affirmative action bans, sought to uphold diversity in legally prescribed color-blind means. This occurred through attempts to widen the admissions pool and expand recruitment. Texas legislators went beyond increasing outreach by targeting race through interactions between race and class in the state, which ultimately benefited Black, Latino, and White working-class students. These efforts illustrate that diversity is still the hegemonic racial logic at institutions where affirmative action has been eliminated. Still, there are a variety of ways that diversity is rhetorically framed and marketed beyond policy and program development as racial practice.

The principles of colorblindness and diversity shape, limit, and expand the policy landscape of affirmative action and open admissions. The colorblind open admissions policy at CUNY produced a diverse student body due to the relaxed admissions standards and the race and class composition of New York City. The restructuring of CUNY, including the abandonment of open admissions, reflected a neoliberal educational landscape, where administrators desired a higher ranking and more affluent students as a means to increase revenue streams. CUNY intentionally worked to engage middle-class students while dismantling efforts to include working-class Black and Latino students. However, using a colorblind admissions policy at a less selective institution meant that CUNY could maintain high levels of students of color, even with institutional reform. Importantly, limiting broad access has threatened CUNY's institutional mission. On the other hand, the colorblind logic expressed through affirmative action bans at selective public universities predictably resulted in drops in Black and Latino enrollment across the board. Administrators engaged in defensive innovation, working between the boundaries of diversity and colorblindness to develop practices that would produce diversity through colorblind methods. These attempts to recover and maintain moderate numbers of Black and Latino students were sometimes successful and sometimes unsuccessful, with UCLA's minority recruitment infrastructure resulting in the highest numbers of Black and Latino students among the selective universities considered here. As diversity remains hegemonic in the field of higher education, administrators will continue to explore legally defensible colorblind methods to pursue student body diversity at selective universities.

CONSTRUCTING A PUBLIC DIVERSITY DISCOURSE

Administrators not only revised programs but also discursively defended race-conscious admissions and campus diversity. Through diversity discourse, as expressed in university addresses, public appearances, and articles, administrators worked to define diversity in higher education, engaging in their own form of race making. In defining and mobilizing diversity at their institutions, administrators focused on American values, the mission of public universities, and the progressive nature of modern liberal arts education. These frames reflect the ways that diversity is utilized as a defense of race-conscious admissions, even after affirmative action bans, and convey how administrators attempt to market diversity to the public.

AMERICAN VALUES AND DEMOCRACY

The American values frame claims diversity is integral to American democracy—and thus meaningful for college campuses. Supreme Court decisions supported the creation of diverse campuses as a compelling state interest, and this frame elaborates on that principle by situating diversity as a persistent feature, and strength, of American culture. While administrators reference the difficulty of having meaningful national conversations about race, diversity discourse communicates familiar tropes of American multiculturalism and assimilation.

UC Berkeley Chancellor Chang-Lin Tien's references to American democracy center on his experience as an immigrant from China. Rehearsing the narrative of America as a nation of immigrants, he said, "As an immigrant, I know America is the land of opportunity. Unlike any other nation in history, America has taken pride in being built by immigrants and allows foreign-born people like me to participate in the world's greatest democracy."[83] Having described immigrants as the heart of American democracy, Tien later suggested that campus diversity was a solution to racial conflict in the larger society. His explication frames diversity as an American value, rooted in the immigrant narrative of opportunity and success.

Other administrators referenced the civil rights movement as integral to the realization of American democracy. UT Austin President Bill Powers, in an editorial in the *Wall Street Journal*, traced the significance of the Supreme Court's decision in *Sweatt v. Painter*, which desegregated UT Austin, as central to the *Brown v. Board of Education* case. In this piece, he highlighted UT Austin as a trailblazer—as one of the first flagship universities in the former Confederacy to integrate—and he placed contemporary Black students within this legacy: "While our 1950 policy aimed to keep certain people out, our 2012 policy is aimed at permitting most of their grandchildren to enter."[84] His references clearly situate affirmative action as a legacy of the civil rights movement and credit that movement for forcing America to live up to its promise of democracy. Notably, this comment references an earlier justification of affirmative action as a racial compensatory policy; this framing has largely been abandoned by administrators, as it is no longer legally defensible. Powers's position at a southern university specifically informs this kind of framing, as the other featured institutions never operated under de jure Jim Crow. Texas's affirmative action policy and then the Ten Percent Plan did not grant access to "most of the grandchildren" of those disadvantaged by the system of Jim Crow, but Powers's comments harnessed the idea of equal opportunity to American values.

This defense of diversity emerged as a response to legal attacks on affirmative action. By framing diversity as integral to American democratic practice, the campus inclusion of students of color and a multicultural curriculum become commonsense and uncontroversial. As Ellen Berrey argues, diversity discourse serves to signal compliance with the law while also codifying diversity as a "racial orthodoxy," or a set of beliefs that organize official, commonly recognized racial meanings.[85] Through this diversity discourse, hegemonic over the field of higher education, administrators render diversity a feature of American culture.

THE MISSION OF PUBLIC INSTITUTIONS

Administrators also define diversity as a core mission of public higher education and highlight the specific responsibility of their institutions to educate a state population with a racially diverse constituency. Robert Berdahl, UC Berkeley Chancellor and former president of UT Austin during *Hopwood v. Texas*, in an address to the nonprofit education forum the Commonwealth Club, framed affirmative action as important to "redeeming the social contract as it appli[es] to minorities who historically [have] been left out."[86] Here, Berdahl links together public higher education and the responsibilities of the state and citizenry to society. He speaks about the inclusion of the racially marginalized in higher education as a responsibility of the state because of historical exclusion.

Other administrators emphasized diversity as a core element of their specific institutional missions. UM President Mary Sue Coleman, in a speech given after the passage of the Michigan Civil Rights Initiative, said, "I am standing here today to tell you that I will not allow this university to go down the path of mediocrity. That is not Michigan. Diversity makes us strong, and it is too critical to our mission, too critical to our excellence, and too critical to our future to simply abandon."[87] Here, Coleman framed diversity as so central to the mission of the university that the institution risks decline without it. Although these kinds of statements highlight the importance of diversity to the university mission, the omission of why diversity became important, in the context of historical institutional exclusion of the racially marginalized, points to the ways that the historical political struggle over racial equality often disappears from narratives of campus diversity.

Finally, as most public universities have specific mandates to educate the state population, many administrators remind the public of these responsibilities, particularly in large, racially diverse states. Along these lines, UT Austin President Bill Powers said, "We live in a very diverse state and it is critical that we have pathways to leadership and provide education to people from all backgrounds and all ethnicities. Having a diverse campus so that we're training and educating a diverse group of leaders, I think, is critical for our state."[88] Here, he references a significant task of flagship public universities, in particular—that is, to train state leaders. In Texas, much of the state political leadership comes from UT Austin and Texas A&M, and one of the core elements of UT Austin's mission is public service. Thus, diversity is mobilized in relationship to public service and state leadership.

As scholars Dina Maramba, V. Thandi Sulé, and Rachelle Winkle-Wagner convey,[89] after the affirmative action ban and emergence of the Ten Percent Plan in Texas, universities pivoted to claim institutional responsibility for diversity as a means to maintain institutional autonomy over decision-making, rather than submitting to external policy intervention, as interest in race-conscious admissions waned. Administrators articulate this institutional responsibility through the mission of public universities frame: diversity is central to the public responsibility of these institutions, even when many of them have not formally included diversity as a component of their mission or have only recently articulated diversity as a priority.

MODERN LIBERAL ARTS EDUCATION

Many universities specifically frame diversity as integral to a modern liberal arts education, suggesting that diversity is important in both the content of the curriculum and the character of campus life at an elite, modern university. Lee Bollinger, former president of UM, has been at the forefront in mobilizing this frame throughout his writings on affirmative action. In explaining why diversity is important, he wrote, "Far from being optional or merely enriching, [diversity] is the very essence of what we mean by a liberal or humanistic education." He further argued that affirmative action programs encourage a "comprehensive diversity" and thus aid universities in achieving their mission, in addition to the policy being "the right thing to do." This frame centers diversity as essential to a well-rounded education that prepares students for a vigorous pursuit of knowledge and active participation in society.

Challenging the idea of college acceptance as an entitlement or a prize for past academic achievement, Bollinger said, "We in higher education understand that the admissions process has less to do with rewarding each student's past performance—although high performance is clearly essential—than it does with building a community of diverse learners who will thrive together and teach one another . . . with students displaying the daring, curiosity, and mettle to discover and learn entirely new areas of knowledge."[90] This framing of the work of the admissions office, as determining the composition of entering classes rather than rewarding individuals, also serves to defend admissions processes that give great weight to the nonnumerical character traits, interests, and activities of applicants. In the early twentieth century, Ivy League institutions used the ambiguous criterion of "character" in admissions as a cover to discriminate against

Jewish students,[91] and conservatives now use character evaluation to charge selective universities with discrimination against Asian applicants.[92] Here, diversity (vaguely defined) can now serve as a source of character in a modern liberal arts education.

While Bollinger's take on diversity and its relationship to liberal arts draws from a humanities perspective, other framings highlight the benefits of diversity in a global economy and the need to train students effectively for twenty-first century careers. UC Berkeley Chancellor Tien reflects this aspect in a speech on affirmative action:

> Let me ask you, the students in our audience, how America's diversity will affect your careers. If you are an education student, who will you teach? It is likely you will teach many youngsters born in different countries. If you are a medical student, who will you treat when you enter practice? Most likely you will treat many patients with beliefs and attitudes about medicine different from the Western outlook. If you are students of engineering or business, what will be your objectives? If you work for major corporations, you will be expected to design, develop, and market products that sell not just in the U.S. but in markets around the world.[93]

Tien's framing of diversity here, referring to people with divergent belief systems, attitudes, nationalities, and consumption patterns, is broad enough to encompass "difference" without specifying historical disadvantage—a common way universities publicly represent diversity. He frames a diverse educational experience, and especially American diversity, as necessary to the future career success of UC Berkeley's students. Along with university resources and networks, renowned academic programs and research, and campus social activities, diversity is a commodity made available to students so they can graduate as well-rounded, sophisticated, and employable adults. Thus, particularly in the context of a modern liberal arts education and the global university, diversity becomes a way to market selective institutions.

The dominance of the American values, public university mission, and modern liberal arts education frames suggests that defining and defending diversity at the administrative level depended on framing it as universal, inclusive, and an important part of rigorous university training. Administrators' diversity discourse drew on common, recognizable frames that rendered it unthreatening, familiar, and appealing to a larger audience of potential students and investors, alumni, peer institutions, and admirers. By pairing diversity with these familiar ideas, administrators shaped diversity within the prescribed legal and political limits, while defining their own replicable diversity frames. Frames that were less recurrent, but significant for how they engaged policy revision, mobilized personal narrative and opposition to reform. These frames rejected the retrenchment of affirmative action and open admissions, drawing on firsthand examples that communicated the benefits of diversity and also conveyed internal disagreement over policy change.

PERSONAL NARRATIVE

This frame engages the personal narratives of administrators in explaining their support of affirmative action policies. In this way, they point to the ways that race-conscious admissions practices work to counter elements of racism in an academic setting. Only one university president used his personal experience to explain this significance, likely because only one university or system president in office during and after these challenges identified as a racial minority—UC Berkeley Chancellor Tien.

Tien, a Chinese immigrant, speaks at length about attending graduate school in Kentucky during Jim Crow and walking (rather than taking the segregated buses) to class. Viewing the complicated positionality of Asians in the affirmative action debate as akin to his societal position in graduate school, he said, "Just where exactly did an Asian fit in? I too have a skin color but I am not black. And if I chose the front section [of the bus], what kind of statement was I making about the black men, women, and children relegated to the rear?"[94] In a later speech, he continued to use his own personal experiences of marginalization in graduate school to explain how racial inequality manifests:

My first months in the U.S. reflect how opportunity and racial intolerance can be linked. I served as a teaching fellow for a professor who refused to pronounce my name and only referred to me as "Chinaman." One day the professor directed me to adjust some valves in a large laboratory apparatus. When I climbed a ladder, I lost my balance and instinctively grabbed a nearby steam pipe. It was so hot that it produced a jolt of pain that nearly caused me to faint. Yet I did not scream out. I stuffed my throbbing hand into my coat pocket and waited until the class ended. Then I ran to the hospital emergency room where I was treated for a burn that had completely singed the skin off my palm. My response seems to fit the Asian model minority myth: Say nothing and go about your business. Yet my silence had nothing to do with stoicism. I simply did not want to endure the humiliation of having the professor scold me in front of the class.[95]

Tien later suggested that the civil rights movement produced conditions in which racial minorities on college campuses were not "forced into silence," and he also argued that affirmative action helped to dismantle racial division in the United States. Here, discrimination and his resulting silence, which he views as specific to the "model minority" stereotype, would have persisted without political struggle and subsequent affirmative action policies. Rather than simply promoting multiculturalism, he illustrated, through his own experience with discrimination and an unwelcome campus racial climate, the importance of political activism in producing societal progress and affirmative action's contribution to this progress.

UM President Coleman did not use her own narrative to explain why racial diversity is important. Rather, she referenced the narrative of an alumna in her remarks at a public gathering during the political struggle over the Michigan Civil Rights Initiative (Proposal 2):

> Last week I received an email from Miranda Garcia, a Michigan graduate who shared my concern about the dangers of Proposal 2, and how it jeopardizes the fiber of our university. "My four years in Ann Arbor," she said, "were a life-changing experience. I met students from every area of the country, from all different socioeconomic and cultural backgrounds." She was blunt in saying her life-changing experience would not have been possible without affirmative action.[96]

President Coleman used the experience of a member of the UM community to highlight the significance of campus diversity in the lives of students. This student is coded as Latina, by the use of the surname Garcia, though she could presumably identify as White, Black, or Asian or come from multiracial lineage. Here, socioeconomic class and culture constitute the boundaries of diversity. This socioeconomic and cultural diversity is framed not only as central to this student's "life-changing experience" but also as an important element of the "fiber" of the university. In this narrative, the elimination of diversity threatens to undermine the institutional identity of UM. In contrast to Tien, who drew on personal examples from his past to argue for campus diversity, Coleman connected the legally defensible justification of diverse campuses to the institutional identity of UM. It is notable that the university presidents from underrepresented groups (relative to their leadership positions) utilized personal narrative to encourage support for affirmative action and the diversity logic.

Social movement scholars have illustrated the importance of storytelling, and oftentimes personal narrative, in recruiting people to a cause.[97] Similarly, these personal narratives are aimed to be persuasive defenses and endorsements of race-conscious admissions. They attach vulnerability and personal experience to diversity discourse, working to compel a broad audience to see universality in expanded educational opportunities. This frame was not common because most university representatives, who were primarily White men, did not speak from their experiences in narratives about diversity. Instead, the Chinese university chancellor and the female university president used personal narratives to drive home the importance of diverse campus settings.

OPPOSITION TO REFORM

As university presidents are tasked with assuaging the public's fears or doubts about potential challenges facing their institution, most administrators did not engage in open conflict with or exhibit hostility toward trustees, voters, or the Supreme Court in public appearances. However, the opposition to reform frame highlights the few instances of open disagreement among faculty and trustees and the upfront rejection of the use of percent plans.

While university presidents addressed concerns regarding challenges to and eliminations of affirmative action policies, CUNY administrators were far more silent on the matter and generally have not made their speeches and statements regarding open admissions publicly accessible—pointing to the lack of transparency that many critics of CUNY leadership have cited. Chancellor Tien is the only university administrator to publicly acknowledge disagreement with trustees, saying "My personal view about using race, ethnicity, and gender as one of many factors in student admissions has put me at odds with many, including the majority of the regents of the University of California who govern my campus."[98]

Michigan Presidents Bollinger and Coleman both rejected outright the Texas Ten Percent Plan and colorblind class-based affirmative action plans. Bollinger remarked that it was a myth that these methods could restore racial diversity, pointing to the drastic drops in Black and Latino enrollment at UC Berkeley. He continued to explain why he did not believe that percent plans could work:

> There are several problems with this approach: first, this approach is completely ineffective for graduate schools and professional schools. Second, it would result in admitting some top students from weak high schools who may not be academically prepared to do the work, and reject very able students who are below the cut-off at a very strong school. Third, all opportunity for individual evaluation and assessment of the candidate is lost . . . And fourth, for such an approach to work, de facto segregation would have to continue in high schools, which, given the purposes of such an approach, would be ironic in the extreme.[99]

Bollinger distinguished selectivity among elite institutions and suggested that the inclusion of poor and possibly unprepared students is not a priority of elite universities. In effect, his articulation of diversity rests on class-homogenous, middle-class Black and Latino students who had access to an elevated level of educational resources and would thus be "prepared" for an elite educational institution.

This implicit rejection of class diversity at UM is not surprising, as it is the least class diverse among the institutions examined in this book and one of the least class diverse among public universities in the nation. Bollinger critiqued the overdetermination of percent plans that minimize institutional processes of assessment and found these plans ineffective for graduate schools in particular.

Coleman also critiqued percent plans and spoke at length about why she opposes them in a statement to the Board of Regents:

> I want to talk a bit about the percentage plans now in place in a couple of states. They are not a panacea, and I firmly believe they would not work at all here at Michigan and for most other highly selective universities across the country. . . . We are an individual institution, not part of a system. And we simply wouldn't be able to guarantee admission to a certain percentage of students from every high school in the state. We have over 25,000 applications for about 5,000 seats. . . . If the nation's goal is to end segregation as identified in *Brown v. Board of Education*, how can we be in the business of relying on it for college diversity?[100]

Coleman went on to critique admission based solely on high school grades and called attention to percent plans as hardly an "unqualified success," particularly in graduate programs. Her pointed comments indicate that she shares with Bollinger a discomfort with admissions dependent on high school segregation. While she claimed that "many K–12 schools in Texas are racially segregated" without acknowledging that Michigan has some of the highest levels of segregation in the country, she raised a significant point of departure in the actual mechanics of the Ten Percent Plan: the plan's effectiveness is dependent on a large, multicampus university system and a large number of admission seats at the flagship campus.

While admission to UT Austin is the most competitive among public institutions in the state, with over 8,000 freshman admitted (and over 47,000 applications), both UM and UCLA admit fewer than 7,000 freshmen (with over 59,000 applications at UM and over 102,000 at UCLA). While UC Berkeley admits 5,000 more freshmen than UT Austin, it also receives almost 38,000 more applications, thus making it more selective than UT Austin. UM has only three campuses (its other two less-selective campuses are primarily commuter schools with larger populations of part-time students), as compared to nine in Texas and ten in California. Additionally, as the differing percent plans in Texas and California suggest, a one-size-fits-all approach to percent plans will not necessarily result in higher representation of Black and Brown students, and neither will a denial of the role of K–12 racial segregation in university admissions.

These rejections of percent plans draw boundaries around institutionally specific and acceptable ways to produce and define diversity. Even among selective public universities, the classification of the types of mechanisms used to ensure diversity may serve to indicate higher levels of selectivity and prestige.

The CUNY conflict played out in the media—but mainly through the remarks of disgruntled professors who rejected CUNY reform under Herman Badillo, vice chair of the CUNY Board of Trustees, and Benno C. Schmidt, CUNY Advisory Task Force chair and later CUNY board chair. When the CUNY Master Plan of 2000–2005 ushered in a new era at the institution, it was faculty, rather than administrators, who were most publicly critical of these changes. The CUNY Advisory Task Force's report, *The City University of New York: An Institution Adrift*, provided much of the strategic basis for CUNY's new direction before the release of the 2000–2005 strategic plan, so it was also a target of critique. Barbara Bowen, Queens College English professor and president of the CUNY Faculty Union, said of Badillo, "Badillo himself helped to create the perception that CUNY was an 'institution adrift.' The truth was that CUNY had been greatly underfunded for 20 years or more, and Badillo had not spoken out on the need for CUNY to recover from years of disinvestment."[101] Here, Bowen raised the financial constraints that befell CUNY as a central factor in its institutional change over time, rather than blaming open admissions and underprepared students as the culprits—which trustees and task force members claimed in media discourse. This oppositional frame does not serve as a kind of diversity discourse but instead critiques CUNY leadership and institutional reform.

Matthew Goldstein, president of Baruch College, publicly supported the end of open admissions and had already begun to implement higher standards in the admissions processes at his college. In a speech at the Harvard Club, he said of open admissions: "It is sad but true that what the public perceives as 'open admissions' at CUNY has been the unwitting agent for lowered standards and diminished expectations in New York City public schools."[102] In his remarks before an audience associated with the conservative think tank that supported the end of open admissions (the Manhattan Institute for Policy Research) and the alumni club of the most selective university in the country (the Harvard Club), Goldstein supported policy change at CUNY. This oppositional frame, in contrast, challenges the historical decision-making at CUNY and signifies enthusiastic consent to the new policy regime. After the CUNY Advisory Task Force issued the report, Goldstein was promoted to chancellor of the CUNY system. At CUNY, administrators were more likely to publicly support open admissions or remain silent about their concerns, rather than expressing outright opposition to institutional decision-making. Thus, their oppositional frames focused on discourse about institutional decision-making rather than diversity.

CONCLUSION

Administrators pursued the objective of racial and ethnic diversity even after they were legally barred from using race in admissions. Diversity, as a principle and a practice, has become so important an aspect of campus life that administrators devised plans and allocated resources to maintain and increase the representation of underrepresented racial minorities. However, their understanding of the value of diversity was limited to the analogy of the American melting pot—a multiculturalism which can be adapted to universal themes and specific institutional identity. Thus, as cultural studies scholar Sara Ahmed argues, diversity can be understood as an "empty container," which allows people to define or use diversity in ways that enable them to accomplish whatever it is that they desire.[103] In a university setting, administrators used diversity to present their universities as academically rigorous, progressive, and in service to the greater society.

Successes at UT Austin suggest that a combination of percent plan measures and traditional methods that incorporate race has worked to raise the representation of Black and Latino students at elite flagship college campuses. In some cases, heavy recruitment of Black and Latino students has also worked to raise their representation on selective campuses. Still, in the context of scholarship that argues diversity efforts often impede racial reform[104] and conceal White domination,[105] campus diversity efforts after retrenchment may be limited in their ability to attract, admit, and retain racially marginalized students. Proportionately large numbers of Asian students at all of these institutions complicate our understanding of race and class marginalization, and the use of Asian plaintiffs in upcoming legal challenges to affirmative action may further weaken policy persistence.

Defensive innovation illustrates how social actors adapt within constraints. Through defensive innovation after policy retrenchment, administrators deployed new conceptions of race and class in discourse and action, bounded by a colorblind legal logic and shaped by a diversity logic that was hegemonic across the field of higher education. Administrators constructed diversity through policy development and discursively defined it in the public sphere. While future lawsuits continue to assert colorblindness in higher education and beyond, higher education is likely to keep the principle of diversity alive. How diversity will change and adapt to shifting political conditions is a question that will continue to shape the racial landscape.

CONCLUSION

We demand initiation of a program in the same format as High Potential Program joining the efforts of the Academic Supports Program and SHAPE. The High Potential Program was founded in 1967 for the purpose of increasing the enrollment and retention of Black and Brown students. The organization hired students of color to recruit and directly enroll these students. The program also fostered empowerment through a model that increased retention of all students. The provision we are requiring is the special admissions provision of the program. The link would allow SHAPE to facilitate special admissions for a limited amount of students fitting certain alternative admissions criteria. The Academic Supports Program would then offer special services (possibly including special classes) for a transitional period after which these students would be integrated into the regular admitted student population, courses and curricular program.

—From the May 2017 Demands of the Afrikan Student Union
at University of California, Los Angeles

THOUGH MOST selective universities would claim that challenges to affirmative action have not undermined institutional commitments to diversity, Black students at predominantly White institutions are still making demands on their administrations. The Afrikan Student Union (ASU) at UCLA, a Black student organization, released a list of eight demands during the 2017 spring quarter in response to the "poor racial climate" on campus, marked by frequent instances of White students using stereotypes to caricature Black, Latino, and Asian students at fraternity parties, on t-shirts and stickers, and on social media.[1] These demands focused on the need for

increased resources for Black students on campus (including financial aid, housing, and campus employment), as well as heightened
recruitment and retention efforts. As noted in the epigraph to this
conclusion, Black students had previously created their own programs
to prepare Black youth in Los Angeles to attend college—SHAPE
(Students Heightening Academic Progress through Education), established after the UC affirmative action ban, and the Academic Supports Program, formed to retain Black students at UCLA.

Drawing inspiration from their predecessors' models, members of the ASU hoped to acquire the resources to recruit Black students themselves, leveraging their own structural interventions to
transform university life. These efforts echoed early experimental
affirmative action and open admissions programs, in which students themselves led recruitment efforts and colleges suspended
traditional admissions criteria. The closing lines of ASU's demands
ground them in a Black Lives Matter moment while drawing on a
1970s iteration of Black radicalism: "It is our duty to fight for our freedom, it is our duty to win, we have nothing to lose but our chains."
This quotation, taken from an open letter penned by Black radical
Assata Shakur while incarcerated in 1973, is a common refrain at
Black Lives Matter mobilizations, used to encourage and unite protestors fighting police brutality and anti-Black racism.

In 2014, the Black Lives Matter movement captured national attention and galvanized young African Americans. Black college students,
some of whom had participated in Black Lives Matter protests off campus, brought the struggle to their universities by connecting larger
movement claims to the Black experience at their universities. More
than eighty groups nationwide demanded the removal of statues and
the renaming of buildings that commemorated slaveholders; the
improvement of mental health resources available to Black students;
increased numbers and retention of Black students, faculty, and staff;
expanded resources for Black student organizations; the removal of
university administrators; and more. In one of the more successful
protests, which included the labor strike of Black football players at
the University of Missouri, the president of the university system and
the chancellor of its main campus in Columbia both resigned.[2] Other
universities have pledged to remove the names of slave owners from
their buildings, increase Black faculty, and even provide scholarships

to the descendants of enslaved people owned by the institutions.[3] However, the wide-scale implementation of this range of student demands would require a fundamental restructuring of universities.

Renewed protests against racism on campus and in the world reveal the failure of colorblind and diversity logics to dismantle racial inequality in the post–civil rights period. While diversity may function as a defense of the consideration of race in admissions, it does not challenge racial inequality or transform systems of oppression. The colorblindness rationale simply discards the existence of racial inequality, if only to reframe Whiteness as a victimized identity. Black and Latino students will always be caught between the contradictions of the struggle over race- and class-access policies. Still, affirmative action is a narrow but clear path of access for Black and Latino students in elite educational spaces; ending these policies nationally will limit the social mobility pipeline for members of racially marginalized groups. Black students who do not gain admission to elite public institutions are likely to still reap the benefits of a college education elsewhere,[4] though sociologist Sigal Alon illustrates that beneficiaries of affirmative action at elite institutions are more likely to graduate and to participate in academic and campus social life than are their counterparts at less selective institutions.[5] Black students have suffered the most losses where affirmative action and open admissions have been eliminated, and they stand to lose the most if affirmative action is abolished.

This conclusion considers the racial political landscape of the contemporary period and the likelihood of the federal elimination of affirmative action. First, I revisit the intellectual contributions of this book, and then I discuss factors that make the racial political environment hostile to the persistence of affirmative action. I conclude by contemplating the resistance of White supremacy and the rise of fascism in the twenty-first century.

ADVANCING RACIAL FORMATION
AND SOCIAL MOVEMENTS

Throughout this book, I have provided insight on how political struggle over affirmative action and open admissions propels racial formation in the post–civil rights period. The courts eliminated racial remedy as a permissible goal of affirmative action, rejecting policy explicitly attending to an entrenched history of racial inequality. As a result, the State has no legal responsibility to atone for past and persisting discrimination. At the same time, conservative court challenges and ballot propositions legally legitimated Whiteness as a victimized identity, even when the courts upheld the state interest of diversity. As the federal courts limit the means by which universities can create moderately diverse classes, their rulings communicate a waning tolerance of affirmative action that will likely cease with new court appointments.

Racial political strategy specifies the racial dimensions of political strategy. It is attentive to the manner in which racial coding and principles appear in the discourse of political actors. Racial political strategy also attends to the ways that racial signification and practice appear in the goals and activities of political actors, whether through the appropriation of particular tactical repertoires, the appointment of spokespersons and figureheads, the selection of fields of conflict, or other action. As political struggle advances racial formation, it is important to pinpoint where and how political actors do this through racial political strategy. Conservatives' use of racial political strategy and assessment of political opportunity produced many more victories than losses in their quest to eliminate race- and class-inclusive admissions. Importantly, grassroots coalitions also used racial political strategy and took advantage of political opportunity, interrupting conservative rearticulation in a few states. These victories (and losses) demonstrate that organized resistance using grassroots "outsider" tactics, as well as more elite "insider" tactics, is necessary to stave off conservative retrenchment.

Attention to the role of articulation in conflict over affirmative action and open admissions demonstrates how language and cultural symbols become sites of political struggle. Elites' articulation of civil rights discourse—particularly the terms *colorblindness, discrimination/nondiscrimination*, and *civil rights*—and their use of civil rights iconography—such as invocations of Martin Luther King Jr. and his "I Have a Dream" speech—illustrate how the powerful manipulate culture in order to roll back reform and maintain political power.

However, whether this articulation successfully translates to a mainstream audience as common sense or is interrupted by opposing discourse and action is important for how racial hegemony transforms.

Limited by the law, administrators and legislators engage in defensive innovation, actively producing diversity in discourse and through university policy. As universities are primary sites in the public sphere that define diversity, they often serve as standard-bearers, helping the public understand and interpret the racial landscape. Liberal university administrators articulated diversity as an element of American democratic inclusion and integral to the institutional mission of elite public universities. Liberal efforts to maintain minimal levels of diversity at elite institutions after affirmative action bans have been uneven. Even widely touted percent plans, as employed in Texas, work best in combination with the consideration of race in universities. Rigorous research comparing race- and class-oriented affirmative action models suggests that a framework that nests race within class produces the most racial and socioeconomic diversity.[6] While defensive innovation is necessary, it will remain limited in impact without an offensive strategy to combat racial inequality. Significantly, student mobilization suggests that diversity efforts have failed at institutions with and without formal affirmative action bans. Though student protest aimed at defending affirmative action and open admissions was unsuccessful, it contributed to the formation of activist relationships and networks that contributed to left cultural spaces and social movements. These networks will continue to be important in resisting the Right in the Trump era.

Colorblindness and diversity, the primary logics that the State and the public use to make sense of race, have not disrupted racial domination. Social actors who promoted colorblindness reinforced racial inequality by denying its existence. In practice, many of these social actors engaged in racial tokenization in order to visually communicate racial tolerance. Social actors who promoted diversity, particularly administrators, sought minor levels of underrepresented minorities to incorporate into elite institutions, rather than mounting a wide-scale challenge to racial hierarchy. Elite universities cannot legally remedy historical and persisting racial inequality in society, and university endowments, selectivity, and elite status can accommodate only *minimal* diversity. In other words, even doubling the number of underrepresented minorities at elite institutions would result in fewer tuition dollars, smaller alumni donations, and would require less dependence on standardized tests, the robust college preparatory industry, and the web of elite feeder schools that populate selective institutions. This kind of inclusion would work to deconstruct elite spaces.

While colorblindness and diversity do not challenge racial domination, both logics appear moderate in the face of blatant White supremacy in the Trump era. However, conservative elite challenges to policies such as affirmative action and the legitimation of "reverse racism" in public discourse and the law paved the way for Trump by providing a basis for Whites to embrace racial victimization—and for some to return to White nationalism. Though distrust of authority and the rejection of northern elites are important elements that make up the identity of President Trump's base of support,[7] White racial victimization is central to how his supporters understand their circumstances and make political decisions. The embrace of the diversity logic made the realization of an African American president possible, but even minimal diversity in the seat of American power awakened the racial backlash that made a Trump presidency possible. The ascendance of the Trump administration further threatens the persistence of affirmative action.

THE END OF AFFIRMATIVE ACTION (AND ITS PRECARIOUS PERSISTENCE)

The cases explored in this book convey that race- and class-inclusive admissions, as political concessions, were inherently vulnerable to later challenges when large-scale social movements no longer pushed the boundaries of the racial political field. Affirmative action does not require federal elimination in order for underrepresented minorities to experience negative impact. Yet, in the contemporary moment, a conservative and reactionary band of politicians controls the executive and judicial branches of the U.S. government; thus, it is likely that affirmative action will be eliminated. This section discusses the

likelihood of affirmative action's end and the factors that may contribute to its waning persistence. Impending legal challenges, the
Trump administration, and the liberal retreat from affirmative action
contribute to an environment hostile to the policy, while the persistence of the diversity logic in higher education and the lack of conservative consensus allow the policy to persevere.

LEGAL CHALLENGES

As of 2018, Edward Blum, the conservative activist behind the two
Fisher v. University of Texas cases, continues to challenge affirmative
action in the federal courts. After losses in the Supreme Court, he
has refiled *Fisher*, but this time in Texas state court as *Students for
Fair Admissions v. University of Texas at Austin*, arguing that affirmative
action violates the state constitution of Texas.[8] His organization, Students for Fair Admissions, has filed other federal lawsuits concerning
the use of race in admissions at Harvard College[9] and the University
of North Carolina.[10] Blum is also in the process of accessing Princeton University's admissions files for the preparation of yet another
anti–affirmative action lawsuit.[11]

In the new cases, Blum argues that affirmative action discriminates against Asian applicants, mobilizing the model minority myth
in political struggle over affirmative action. The evidence of discrimination against Asians in the University of California system in the
1980s and subsequent legal scholarship on "negative action" suggest
that Asian students are held to higher standards than White students
at elite universities.[12] As Asian students are largely not underrepresented at elite schools anymore (and, in fact, may be overrepresented
relative to state and regional population demographics), they do not
benefit from affirmative action as a whole; rather, they perform better academically than White students but are admitted at lower rates
than those White students. Still, Asians that are class disadvantaged
may benefit from affirmative action and its holistic review of applicants, in particular. Selecting Asian plaintiffs to dismantle affirmative
action is a tactically savvy move that conflates Asian discrimination with perceived White victimization and obscures the fact that
Asians would likely still be disadvantaged as compared to Whites in

admissions even with the termination of affirmative action. Though organizations representing Asian Americans have offered arguments on both sides of the affirmative action debate in the past, their role in current and future contention may prove instrumental in its endurance or demise. Recent events likely foreshadow the policy's end: a complaint filed with the U.S. Department of Justice in 2015 by a coalition of sixty-four Asian American organizations claims that Harvard University discriminates against Asian applicants; they hold affirmative action responsible for this discriminatory treatment. In this complaint, the coalition also argues that Whites have suffered discrimination due to the use of affirmative action.[13] As of December 2018, the *Students for Fair Admissions v. Harvard* trial had concluded, with the federal district court's decision expected in the spring of 2019. It is likely that the losing party will appeal.

The Powell decision in *Regents of the University California v. Bakke* established Harvard College's plan, characterized by individualized holistic review and "race as plus factor" but not the predominant criterion in admissions, as the model for the use of affirmative action. This precedent continues to inform affirmative action programs today and further solidifies the extant pattern of institutional isomorphism with respect to the use of affirmative action in university admissions. A successful challenge to Harvard's program, in particular, has the potential to eliminate affirmative action programs across the field of higher education.

All of these challenges together occur during a political period in which the already rightward leaning Supreme Court may be made more conservative, given the aging court, the power of President Donald Trump to nominate justices, and the Republican control of the Senate, which approves those nominations. Though liberal Justices Sotomayor, Kagan, and Ginsburg are supportive of affirmative action, conservative Justices Thomas, Alito, and Roberts have all ruled against it. The most recent appointments, conservative Justices Gorsuch and Kavanaugh, will rule against affirmative action, creating a legal environment advantageous for anti–affirmative action crusaders.

The U.S. Justice Department also appears to support the dismantling of affirmative action. An internal memo made public in August 2017 confirms that its Civil Rights Division sought attorneys to investigate "intentional race-based discrimination" in college and university admissions.[14] Though the department claimed that this internal announcement referred to only one case, the complaint filed by the coalition of sixty-four Asian American organizations against Harvard University and pending lawsuits filed by Blum and Students for Fair Admissions mean that the department may take on multiple cases. The administrations of Ronald Reagan and George W. Bush intervened in affirmative action cases by filing amicus curiae briefs that supported the anti–affirmative action claimant. However, the department could also aggressively intervene by joining a lawsuit on the side of the plaintiffs or by filing its own lawsuit. Although this kind of direct interference on the part of the federal government is unprecedented in affirmative action cases, the Trump administration is unpredictable. The U.S. Departments of Justice and Education have already eliminated Obama-era guidelines for considering race in admissions, documents that universities used to stay in compliance with federal law.[15]

In response to numerous challenges to affirmative action over the years, some universities have preemptively dismantled scholarships, programs, and outreach initiatives targeting underrepresented students for fear of facing costly lawsuits. Amherst College and Mount Holyoke College ended special open house programs for students of color. Williams College broadened a graduate fellowship and a prefreshman program to include Whites. Carnegie Mellon University, Princeton's Woodrow Wilson School of Public Policy and International Affairs, and Massachusetts Institute of Technology all expanded minority-focused summer or extracurricular programs to include Whites; Carnegie Mellon also expanded a full-tuition scholarship to include Whites. Southern Illinois University, facing action from the Justice Department, negotiated a consent decree to open graduate fellowships targeted at minorities and women to Whites and men. Washington University in St. Louis, also under threat from the Justice Department, broadened a minority scholarship, endowed in memory of the university's first Black dean, to White students. The State University of New York system broadened its $6.8 million in scholarships for minority students to include Whites.[16]

The fears of university administrators cannot be seen as excessive, since conservative groups promise lawsuits if these institutions do not retreat from using race in outreach practices and financial award decisions. The Center for Equal Opportunity (CEO), a conservative think tank, and Ward Connerly's American Civil Rights Institute sent out more than two hundred letters to universities that utilized race-conscious outreach and admissions after the *Gratz* decision. In their letters, the two groups demanded that the universities end race-conscious programs and outreach and/or expand them to White students. They also threatened to file complaints with the Office for Civil Rights if the universities did not respond adequately within three weeks.[17] The Office for Civil Rights can deny federal funding to universities that are found to discriminate on the basis of race and gender, and many universities work to change programs in the face of that threat alone, rather than risk losing funding or engaging in costly defensive lawsuits. Litigation in the *Gratz* and *Grutter* cases cost the University of Michigan $10 million.[18] Persisting legal challenges, conservative political power, and universities' fear of lawsuits all contribute to an advantageous legal environment for the anti–affirmative action movement.

THE LIBERAL RETREAT FROM AFFIRMATIVE ACTION

While liberal politicians may not express hostility to affirmative action, there is notable liberal opposition to the policy. Of the many arguments that liberal opponents of affirmative action use, including claims that it sets Black and Latino students up for failure and stigmatizes them in elite universities,[19] a class-based argument has begun to take hold. This argument suggests that affirmative action is unfair because it simply admits unqualified, but relatively privileged, Black and Latino students to elite schools ahead of more qualified White working- and middle-class students. They argue that race-based affirmative action should be dismantled in favor of class-based affirmative action, a colorblind admissions policy that gives more weight to family income.

Sociologists such as William Julius Wilson have advocated this position, suggesting that those who want to improve the socioeconomic condition of Black people should advocate class-based programs that reach low-income groups across race.[20] One of the most vocal opponents of race-based affirmative action, Richard Kahlenberg, a fellow at the liberal think tank Century Foundation, argues that class-based affirmative action better approximates merit than race because race matters less than class in predicting social outcomes.[21] Kahlenberg, an education researcher who also studies class integration in K–12 schools and encourages the adoption of charter school models, insists that race-neutral class-based affirmative action is the only method that ensures meritocratic higher education. Pointing to affirmative action's political vulnerability and the poor public opinion that surrounds it, he suggests that race neutrality is not only the most sound social and political choice but also the most moral. Researchers such as Kahlenberg and Duke University's Peter Arcidiacono have testified in support of Students for Fair Admissions in the Harvard College lawsuit.[22]

Many who advocate class-based affirmative action have not reached consensus on how to measure class in university admissions.[23] Colorblind class-based affirmative action programs have been envisioned as percent plans (as used at the University of Texas at Austin), increased financial aid and scholarships for low-income students, outreach to low-income students, and the use of admissions criteria that take into account factors such as family income, wealth, and neighborhood poverty levels; single-parent status; home language; and parents' educational attainment. As my review of the University of California system's percent plan suggests, such efforts may or may not include sufficient indicators to protect access for underrepresented minorities. Additionally, Alon suggests that percent plans are not true examples of class-based affirmative action; among a variety of reasons for this, she highlights how the Texas Ten Percent Plan increased geographic diversity but not socioeconomic diversity at the two flagship campuses. The segment of applicants and admits from poor high schools who were admitted to the University of Texas at Austin and Texas A&M University actually decreased after the adoption of the Ten Percent Plan.[24] In percent plans, affluent and working-class students receive the same consideration if they are able to fulfill stated requirements; there is no "plus factor" for being nonwealthy.

Admissions policies at elite universities should consider class. In fact, one positive outcome of efforts to promote class-oriented policies is that some universities have eliminated legacy preferences.

However, measurements of class are not necessarily more precise than the boundaries of race. Race continues to play a significant role in shaping the class status of Americans; thus, class-oriented measures should be employed not at the expense of race but in addition to race considerations. As seen at the City University of New York, even the less selective institutions that serve working-class students have experienced decreases in Black and Latino students. Class-sensitive policy alone does not adequately address racial inequality.

Liberal researchers' abandonment of affirmative action provides a basis for liberals and conservatives to withdraw support of the policy. The political and legal environment may produce an affirmative action ban, but the persistence of the diversity logic in the field of higher education and the lack of conservative consensus may contribute to policy persistence.

THE DIVERSITY LOGIC AND HIGHER EDUCATION

As illustrated in chapter 5, selective universities are committed to producing and maintaining moderate campus diversity. Along with other university programs and policies, the diversity management of elite universities is hegemonic over the field of higher education. Thus, structures, programs, and roles related to ensuring diversity are institutionalized throughout the field of higher education. Less selective universities also participate in this diversity management, along with nonprofit support organizations with relationships to colleges and K–12 schools. Universities promote diversity as part of the campus culture and utilize significant resources to ensure moderate racial representation, even when legally barred from considering race in college admissions. As a marker of modern, sophisticated elite institutions, diversity is essential to the institutional identity of higher education. Universities will fight attacks on diversity but also on their institutional autonomy.

Because the bureaucracy of elite institutions and the larger field of higher education have incorporated the logic of diversity, unraveling diversity management cannot be a quick or seamless process. As literature on organizations explains, bureaucratic organizations are slow to change and are designed to resist it.[25] Universities' monetary and social investment in diversity have played the most significant role in the persistence of affirmative action. However, the endurance of affirmative action may depend on the fate of further court challenges and the state of public opinion.

CONSERVATIVE CONSENSUS

A lack of consensus among conservatives has also contributed to the persistence of affirmative action in higher education. Lobby groups are key influencers in American political decision-making, and there are currently no citizen or business lobby groups organized for the sole purpose of opposing affirmative action. Accordingly, many conservatives do not consider affirmative action to be a high priority on their political agendas. In 1995, after Republicans gained majorities in the U.S. House and Senate and presidential hopefuls began organizing campaigns, affirmative action temporarily became a national issue. President Bill Clinton, General Colin Powell, Senator Bob Dole, and California Governor (and presidential hopeful) Pete Wilson all weighed in on the issue, and global news publications highlighted coverage and analysis of California's affirmative action ban. However, since then, conservatives have spent more time, money, and energy fighting other issues, such as health care reform, immigration, gay rights, and economic policy.[26]

Affirmative action is a relatively low-cost government regulation in comparison to environmental or health care policies.[27] And while Whites largely vote against affirmative action in statewide elections, greater concern over employment, health care, and taxes means that affirmative action is likely a low-salience issue for many. However, the growing mobilization of White supremacists in the Trump era may mean that affirmative action will become a high-priority issue. President Trump often deflects from major political concerns (such as possible war with North Korea, attempts to repeal the Affordable Care Act, immigrant detention camps, and the humanitarian crisis in Puerto Rico) by riling up his supporters over issues such as football players' kneeling protests or "fake news," and affirmative action is a divisive, racially symbolic issue that could energize these supporters.

Business interests have not dedicated much attention to opposing affirmative action in recent years. Many corporations, including General Motors, IBM, and DuPont, filed amicus curiae briefs *in support of* affirmative action in the University of Michigan Supreme Court cases, claiming that diversity is a great asset to their companies— and is crucial for American business and the global economy.[28] A 2015 PricewaterhouseCoopers survey of CEOs across the world found that, of those polled whose companies have a formal diversity strategy (64 percent), 85 percent claimed that these diversity strategies have enhanced business performance.[29] Businesses that do not support affirmative action have largely remained silent on the issue, wanting to avoid boycotts of their products.[30] Thus, while politicians and think tanks have been central to the retrenchment of affirmative action, the business community has not reached consensus on the issue.

Past and current anti–affirmative action campaigns are comparatively underfunded in relationship to other conservative causes. For example, while supporters of California's Proposition 209 spent about $5.5 million on the campaign in 1996 (or about $7.5 million in 2008 dollars), supporters of the anti-gay marriage Proposition 8 spent about $42 million in 2008.[31] In Arizona, supporters raised less than $200,000 for the successful anti–affirmative action Proposition 107, and most of these funds came from the American Civil Rights Institute. Yet, during the same election, supporters of the failed Proposition 109, aimed at declaring hunting, fishing, and the harvesting of wildlife a constitutional right of Arizonans, raised more than twice that amount.[32] Though anti–affirmative action ballot measures have garnered support in many states, funding for these campaigns has been considerably more modest than for other conservative causes. As current efforts to limit affirmative action have already resulted in significant decreases of Black students, in particular, and have placed universities in a defensive position, conservatives may decide that their efforts are succeeding and do not require more resources. Conservatives may believe that the current numbers of racially marginalized students in selective universities will continue to dwindle on their own or are already meager enough that there is no need to pursue a formal elimination of affirmative action.

Even with the institutionalization of diversity in the field of higher education and the lack of conservative consensus, consistent challenges to affirmative action will likely result in elimination. This probable elimination forces us to consider a range of tactics and strategies to fight White supremacy and alternative means of educating Black and Brown students.

NEW VISIONS

Our current political-economic system guarantees racial inequality. As a number of scholars illustrate, the exploitation of non-White people has been a central element of global capitalism, even as non-elite Whites are differentially exploited.[33] Thus, a more humane society requires new political, economic, and social systems. While I cannot provide a road map for revolution here, I will offer some thoughts on resisting persistent inequality and on creating new systems.

In light of our current sociopolitical conditions, progressive organizations and politicians have to be willing to mount a coordinated effort to push back on conservative retrenchment and the rise of fascism. This coalition will, of course, include groups that may not always share the same political line but that are united for the purpose of immediate defense. Such a coalition could focus on supporting progressive political candidates at the local and national levels, lobbying for the nomination of progressive federal court judges, coordinating a legal strategy to challenge discriminatory laws, and cultivating leaders to take roles on public university boards of trustees and in other kinds of powerful nonprofit institutions. Conservatives have been strategic in recruiting teenagers and college students for their organizations, funding student publications and doctoral fellowships, and producing conservative-influenced research, and progressive organization have an opportunity to do the same, even with fewer resources. These groups can work to develop young political leaders with new ideas and give them a platform from which to engage in formal political activity.

In regard to efforts to resegregate elite higher education, progressive politicians need to push for increased resources for and attention to spaces that educate most Black and Brown people. This effort should include a complete overhaul of K–12 education, especially in Black and Brown communities, so that it moves away from market-based models to public, transparent decision-making and to an education that cultivates in students the capacity to form a new world. Ths includes federal investment in the public, less selective institutions of higher education in which most American college students are enrolled. This includes a public commitment to sustaining Historically Black Colleges and Universities, Hispanic-Serving Institutions, and tribal colleges, as these are the spaces historically committed to cultivating underrepresented college students. This requires the ban of predatory, for-profit colleges that exploit vulnerable student populations. And this most certainly requires the elimination of crushing student debt, which has produced its own crisis among borrowers.

Beyond the realm of formal politics, the Left should draw attention to the primacy of language and culture, as consent to regressive economic policies is often first secured in the cultural realm. Central to political struggle over race- and class-inclusive admissions is the deployment and manipulation of recognizable language. Trump's ascent is due, in part, to his use of plain and catchy rhetoric; for example, his references to "fake news," while deceptive, communicate a clear distrust of authoritative mainstream news organizations, which aligns with the worldviews of many in and beyond his base. Language is an important part of how people understand the world; thus, it is an important site of political struggle. As Antonio Gramsci, and later Stuart Hall, would articulate, in moments of "organic crisis," when the fundamental contradictions of the social order are glaring to the public and there is a distrust of established political parties and traditional decision-making, even "common sense" changes.[34] There is an opportunity for those committed to a radically just world to shape new notions of common sense, along with different ways of governing and alternative social relations, that speak to people's lived experiences and problems. Whereas diversity and colorblindness anchored racial hegemony at the close of the twentieth century, there is an opportunity for those not incorporated into these logics, at the margins of society, to project a new vision for the twenty-first century.

APPENDIX A

Situating Political Struggle Over Affirmative Action and Open Admissions

SCHOLARSHIP ON political contention over race- and class-inclusive admissions can be broadly organized into texts concerned with (1) the history of policy development and implementation, (2) the period of retrenchment at specific sites, and (3) group-specific engagement in debate and contestation. Little has been written on open admissions in four-year institutions—and even less on the political struggle over these policies.

The most comprehensive accounts of political contention over affirmative action concern the cultural and political origins of the policies and practices and the resulting backlash. In examining the logics of action in the development of social welfare policy, scholars argue that, while the public largely commended GI benefits, which granted educational access to mostly White working-class men, affirmative action was widely controversial because it benefited racial minorities.[1] Although affirmative action has long been the subject of debate, scholars argue that its implementation served a political function in demobilizing civil-rights-era social unrest.[2]

Terry H. Anderson roots the origins of affirmative action in demands for Black inclusion in defense industry employment by A. Phillip Randolph's March on Washington Movement during World War II and in subsequent state concessions.[3] Lisa M. Stulberg and

Anthony S. Chen specifically locate the implementation of affirmative action policies at selective institutions in a first wave of early adopters that created policies in response to the southern civil rights movement and in a second wave of late adopters that developed policies after widespread urban riots and campus protest in the North.[4] Their analysis, which focuses on the universities themselves rather than the State, also suggests that institutional isomorphism,[5] or the development of shared institutional practices across a field, played a role in affirmative action policy adoption in elite colleges and universities. Jerome Karabel's work on Ivy League admissions and the construction of "merit" as a means to maintain the elite status of universities also suggests that elite university administrators developed affirmative action programs in response to the American racial landscape of the 1960s and requests by President John F. Kennedy, who called on the presidents of a number of top universities to "make a difference" and model practices for other universities to implement.[6]

Other literature considers the early backlash to affirmative action; in particular, Dennis A. Deslippe recounts the outcry and mobilization against affirmative action among labor unionists, colorblind liberals, and conservatives—as well as the deterioration of the Black-Jewish civil rights coalition.[7] Stephen Steinberg also highlights the emergence of neoconservatism,[8] led by liberals turned conservatives, and its role in anti–affirmative action debates, along with liberals' retreat from supporting affirmative action.[9] Lee Cokorinos importantly documents the role of think tanks such as the Heritage Foundation, Center for Equal Opportunity, and Federalist Society in Reagan-era policy retrenchment.[10]

Critical race theorist and legal scholar Derrick Bell has analyzed affirmative action from a variety of perspectives—highlighting how minority representatives were ignored in their attempts to intervene in *Regents of the University of California v. Bakke*; how debate over affirmative action tends to center on its costs to Whites, rather than its benefits to the racially marginalized; and what the legal pitfalls and limitations of the diversity rationale are.[11] Bell's interest convergence theory[12]—which suggests that the decision in *Brown v. Board of Education* resulted when Black demands for desegregation converged with White elite interests in demobilizing Black resistance, plans for further industrializing the South, and furthering Cold War public relations—also has implications for the implementation and retrenchment of affirmative action. The rollback of affirmative action is but one example of how group interests of desegregation diverged after the post-civil rights period.

Most literature on the post-*Bakke* period of retrenchment includes historical, sociological, legal, and journalistic accounts of specific cases, especially the *Gratz v. Bollinger* (2003) and *Grutter v. Bollinger* (2003) Supreme Court cases,[13] and of the ballot contests in Michigan[14] and California.[15] Robert Rhoads, Victor Saenz, and Rozana Carducci use a social movement framework to argue that the spread of affirmative action throughout higher education and the collective actions in support of and against the policy are examples of social movements.[16] Critical race theorists have focused on the needs to identify race in the legal rationales operating in attempts to save and end affirmative action[17] and to develop "political race" as a basis for a coalition strategy to preserve methods for achieving diversity.[18] Critical race theory's emphasis on antiracist legal and political action provides potential strategies and ideological justifications for the defense of affirmative action.

A considerable amount of outcome-oriented research on affirmative action was presented in amicus curiae briefs and expert testimony in *Gratz v. Bollinger* (2003), *Grutter v. Bollinger* (2003), *Fisher v. University of Texas* (2013), and *Schuette v. Coalition to Defend Affirmative Action (BAMN)* (2014).[19] Other work contributes to the assessment of the Texas Ten Percent Plan (a diversity intervention adopted after the affirmative action ban in Texas).[20] In the recent anti–affirmative action lawsuit against Harvard, *Students for Fair Admissions v. Harvard*, conservative activist Edward Blum has used the expert testimony of Richard Kahlenberg,[21] who advocates for the inclusion of class measures rather than race measures in admissions, and Peter Arcidiacono,[22] a proponent of mismatch theory, which argues that selective universities harm ill-prepared beneficiaries of affirmative action.

Other literature highlights group-specific experiences of political contestation and debate over affirmative action. Most literature related to Black students' demands for affirmative action center on campus movements for Black studies, which often included specific demands for affirmative action for student and faculty bodies.[23] David R. Dietrich examines the construction of White racial identity in the era of affirmative action rollback through the protest activity of anti–affirmative action bake sales, where conservative campus organizations charge White men a higher price for baked goods than Blacks and Latinos are charged to demonstrate the unfairness of affirmative action.[24]

Scholarship also examines the role of elite mobilization in affirmative action defense and rollback. Ellen Berrey's account of the Coalition to Defend Affirmative Action, Integration and Immigrant Rights, and Fight for Equality By Any Means Necessary (known as BAMN) highlights how the organization managed its activist outsider status in elite legal mobilization to defend affirmative action by making civil rights claims.[25] In framing legal battles over affirmative action as elite contests, Tomiko Brown-Nagin questions whether law can be compatible with social movements and ultimately argues that social movement organizations like BAMN that define themselves through the law threaten their insurgent role and become less effective at achieving their goals.[26] However, Wayne A. Santoro and Gail M. McGuire argue for the consideration of "institutional activists," or state actors who seek social movement goals through conventional political routes, in affirmative action mobilization.[27]

White women and Asians, both groups that have benefited from affirmative action but have not been central to the political debate until recently, figure in the literature as well. Researchers have examined the representation (and absence) of White women in policy discourse,[28] the minimal gains of women in employment due to the absence of affirmative action enforcement,[29] the benefits to women as a result of affirmative action,[30] and the role of White female strategists in organizing against affirmative action bans.[31] Still, there is no literature that considers the positionality of White women in debate and political mobilization.

A focus on the relationship of Asian Americans to affirmative action points to the absence of Asians in popular discourse about these race- and class-inclusive educational policies,[32] the ways that Asians are socially constructed in regard to Left and Right framings of affirmative action,[33] and the danger of model minority myths deployed in battles over affirmative action.[34] However, Asian Americans are active in the mobilization over affirmative action, making claims as organizations, political actors, and university administrators[35] and projecting a coalition perspective in framing the benefits of affirmative action for Asian American students.[36] William C. Kidder's discussion of "negative action"[37] (in that Asians are still disadvantaged in elite admissions as compared to Whites) offers suggestions on how Asians could articulate legal claims of admissions discrimination in relationship to White students, rather than Black or Latino students.[38] More scholarship on the intersection of these populations and affirmative action in higher education is needed, especially as conservative organizations utilize White female and Asian plaintiffs in federal lawsuits challenging affirmative action.

There is an absence of academic literature on political contention over open admissions. As the City University of New York (CUNY) is the largest university to employ open admissions in four-year undergraduate colleges, the literature concerning policy implementation, political mobilization, and outcomes necessarily centers on CUNY. Comprehensive studies by David E. Lavin, Richard D. Alba, and Richard A. Silberstein[39] and by Jack E. Rossmann, Helen S. Astin, Alexander W. Astin, and Elaine H. El-Khawas[40] on the initial outcomes of open admissions at CUNY, as well as a follow-up study regarding the positive outcomes of open admissions graduates,[41] are some of the most thorough empirical studies on the CUNY's policy. Christopher Gunderson's account of the CUNY student movement[42] and personal accounts by professors and open admissions policy makers provide insight specific to the open admissions struggle at CUNY.[43]

While most literature on the political origins of open admissions at CUNY focuses on the 1969 City College occupation, Martha Biondi's work on the police repression of student activists at Brooklyn College and the demand for open admissions at San Francisco State College (and at other educational institutions across the country) is a meaningful contribution to the literature on race, politics, and higher education access.[44] Finally, Alice O'Connor's history of the Manhattan Institute for Policy Research, a conservative think tank central to attacks on open admissions at CUNY, traces how the organization connected "urban decline" and the parallel "moral decline" of the city as a means of promoting neoliberal policy interventions, including the elimination of open admissions.[45] Accounts of the development, implementation, and political struggle over the adoption of these policies shed light on the genealogy of contemporary political controversy and provide an opportunity to extend analysis to the present day.

To Fulfill These Rights complements this body of work by examining shifts in the racial landscape in the post–civil rights neoliberal period. I explore how race is articulated and practiced in policy development, youth protest, elite mobilization on the Right and Left, and efforts to preserve campus diversity after affirmative action elimination. Through an exploration of universities representing the four regions of the United States, I present a national story about how racial discourse and practice are formed, challenged, and remade through the political struggle over affirmative action and open admissions.

APPENDIX B

Research Methodology

THE QUALITATIVE and interpretive research design of this study focused on stages of policy development and political mobilization over a fifty-year period. Throughout, I drew attention to the elements that pushed forward these racial political projects at each site—social movement tactics and strategies, political agendas, public discourse, and the greater political context. I examined the activities of a variety of political actors: conservative think tanks and legal defense organizations, university boards of trustees and administrators, politicians and federal court judges, student activists and community organizations. Focusing on these elements of social movement mobilization and categories of political actors, I identified commonalities and differences among the cases studied, the relationships among actors and institutions across sites, and, ultimately, the means by which social change collectively occurred on a national level.

Fligstein and McAdam's "strategic action fields" provided a framework with which to analyze the conflict over race- and class-inclusive admissions.[1] As mobilization against affirmative action and open admissions has mostly involved the action of elites, I examined elite "insider tactics," or collective actions that exert influence within the formal political system.[2] Whereas much social movement research emphasizes the tactics of grassroots activists who necessarily employ disruption and alternative methods of political engagement, elites' efforts at collective organization to change law, harness power, and influence the public have incredible consequences for the social world. Thus, I investigated how conservative elites used the law (organizing lawsuits and interpreting legal precedent), how they created law (mounting ballot proposition campaigns and influencing voters), and how they shaped university-level policy (gaining appointments to trustee boards and developing external committees of influence). I also explored the role of university professors in supporting conservative elite efforts to challenge race- and class-inclusive admissions. On the other hand, I considered the ways that liberal politicians, administrators, and faculty attempted to defend against court, ballot, and institutional challenges and how they developed alternative policies after the end of affirmative action and open admissions. Finally, I explored how student activists and community coalitions mobilized to defend affirmative action policies and how their efforts did not save these policies but oftentimes led them to become lifelong activists. In addition to focusing on the collective actions of public figures, organizations, and universities, I assessed the racial discourse deployed in mobilization, concentrating on how social actors communicated ideas about race.

This research is based on historical evidence, retrieved from archival, media, interview, and historical sources. These sources include materials such as organizational reports, press releases, and media produced by conservative think tanks; federal court proceedings, case files, and legal decisions; university trustee board minutes and strategic plans; state educational policies and reports; media accounts of mobilization and policy reform; speeches and public interviews with administrators; twenty-six interviews of student activists and organizational materials of student organizations; and first-person accounts written by political actors engaged in political contestation. The triangulation of these data sources allowed for the development of a detailed and extensive account of mobilization and policy reform over a fifty-year period.

NOTES

INTRODUCTION

1. WeTheProtestors (2015).
2. Johnson (1965), p. 1.
3. National Center for Education Statistics (2016).
4. Toldson and Lewis (2012); Patton (2012); National Center for Education Statistics (2015); McMillan-Cottom (2017). In its 2000 report "Cellblocks or Classrooms: The Funding of Higher Education and Corrections and Its Impact on African American Men," the Justice Policy Institute claimed that one-third more African American men (that is, 100,000 more men) were incarcerated than were enrolled in college. Toldson (2013) argues that the report is based on insufficient data. More than 1,000 universities (including several historically Black colleges and universities and urban universities that enroll significant numbers of African American male students) did not report demographic information.
5. Looney and Yannelis (2015).
6. Smith and Parrish (2014).
7. Massey et al. (2006); Charles et al. (2009); Fischer (2010).
8. Lavin and Hyllegard (1996); Bowen and Bok (2000); Torche (2011).
9. Mouw (2003); Clauset, Arbesman, and Larremore (2015).
10. Anderson (2004).
11. Dale (2005); Stulberg and Chen (2014).
12. Dale (2005); Shaw (2017).
13. Shaw (2017).

14. Malveaux (2004); Perry (2007).
15. Hirschman and Berrey (2017).
16. Grodsky (2007); Lipson (2007); Hirschman and Berrey (2017).
17. Cohen and Kisker (2009).
18. Apodaca (2009); Cohen and Kisker (2009).
19. Van Deburg (1992); Rogers (2012).
20. Movement for Black Lives (2016).
21. Nguyen Barry and Dannenberg (2016).
22. *Washington Post* (2017).
23. Deslippe (2012).
24. Refer to *Firefighters Local Union No. 1784 v. Stotts* (1984), *Wygant v. Jackson Board of Education* (1986), *Johnson v. Transportation Agency, Santa Clara City* (1987), *City of Richmond v. J. A. Crosson Company* (1989), *Wards Cove Packing Co. v. Atonio* (1989), *Martin v. Wilks* (1989), *Lorance v. AT&T Technologies, Inc.* (1989), *Jett v. Dallas Independent School District* (1989), and *Patterson v. McLean Credit Union* (1989).
25. Refer to *Bush v. Vera* (1996), *Reno v. Bossier Parish School Board* (2000), and *Evenwol v. Abbott* (2016).
26. The Supreme Court rejected challenges to the Voting Rights Act in *South Carolina v. Katzenbach* (1966), *Georgia v. United States* (1973), *City of Rome v. United States* (1980), and *Lopez v. Monterey County* (1999), but in *Shelby County v. Holder* (2013), it struck down section 4(b) and made section 5 unenforceable.
27. For example, the decision in *San Antonio Independent School District v. Rodriguez* (1973) concluded that education is not a fundamental right and not protected by the U.S. Constitution. Voter ID laws and felony disenfranchisement are also significant mechanisms of voter disenfranchisement in the post–civil rights period.
28. Berrey (2015a), p. 3.
29. Guinier and Torres (2003).
30. Green, Apuzzo, and Benner (2018).
31. See *Washington Post* Editorial Board (2017); Garris (2006); Colson (2017).
32. See Bowen and Bok (2000); Massey et al. (2006); Niu, Sullivan, and Tienda (2008); Charles et al. (2009); Espenshade and Radford (2009); Harris and Tienda (2010).
33. Hall and O'Shea (2013), p. 12.
34. Omi and Winant (2015).
35. Ruth Wilson Gilmore provides an apt definition of racism, "the state-sanctioned or extra-legal production of group-differentiated vulnerability to premature death," in *Golden Gulag: Prisons, Surplus, Crisis, and Opposition in Globalizing California* (2007), p. 28.
36. Omi and Winant (2015).
37. Cowie (2012); Baumeister and Kilian (2016); Bureau of Labor Statistics (2017).

38. Harvey (2009).
39. Ibid.
40. Anderson et al. (2006).
41. Whitney (2006).
42. Cohen and Kisker (2009); Stefancic and Delgado (1996); Giroux (2014); Mayer (2017).
43. Siegel (2000). See Judge Harlan's dissent in *Plessy v. Ferguson* (1896).
44. Haney-Lopez (2013); Siegel (2000).
45. Obasogie (2013).
46. *Parents Involved in Community Schools v. Seattle School District No. 1* (2007), 40–41.
47. Haney-Lopez (2007); Guinier and Torres (2003); Bonilla Silva (2006); Doane (2007); Obasogie (2013); Manning, Hartmann, and Gerteis (2015).
48. Bonilla Silva (2006); Doane (2007).
49. Moore and Bell (2011); Collins (2011); Berrey (2015a).
50. Moore and Bell (2011).
51. Micklethwait and Wooldridge (2004).
52. "Top Public Schools—National Universities" (n.d.); "Best Public Universities in the United States 2018" (2018).
53. Chetty et al. (2017).
54. Shaw (2016).
55. Hall and Grossberg (1996).
56. Omi and Winant (2015).

1. A RIGHT OF POSTWAR CITIZENSHIP: THE EMERGENCE OF MASS HIGHER EDUCATION AND RACE- AND CLASS-INCLUSIVE ADMISSIONS

1. Marshall (1950).
2. Jenson (2013).
3. Cohen and Kisker (2009).
4. ASHE (2010).
5. Cohen and Kisker (2009).
6. Boyd (2007).
7. Karabel (2005).
8. Ibid.
9. Steinberg (1974); Karabel (2005).
10. Karabel (2005), p. 132.
11. Karabel (2005).
12. Cohen and Kisker (2009).
13. Cohen and Kisker (2009); Hinsdale (2010).
14. Hinsdale (2010).

15. Hinsdale (2010); Dettmer (2012).

16. Helfand (2002).

17. Roff, Cucchiara, and Dunlap (2000).

18. Roff, Cucchiara, and Dunlap (2000); Morris (1995); Calkins (2002).

19. Duren and Iscoe (1979).

20. Olson (1973).

21. Roosevelt (1943), p. 1.

22. Olson (1973).

23. Murray (2002).

24. Brodkin Sacks (1994).

25. Skrentny (1996); Katznelson (2005).

26. Brodkin Sacks (1994); Katznelson (2005).

27. Brodkin Sacks (1994).

28. Onkst (1998).

29. Brodkin Sacks (1994).

30. Brodkin Sacks (1994); Wynn (1976).

31. Bound and Turner (2002); Cohen and Kisker (2009).

32. Johnson (1966).

33. Chomsky et al. (1998).

34. Cohen and Kisker (2009).

35. Newfield (2011).

36. Soares (2011).

37. California State Department of Education (1960).

38. Ibid.

39. Kerr (2001).

40. Thelin (2011).

41. Kerr (2001).

42. Cohen and Kisker (2009).

43. Du Bois (1998).

44. Ware (2001).

45. Ware (2001); Tushnet (1994).

46. Ware (2001).

47. *Brown v. Board of Education of Topeka*, 347 U.S. 483, p.3 (1954) (Warren opinion).

48. Ware (2001); Tushnet (1994).

49. Litolff (2007); Shaw (2016).

50. See the following partial list: *Cooper v. Aaron*, 358 U.S. 1 (1958); *Griffin v. County School Board of Prince Edward County*, 377 U.S. 218 (1964); *Green v. County School Board of New Kent County*, 391 U.S. 430 (1968); *Alexander v. Holmes County Board of Education*, 396 U.S. 19 (1969); *Keyes v. School District No. 1*, 413 U.S. 189 (1973); *Adams v. Richardson*, 356 F. Supp. 92 (D.D.C. 1973); *Dayton Board of Education v. Brinkman*, 443 U.S. 526 (1979); *Columbus Board of Education v. Penick*, 443 U.S. 449 (1979).

51. Examples include James Meredith's desegregation of the University of Mississippi in 1962 and Governor George Wallace's obstruction of Vivian Malone's and James Hood's enrollment at the University of Alabama in 1963.
52. Painter (2006); Burnham (2015).
53. Anderson (2004).
54. Dale (2005).
55. Shaw (2016).
56. Dale (2005); Litolff (2007); Shaw (2016).
57. Deslippe (2012).
58. Anderson (2004).
59. These were the states of Alabama, Arkansas, Delaware, Florida, Georgia, Kentucky, Louisiana, Maryland, Mississippi, Missouri, North Carolina, Ohio, Oklahoma, Pennsylvania, South Carolina, Tennessee, Texas, Virginia, and West Virginia.
60. Litolff (2007).
61. Litolff (2007); Herbers (1970).
62. Litolff (2007); Shaw (2016).
63. Shaw (2016).
64. Ibid., p. 176.
65. See Bowen and Bok (2000); Anderson (2004); Orlans (1992); Wilkinson (1979).
66. Hinton (2016).
67. National Advisory Commission on Civil Disorders (1968).
68. Orlans (1992).
69. Stulberg and Chen (2014).
70. Biondi (2014); Deslippe (2012).
71. Deslippe (2012); Gordon and Wilkerson (1966)
72. Duren and Iscoe (1979).
73. Cohen and Kisker (2009).
74. Moll (1986).
75. Satija and Watkins (2017).
76. Tushnet (1994).
77. *Sweatt v. Painter*, 339 U.S. 629 (1950).
78. Shabazz (2004).
79. Duren and Iscoe (1979).
80. *Daily Texan* Editorial Board (2012).
81. Duren and Iscoe (1979).
82. Ibid., p. 20.
83. Ibid.
84. Ibid.
85. Ibid., p. 27; Barrera (1998).
86. Duren and Iscoe (1979).

87. Duren and Iscoe (1979); Carter (1969).
88. Duren and Iscoe (1979).
89. Ibid.
90. Laycock (2001).
91. Biondi (2014).
92. Karabel (1999).
93. Biondi (2014).
94. Berdahl (2000).
95. Biondi (2014), p. 52.
96. Biondi (2014).
97. Wang (1997); Taylor (2010).
98. Dong (2009); Taylor (2010).
99. Wang (1997).
100. Ibid.
101. Taylor (2010).
102. Assembly Concurrent Resolution 151 (1974); Assembly Concurrent Resolution 83 (1984).
103. Lipson (2007).
104. Karabel (1989).
105. Berdahl (2000).
106. Karabel (1989); Committee on Admissions, Enrollment, and Preparatory Education (2002).
107. Perry (2007).
108. Greenland, Chen, and Stulberg (2010).
109. Hirschman, Berrey, and Rose-Greenland (2016).
110. Perry (2007); Glenn (2010).
111. Glenn (2010).
112. Black Action Movement (1970–1987), box 107.
113. Glenn (2010).
114. Ibid.
115. Perry (2007); Anderson (2007).
116. Perry (2007).
117. Black Action Movement (1970–1987), box 109.
118. Meachum (1975).
119. U.S. Census (2006).
120. Perry (2007); Anderson (2007).
121. Perry (2007).
122. Black Action Movement (1970–1987), box 22.
123. Ibid.
124. Roff, Cucchiara, and Dunlap (2000); Cohen and Kisker (2009).
125. Gunderson (2003).
126. City College of New York (n.d.).
127. Women's City Club of New York (1975).

128. Ballard (1973).
129. Birnbaum and Goldman (1971).
130. Ballard (1973).
131. Biondi (2014).
132. Ballard (1973).
133. Steinberg (2018).
134. Ballard (1973); Biondi (2014).
135. Ballard (1973); Gunderson (2003).
136. Ballard (1973); Gunderson (2003); Renfro and Armour-Garb (1999).
137. Gunderson (2003).
138. Lipson (2011).
139. *Regents of the University of California v. Bakke*, 436 U.S. 265 (1978).
140. Powell (1971).
141. Berrey (2011).
142. Shinar (2013).

2. LEGAL MOBILIZATION:
RACIAL POLITICAL STRATEGY AND AFFIRMATIVE ACTION RETRENCHMENT IN THE FEDERAL COURTS

1. *Bush v. Vera*, 517 U.S. 952 (1996).
2. *Evenwel v. Abbot*, 578 U.S.__(2016).
3. *Northwest Austin Municipal Utility District No. 1 v. Holder*, 557 U.S. 193 (2009); *Shelby County v. Holder*, 570 U.S. 529 (2013).
4. Maney et al. (2012), p. xvii.
5. Maney et al. (2012); Meyer and Staggenborg (2012).
6. Omi and Winant (2015).
7. Ibid.
8. Ibid., p. 164.
9. Teles (2008).
10. Ibid.
11. Ibid
12. Ibid., p. 22.
13. Powell (1971).
14. Ibid., p. 6.
15. Vassar (2015).
16. Stahl (2016), p. 62.
17. Mayer (2017).
18. Stefancic and Delgado (1996).
19. Skrentny (1996).
20. Anderson (2004); Perry (2007).
21. Paul (1990).

22. Fried (1990); Anderson (2004).

23. Lewis (1992).

24. Such as *Firefighters v. Cleveland* (1986), *Sheet Metal Workers v. EEOC* (1986), and *United States v. Paradise* (1987).

25. Refer to *Firefighters Local #1784 v. Stotts* (1984); *Wygant v. Jackson Board of Education* (1986); *Johnson v. Transportation Agency, Santa Clara* (1987); *City of Richmond v. J. A. Crosson Company* (1989); *Wards Cove Packing Co. v. Atonio* (1989); *Martin v. Wilks* (1989); *Lorance v. AT&T Technologies* (1989); *Jett v. Dallas Independent School District* (1989); and *Patterson v. McLean Credit Union* (1989).

26. Perry (2007), p. 38. *Adarand Constructors Inc. v. Pena* (1995) is a notable exception.

27. Lewis (1992); Perry (2007).

28. Leadership Conference on Civil Rights (2009), p. 26.

29. Leadership Conference on Civil Rights (2009), p. 24.

30. Amaker (1988).

31. See *Washington v. Seattle School District No. 1* (1982); *School Desegregation: Hearings Before the Subcommittee on Civil and Constitutional Rights* (1981), p. 614 (statement of William B. Reynolds, Assistant Attorney General, Civil Rights Division).

32. See *Grove City College v. Bell* (1984).

33. Johnson (1988).

34. Musgrove (2012).

35. Center for Individual Rights, "Cases" (2011).

36. Center for Individual Rights, "Mission" (2011).

37. Center for Individual Rights, "Cases" (2011).

38. Verhovek (1996).

39. Burka (1996).

40. Center for Individual Rights, "Cases" (2011).

41. Laycock (2001).

42. *Hopwood v. Texas*, 861 F. Supp. 554 (W.D. Tex. 1994).

43. Burka (1996).

44. Laycock (2001); Burka (1996).

45. Leonard (1989); Crenshaw (2007).

46. *Hopwood v. Texas*, 861 F. Supp. 554 (W.D. Tex. 1994), pp. 1–30

47. Shaw (2016).

48. Olivas (2013).

49. Ibid.; Laycock (2001).

50. *Hopwood v. Texas*, 861 F. Supp. 554, 1–30 (W.D. Tex. 1994) (Sparks. memorandum opinion).

51. Perry (2007); Broscheid (2011).

52. *Hopwood v. Texas*, 78 F.3d 932 (5th Cir. 1996).

53. Shaw (2016).

54. Council and Robbins (2002).
55. King (2002); Henary (2002).
56. Perry (2007).
57. Ibid.
58. *Gratz v. Bollinger*, 539 U.S. 244 (2003).
59. *Grutter v. Bollinger*, 539 U.S. 306 (2003).
60. Thorne (2012).
61. *Gratz v. Bollinger*, 122 F. Supp. 2d 811 (E.D. Mich. 1997); *Grutter v. Bollinger*, 137 F. Supp. 2d 874 (E.D. Mich. 1997).
62. *Gratz v. Bollinger*, 122 F. Supp. 2d 811, 1–7 (E.D. Mich. 2001) (Duggan opinion).
63. Perry (2007).
64. *Grutter v. Bollinger*, 137 F. Supp. 2d 874, 840 (Friedman concurring opinion).
65. Perry (2007), p. 76.
66. *Grutter v. Bollinger*, 246 F.3d 631 (6th Cir. 2001).
67. Stohr (2004).
68. Perry (2007), p. 84.
69. *Gratz v. Bollinger*, 539 U.S. 244 (2003); *Grutter v. Bollinger*, 539 U.S. 306 (2003).
70. Perry (2007); Stohr (2004).
71. Garfield (2005), p. 675; *Grutter v. Bollinger*, 539 U.S. 306 (2003).
72. Malveaux (2004); Perry (2007); Stohr (2004).
73. *Schuette v. Coalition to Defend Affirmative Action*, 572 U.S. 291, 2 (2014) (Sotomayor dissenting opinion).
74. *Schuette v. Coalition to Defend Affirmative Action*, 572 U.S. 291, 6 (2014) (Sotomayor dissenting opinion).
75. Hannah-Jones (2013)
76. University of Texas at Austin (2004)
77. Ibid.
78. Opposition to Motion for Preliminary Injunction (May 5, 2008), in *Fisher v. University of Texas*, 645 F. Supp. 2d 587 (W.D. Tex. 2009).
79. Biskupic (2012).
80. Cokorinos (2003).
81. Stohr (2004).
82. Biskupic (2012).
83. Ibid.
84. Kroll (2013), p. 1.
85. Biskupic (2012).
86. Blum, along with lawyers from Wily Rein, also filed suit in *Shelby County v. Holder* (2013), which was heard during the same session as *Fisher v. University of Texas*. *Shelby County* overturned two provisions of the Voting Rights Act that required southern counties with documented discrimination to obtain federal permission to change election laws. In this way, Blum concurrently challenged two civil rights era policies during the same session.
87. *Fisher v. University of Texas*, 645 F. Supp. 2d 587 (W.D. Tex. 2009).

88. *Fisher v. University of Texas*, 645 F. Supp. 2d 587, 1–2 (W.D. Tex. 2009) (Sparks judgement).
89. Sherman (2012).
90. Ibid.; Liptak (2012).
91. Liptak (2012)
92. Transcript of Oral Argument at 34–40, *Fisher v. University of Texas*, 133 S. Ct. 2411 (2013) (No. 11-345).
93. *Fisher v. University of Texas*,1–14 133 S. Ct. 2411 (2013) (Kennedy opinion)
94. Ibid.
95. Ibid.
96. *Fisher v. University of Texas*, 1-4 133 S. Ct. 2411 (2013)(Ginsburg dissenting opinion).
97. *Fisher v. University of Texas (Fisher II)*, 2-41 758 F.3d 633 (5th Cir. 2014) (Higginbothan opinion).
98. Petition for a Writ of Certiorari (February 10, 2015) in *Fisher v. University of Texa (Fisher II)*; Brief in Opposition to Petition for Writ of Certiorari (April 15, 2015) in *Fisher v. University of Texas (Fisher II)*.
99. *Fisher v. University of Texas*, 136 S. Ct. 2198 (2016)

3. BOARD VOTES AND BALLOT INITIATIVES: RACIAL POLITICAL STRATEGY IN TRUSTEE DECISION-MAKING AND STATE ELECTIONS

1. *Sweezy v. New Hampshire*, 354 U.S. 234, 354 (1957). Here, Justice Felix Frankfurter referenced the language of South African scholars fighting segregated university education under apartheid.
2. See *Stronach v. Virginia State* University, 577 F. Supp. 2d 788 (E.D. Va. 2008).
3. Cohen and Kisker (2009).
4. Smith (1996); Duggan (2004); Harvey (2009).
5. Fiske (1976).
6. Paolucci (1970); Maeroff (1974); Cahn (1977).
7. Schmidt et al. (1999).
8. Hevesi (1995); Haumptman (1999); Schmidt et al. (1999).
9. Steck (2006).
10. Solomon and Hussey (1998).
11. Saxon (1999).
12. Arenson (1998b).
13. Solomon and Hussey (1998); Duggan (2004).
14. Arenson (1998a); Solomon and Hussey (1998).
15. Mac Donald (1994, 1996, 1998).
16. Mac Donald (1998)
17. Badillo (2006).

18. Ibid.
19. Graham (1999).
20. Dávila (2004); Badillo (2006).
21. Schmidt et al. (1999).
22. Applebome (1995).
23. Firestone (1997).
24. Waitrovich (2017).
25. Herbert (2000).
26. Uhlig (1987).
27. Arenson (1998b).
28. Schmidt et al. (1999).
29. Arenson (1998c).
30. Arenson (1998d).
31. Arenson (1998c); Graves (1999).
32. CUNY University Faculty Senate (1999).
33. Internationalist (1999); Arenson (1999).
34. Newfield (2011).
35. Ibid.; Chávez (1998).
36. Chavez (1998); Meacham (1995); Impoco (1995).
37. Maharidge (1995).
38. Chávez (1998).
39. Woo (1988).
40. Matthews (1990).
41. *Los Angeles Times* (1989).
42. Wang (1993); UC Berkeley Office of Planning and Analysis (2017b).
43. UC Berkeley Office of Planning and Analysis (2017b).
44. Newman (1995); Chávez (1998).
45. Williams (2001).
46. Rockwell (1995).
47. Ibid.
48. Chávez (1998); Cokorinos (2003).
49. Connerly (2001); Bernstein (1995).
50. Bernstein (1995).
51. Pusser (2004).
52. Connerly (1995a).
53. Pusser (2004).
54. Douglass (1997), p. 6.
55. Douglass (1997)
56. Connerly (1995b); Chávez (1998).
57. Connerly (2001), p. 4.
58. Chávez (1998), Pusser (2004).
59. Rockwell (1995).
60. Wallace and Lesher (1995).

61. Pusser (2004), p. 145. See also Chávez (1998); Wallace and Lesher (1995).
62. Chavez (1998).
63. Pusser (2004), p. 160.
64. Newman (1995); Chávez (1998).
65. Pusser (2004).
66. Chávez (1998), p. 66
67. Chávez (1998)
68. Gamble (1997).
69. Bell (1978); Bowler and Donovan (2001).
70. Gamble (1997).
71. Gayner (1995); Micklethwait and Wooldridge (2004).
72. Stefancic and Delgado (1996).
73. Andrews (1995).
74. Micklethwait and Wooldridge (2004).
75. Krauthammer (1995); Purdum (1995); Chávez (1998).
76. McCarthy (1995).
77. Chávez (1998); Anderson (2004).
78. Organizational History, California Civil Rights Initiative Records, 1990–1996, Bancroft Library, University of California, Berkeley.
79. Chávez (1998).
80. Ibid., p. 7.
81. Ayres (1995).
82. Chávez (1998).
83. Initiative Development, California Civil Rights Initiative Records, 1990–1996, box 1, folders 1–18, Bancroft Library, University of California, Berkeley; School Segregation and Desegregation, California Civil Rights Initiative Records, 1990–1996, box 3, folder 41, Bancroft Library, University of California Berkeley; Chávez (1998).
84. Chávez (1998).; Onishi (2012).
85. Chávez (1998).; Teles (2008).
86. Chávez (1998).
87. Ayres (1995).
88. Taylor and Balz (1995).
89. Chávez (1998), p. 41.
90. Chávez (1998).
91. Ibid.
92. Decker (1995).
93. Chávez (1998).
94. *Lungren v, Superior Court of Sacramento County* (1996), p. 6.
95. Chávez (1998).
96. Ibid., p. 218.
97. Stall and Morain (1996).
98. Chávez (1998).

99. Ayres (1995).

100. Chávez (1998).

101. Ibid.

102. Importantly, opponents of the measure filed a lawsuit aiming to stop the implementation of Proposition 209 (in which the Center for Individual Rights intervened) and temporarily blocked enforcement; however, the Ninth Circuit Court of Appeals overturned this decision in 1997.

103. Perry (2007).

104. Greenberg (1996).

105. Allen (2008).

106. Berrey (2015b).

107. Allen (2008).

108. Ibid, p. xii.

109. Allen (2008).

110. Ibid.

111. Lewin (2006); Stein (2006); Allen (2008)

112. Berrey (2015b).

113. Allen (2008).

114. Michigan Civil Rights Commission (2006), p. 12

115. The Center for Individual Rights, the organization behind *Hopwood*, *Gratz*, and *Grutter*, represented MCRI in this case. See Center for Individual Rights, "Cases" (2011).

116. *Operation King's Dream v. Connerly* (E.D. Mich. 2006).

117. *Operation King's Dream v. Connerly* (6th Cir. 2007).

118. "Yes on Proposal 2" (2006), MCRI television campaign advertisement; "Vote Yes on 2" (2006), MCRI print campaign advertisement.

119. Allen (2008).

120. Savage (2012).

121. XIV Foundation (2012).

122. Smith (2010).

123. Zeveloff (2008).

124. Larson and Menendian (2008).

125. James (2008).

126. Larson and Menendian (2008).

127. Goodman (2008).

128. Ibid.

129. Ibid.; Larson and Menendian (2008).

130. Larson and Menendian (2008); Simon (2008).

131. Colorado Unity (2008).

132. Larson and Menendian (2008); Frosch (2008); McPhee (2008).

133. Ibid.

134. Ibid.

135. Zeveloff (2008).

136. Ibid.; Larson and Menendian (2008).
137. Zeveloff (2008); Larson and Menendian (2008).
138. Slevin (2008).
139. Larson and Menendian (2008).
140. *St. Louis Post-Dispatch* Editorial Board (2008); Zeveloff (2008).
141. Schmidt (2012).
142. Smith (2010).
143. Ibid.
144. Meyers (1999).
145. Chin et al. (1996); Kidder (2006).
146. Balingit (2019).

4. A FORCE OF NATURE:
STUDENT RESISTANCE TO POLICY ELIMINATION

1. D'Emilio (2004); Gunderson (2003).
2. Newfield (1965); Freeman (2001); Biondi (2014).
3. McKinley (1989); Kolbert (1989); Loeb (1994).
4. As discussed in chapter 2, the SEEK program was established in 1966 to facilitate racial integration of the CUNY system. It was a primary mechanism for organizing remedial courses, tutoring, and financial assistance for Black, Puerto Rican, and poor students. Its community college counterpart is College Discovery.
5. Honan (1995); Meyers (1999).
6. Gunderson (2003).
7. Orlando Green, interview by Amaka Okechukwu, New York, February 8, 2014; John Kim, telephone interview by Amaka Okechukwu, February 18, 2014; Kamau Franklin, telephone interview by Amaka Okechukwu, January 15, 2014.
8. Green, interview, February 8, 2014; Franklin, telephone interview, January 15, 2014; Lenina Nadal, interview by Amaka Okechukwu, New York, April 22, 2013.
9. "The World Is Ours" (Student Power Movement pamphlet), Student Liberation Action Movement Collection, 1989–2007, Tamiment Library and Robert F. Wagner Archives, box 1, folder 66, New York University Libraries, New York.
10. Rob Hollander and David Suker, interview by Amaka Okechukwu, New York, January 29, 2014; Nadal, interview, April 22, 2013.
11. Nadal, interview, April 22, 2013; Rachel LaForest, telephone interview by Amaka Okechukwu, August 9, 2013; Green, interview, New York, February 8, 2014; Ramiro Campos, telephone interview by Amaka Okechukwu, January 27, 2014.

12. Campos, telephone interview, January 28, 2014; subways (2015).

13. subways (2015).

14. Hollander and Suker, interview, January 29, 2014; Chris Gunderson, interview by Amaka Okechukwu, New York, February 10, 2014.

15. Vitale (1995).

16. Scherer (1995); Vitale (1995).

17. Gladwell (1995); Meyers (1999); Hollander and Suker, interview, January 29, 2014.

18. Sack (1995); Meyers (1999).

19. Sack (1995); Meyers (1999).

20. Gunderson (2003); Vitale (1995).

21. "SLAM! Structure," Student Liberation Action Movement Collection, 1989–2007, Tamiment Library and Robert F. Wagner Archives, box 8, folder 12, New York University Libraries, New York.

22. Hollander and Suker, interview, January 29, 2014; Green, interview, February 8, 2014.

23. Neha Guatam, interview by Amaka Okechukwu, New York, January 17, 2014; Hank Williams, interview by Amaka Okechukwu, New York, January 14, 2014.

24. Franklin, telephone interview, January 15, 2014.

25. Irini Neofotistos, interviews by Amaka Okechukwu, New York, May 23, 2013 and September 30, 2011; Campos, telephone interview, January 28, 2014.

26. Mariano Muñoz, interview by Amaka Okechukwu, New York, May 15, 2013; Luz Schreiber, interview by Amaka Okechukwu, New York, May 22, 2013.

27. Jesse Ehrenhaft-Hawley, interview by Amaka Okechukwu, New York, January 24, 2014; Jorge Matos, interview by Amaka Okechukwu, New York, August 8, 2014; Rachel LaForest, telephone interview by Amaka Okechukwu, June 6, 2014; Neofotistos, interview, May 23, 2013; Nadal, interview, April 22, 2013; Left Spot (2006).

28. *Hunter Envoy* Staff List, February 3, 1998, Student Liberation Action Movement Collection, 1989–2007, Tamiment Library and Robert F. Wagner Archives, box 2, folder 9, New York University Libraries, New York; Kazembe Balagun, interview by Amaka Okechukwu, New York, May 3, 2013.

29. Walker (1992).

30. McFadden (1993).

31. Jones (1995).

32. Bernstein (1998).

33. *New York Times* (1996).

34. Sandra Barros, interview by suzy subways (digital recording), New York, March 31, 2014; Gunderson (2003).

35. Keith Higginbotham, "Is Education a Right?" *Hunter Envoy*, November 10, 1998, Student Liberation Action Movement Collection, 1989–2007, Tamiment Library and Robert F. Wagner Archives, box 2, folder 11, New York University Libraries, New York.

36. Barros, interview, March 31, 2014; Nadal, interview, April 22, 2013; Kazembe Balagun, interview by Amaka Okechukwu, New York, May 3, 2013.

37. Alex Hogan, "CUNY Is Being Restructured by These People: Who's on the Schmidt Commission?" *Hunter Envoy*, January 28, 1998, Student Liberation Action Movement Collection, 1989–2007, Tamiment Library and Robert F. Wagner Archives, box 2, folder 9, New York University Libraries, New York.

38. Arenson (1998c).

39. Arenson (1998d).

40. Arenson (1999).

41. Internationalist (1999); Arenson (1999).

42. Arenson (1999).

43. "Myths & Facts About CUNY" (flyer), Student Liberation Action Movement Collection, 1989–2007, Tamiment Library and Robert F. Wagner Archives, box 2, folder 3, New York University Libraries, New York.

44. "The Struggle at CUNY: Open Admissions and Civil Rights" by Ron McGuire (special to Hunter *Envoy*), Spring 1998, Student Liberation Action Movement Collection, 1989–2007, Tamiment Library and Robert F. Wagner Archives, box 6, folder 15, New York University Libraries, New York.

45. Badillo (1992); Mac Donald (1994, 1998).

46. Aliyah Khan, "Workfare," *Hunter Envoy*, January 28, 1998, Student Liberation Action Movement Collection, 1989–2007, Tamiment Library and Robert F. Wagner Archives, box 2, folder 10, New York University Libraries, New York.

47. suzy subways, "Thousands Protest Washington Meetings of IMF, World Bank," *Hunter Envoy*, May 16, 2000, Student Liberation Action Movement Collection, 1989–2007, Tamiment Library and Robert F. Wagner Archives, box 2, folder 11, New York University Libraries, New York; subways (2008).

48. "Do You and Your Friends Want to Go to College?" (flyer), Student Liberation Action Movement Collection, 1989–2007, Tamiment Library and Robert F. Wagner Archives, box 2, folder 3, New York University Libraries, New York.

49. "Missing," March 19, 2003, Student Liberation Action Movement Collection, 1989–2007, Tamiment Library and Robert F. Wagner Archives, box 2, folder 14, New York University Libraries, New York.

50. LaForest, telephone interview, June 6, 2014; Neofotistos, interview, May 23, 2013.

51. LaForest, telephone interview, August 9, 2013; Ehrensaft-Hawley, interview, January 24, 2014.

52. Sabrine Hammad, telephone interview by Amaka Okechukwu, January 14, 2014; "Voices for the Voiceless Benefit Concert for Mumia and Victims of Police Brutality," *Hunter Envoy*, May 16, 2000, Student Liberation Action Movement Collection, 1989–2007, Tamiment Library and Robert F. Wagner Archives, box 2, folder 12, New York University Libraries, New York; Aliyah Khan, "Abu-Jamal Death Warrant Signed: Hunter Students Turn Out to Demonstrate Opposition," *Hunter Envoy*, October 26, 1999, Student Liberation Action Movement Collection, 1989–2007, Tamiment Library and Robert F. Wagner Archives, box 2, folder 11, New York University Libraries, New York.

53. Balagun, interview, May 3, 2013; suzy subways, interview by Amaka Okechukwu, New York, January 31, 2014; subways (2010).

54. subways (2010); Aliyah Khan, "Direct Actions Disrupts City: 425 Arrested, Allegations of Police Misconduct," *Hunter Envoy*, September 5, 2005, Student Liberation Action Movement Collection, 1989–2007, Tamiment Library and Robert F. Wagner Archives, box 2, folder 12, New York University Libraries, New York,

55. Anonymous, interview by Amaka Okechukwu, New York, January 15, 2014.

56. Rorabaugh (1989).

57. Wang (1997); Taylor (2010).

58. Khalil Jacobs-Fantauzzi, telephone interview by Amaka Okechukwu, August 30, 2013.

59. Douglass (1997); Goldberg (1997).

60. Pusser (2004).

61. Wallace and Lesher (1995); Goldberg (1997).

62. Wallace and Lesher (1995); Goldberg (1997).

63. Burdman (1996); Pusser (2004).

64. Goldberg (1997).

65. Jacobs-Fantauzzi, telephone interview, August 30, 2013.

66. Sabrina Smith, telephone interview by Amaka Okechukwu, June 1, 2012.

67. Ingrid Benedict, telephone interview by Amaka Okechukwu, August 30, 2013.

68. Bailey (1995); Pusser (2004).

69. Smith, telephone interview, June 1, 2012; Benedict, telephone interview, August 30, 2013.

70. Koury (1995).

71. Jacobs-Fantauzzi, telephone interview, August 30, 2013; Goldberg (1997).

72. Jacobs-Fantauzzi, telephone interview, August 30, 2013; Goldberg (1997).

73. Jacobs-Fantauzzi, telephone interview, August 30, 2013; Goldberg (1997).

74. Jacobs-Fantauzzi, telephone interview, August 30, 2013.

75. Goldberg (1997).
76. Tuomey (1995); Pusser (2004).
77. Goldberg (1997).
78. Newman (1995); Goldberg (1997).
79. Goldberg (1997).
80. Harmony Goldberg, personal communication to Amaka Okechukwu, September 2, 2012; Jacobs-Fantauzzi, telephone interview, August 30, 2013; Berrey (2015b).
81. Berrey (2015b); Allen (2008).
82. Breitman, LeBlanc, and Wald (1996).
83. Goldberg, personal communication, September 2, 2012; Jacobs-Fantauzzi, telephone interview, August 30, 2013.
84. Goldberg (1997); Goldberg, personal communication, September 2, 2012; Jacobs-Fantauzzi, telephone interview, August 30, 2013.
85. Goldberg (1997);.Kim (1995); Berrey (2015b); Jacobs-Fantauzzi, telephone interview, August 30, 2013.
86. Staggs (1998).
87. Ibid.; Goldberg (1997).
88. Goldberg (1997).
89. Anderson (2001).
90. Newman (2003).
91. Staggs (1998).
92. Molina (1996); *Michigan Daily* (2001).
93. *Michigan Daily* (1990).
94. Goldberg (1997).
95. One America Initiative (1997).
96. "The Klan Supports 209" (poster), Political Posters Collection, All of Us or None (AUON) Archive Project, Oakland Museum of California, Oakland.
97. *Revolutionary Worker* (1996); Associated Press (1996).
98. Goldberg (1997).
99. La Voz de Berkeley Newswire (1996).
100. Goldberg (1997); *Revolutionary Worker* (1996).
101. Harris (1997).
102. "School of Unity and Liberation Newsletter," Student Liberation Action Movement Collection, 1989–2007, Tamiment Library and Robert F. Wagner Archives, box 10, folder 16, New York University Libraries, New York.
103. "Critical Resistance: Beyond the Prison Industrial Complex" (conference program), September 25–27, 1998, Student Liberation Action Movement Collection, 1989–2007, Tamiment Library and Robert F. Wagner Archives, box 20, folder 16, New York University Libraries, New York.
104. Soul Summer School Correspondence, Student Liberation Action Movement Collection, 1989–2007, Tamiment Library and Robert F. Wagner Archives, box 3, folder 5, New York University Libraries, New York.

5. THE LIMITATIONS OF DIVERSITY: DEFENSIVE INNOVATION AFTER THE END OF AFFIRMATIVE ACTION AND OPEN ADMISSIONS

1. Lipson (2011).
2. Warikoo (2016).
3. Kahlenberg (1997); Kahlenberg and Potter (2012); Wilson (2012); Gaertner and Hart (2013).
4. Schmidt et al. (1999).
5. Arenson (2000a).
6. Schmidt et al. (1999).
7. Parker and Richardson (2005).
8. Ibid.
9. Romo and Falbo (1995); Jencks and Phillips (1998); McNeil (2000).
10. Schmidt et al. (1999).
11. Parker and Richardson (2005).
12. Treschan and Mehrotra (2012).
13. Ibid.
14. CUNY Office of Institutional Research (2015).
15. Lavin and Hyllegard (1996); Attewell et al. (2009).
16. Chetty et al. (2017).
17. Parker and Richardson (2005); Hebel (2002).
18. Ibid.
19. Opportunity Programs (n.d.).
20. Parker and Richardson (2005).
21. Ibid.; Arenson (2000b).
22. CUNY Office of Institutional Research (2014).
23. Plestis (2011).
24. Jorge Matos, interview by Amaka Okechukwu, New York, August 8, 2014; Hank Williams, interview by Amaka Okechukwu, New York, January 14, 2014.
25. Arenson (2005).
26. Arenson (2006).
27. CUNY Office of Institutional Research (2015).
28. Macaulay Honors College (2018).
29. Hertog Scholars Program (2011).
30. CUNY (2014).
31. New York State (2017b).
32. New York State (2017a).
33. New York State (2017b).
34. Whitford (2017).
35. National Center for Education Statistics (2017a); National Center for Education Statistics (2017b).

36. Hilliard (2018).
37. Tien (1996); Frost (1998).
38. Gilmore (2000).
39. MacLachlan (2007).
40. Watanabe (2016a).
41. Watanabe (2016b).
42. Ibid.; UCLA Undergraduate Admission (2017); UC Berkeley Office of Planning and Analysis (2017).
43. California State Auditor (2016).
44. UC Berkeley Office of Planning and Analysis (2017); UCLA Undergraduate Admission (2017).
45. UC Berkeley Office of Planning and Analysis (2017); UCLA Undergraduate Admission (2017); University of Michigan Office of the Registrar (2017); University of Texas at Austin (2017).
46. Chetty et al. (2017).
47. Hartocollis (2016).
48. University of Michigan (2016).
49. Hartocollis (2016).
50. Fitzgerald (2015).
51. University of Michigan Office of the Registrar (2017).
52. Bastedo, Howard, and Flaster (2016).
53. Bastedo et al. (2017).
54. Bastedo, Howard, and Flaster (2016).
55. Guinier and Torres (2003).
56. Thompson and Tobias (2000).
57. Ibid.
58. Texas Higher Education Coordinating Board (1997).
59. Thompson and Tobias (2000).
60. Guinier and Torres (2003).
61. Thompson and Tobias (2000); Guinier and Torres (2003).
62. Texas Education Agency n.d.
63. Horn and Flores (2003).
64. Ibid.; Guinier and Torres (2003).
65. Texas House of Representatives (1997).
66. Irving (1999); Thompson and Tobias (2000).
67. Thompson and Tobias (2000).
68. Webster (2007).
69. Hannah-Jones (2013).
70. Roush (2012).
71. University of Texas at Austin (n.d.).
72. Tienda et al. (2003); Alon and Tienda (2007); Long and Tienda (2008).
73. Koffman and Tienda (2008).
74. Niu, Sullivan, and Tienda (2008).

75. Tienda and Niu (2006).
76. Long, Saenz, and Tienda (2010).
77. "California Master Plan for Higher Education 2010 Review" (2010).
78. California Postsecondary Education Commission (1997).
79. Horn and Flores (2003).
80. Ibid.; Robinson (2003).
81. Selingo (2001); Atkinson and Pelfrey (2004).
82. Horn and Flores (2003).
83. Alon (2015).
84. Tien (1996), p. 6.
85. Powers (2012).
86. Berrey (2011).
87. Berdahl (1998).
88. Coleman (2006).
89. Taliaferro (2015).
90. Maramba, Sulé, and Winke-Wagner (2015).
91. Bollinger (2007).
92. Karabel (2005).
93. *Students for Fair Admissions v. Harvard College*, Motion for Summary Judgment, June 15, 2018, http://samv91khoyt2i553a2t1so5i-wpengine.netdna-ssl.com/wp-content/uploads/2018/06/Doc-412-Motion-for-Summary-Judgment.pdf.
94. Tien (1996), p. 8.
95. Tien (1995), p. 19.
96. Tien (1996), p. 6.
97. Coleman (2006).
98. Polletta (2006); Polletta et al. (2011).
99. Tien (1996), p. 6.
100. Bollinger (2002).
101. Coleman (2003).
102. Arenson (2001).
103. Saltonstall (1997).
104. Ahmed (2012).
105. Berrey (2015a); Moore and Bell (2011).
106. Bell and Hartmann (2007).

CONCLUSION

1. Afrikan Student Union (2017).
2. Svrluga (2015).
3. Simpson (2017).
4. Tienda, Alon, and Niu (2010).

5. Alon (2015).
6. Ibid.
7. Hochschild (2016).
8. "Press Release: Students for Fair Admissions Files Lawsuit Against Univ. of Texas at Austin," http://samv91khoyt2i553a2t1so5i-wpengine.netdna-ssl.com/wp-content/uploads/2017/06/SFFA-UT-Press-Release-Suit-Filed-1.pdf.
9. *Students for Fair Admissions v. Harvard College*, Motion for Summary Judgment, June 15, 2018, http://samv91khoyt2i553a2t1so5i-wpengine.netdna-ssl.com/wp-content/uploads/2018/06/Doc-412-Motion-for-Summary-Judgment.pdf.
10. *Students for Fair Admissions v. University of North Carolina*, Complaint, http://samv91khoyt2i553a2t1so5i-wpengine.netdna-ssl.com/wp-content/uploads/2014/11/SFFA-v.-UNC-Complaint.pdf.
11. *Students for Fair Admissions v. U.S. Department of Education*, Complaint, October 27, 2016, http://samv91khoyt2i553a2t1so5i-wpengine.netdna-ssl.com/wp-content/uploads/2016/10/Doc-1-Complaint.pdf.
12. Walsh (1990); Kidder (2006); Liu (2008).
13. Coalition of Asian-American Associations, "Complaint Against Harvard University and the President and Fellows of Harvard College for Discriminating Against Asian-American Applicants in the College Admissions Process" (submitted to the Office for Civil Rights, U.S. Department of Education and the Civil Rights Division, U.S. Department of Justice), May 15, 2015, *Chronicle of Higher Education*, http://www.chronicle.com/items/biz/pdf/Final%20Aisan%20Complaint%20Harvard%20Document%2020150515.pdf.
14. *Washington Post* (2017).
15. U.S. Department of Justice, Civil Rights Division and U.S. Department of Education, Office for Civil Rights, "Announcement," July 3, 2018, http://blogs.edweek.org/edweek/campaign-k-12/Embargoed%20Until%204%20p.m.DCL%207.3.18.pdf.
16. Perry (2007).
17. Elson (2009).
18. Perry (2007);Elson (2009).
19. Sander and Taylor (2012); Arcidiacono and Lovenheim (2016).
20. Wilson (2012).
21. Kahlenberg and Potter (2012).
22. *Students for Fair Admissions, Inc. v. Harvard*, Expert Report of Richard D. Kahlenberg, June 15, 2018, http://samv91khoyt2i553a2t1so5i-wpengine.netdna-ssl.com/wp-content/uploads/2018/06/Doc-416-1-Kahlenberg-Expert-Report.pdf; *Students for Fair Admissions, Inc. v. Harvard*, Expert Report of Peter S. Arcidiacono, June 15, 2018, http://samv91khoyt2i553a2t1so5i-wpengine.netdna-ssl.com/wp-content/uploads/2018/06/Doc-415-1-Arcidiacono-Expert-Report.pdf.

23. Alon (2015).
24. Koffman and Tienda (2008); Tienda, Alon, and Niu (2010).
25. DiMaggio and Powell (1983); Powell and DiMaggio (2012).
26. Jones, Bradley, and Oberlander (2014); Steensland and Wright (2014); Klar (2014).
27. Hochschild (1999); Skrentny (2001).
28. Perry (2007).
29. PricewaterhouseCoopers (2015).
30. Skrentny (2001).
31. Chávez (1998); Audi, Scheck, and Lawton (2008).
32. National Institute on Money in State Politics (2015a, 2015b).
33. Du Bois (1998); Robinson (2000); Lowe (2015).
34. Gramsci (1971); Hall (1988); Hall and O'Shea (2013).

APPENDIX A. SITUATING POLITICAL STRUGGLE OVER AFFIRMATIVE ACTION AND OPEN ADMISSIONS

1. Brodkin Sacks (1994); Skrentny (1996); Katznelson (2005).
2. Orlans (1992); Skrentny (2001); Anderson (2004).
3. Anderson (2004).
4. Stulberg and Chen (2014).
5. DiMaggio and Powell (1983).
6. Karabel (2005).
7. Deslippe (2012).
8. Steinberg (2003).
9. Steinberg (1995).
10. Cokorinos (2003).
11. Bell (1979); Bell (2003).
12. Bell (1978).
13. Massie (2004); Stohr (2004); Perry (2007).
14. Benson (2007); Allen (2008).
15. Chávez (1998); Guerrero (2002); Pusser (2004).
16. Rhoads, Saenz, and Carducci (2005).
17. Yosso et al. (2004).
18. Guinier and Torres (2003).
19. Bowen and Bok (2000); Gurin et al. (2004); Massey et al. (2006); Charles et al. (2009); Chang and Rose (2010).
20. Tienda et al. (2003); Long and Tienda (2008); Harris and Tienda (2012); Flores and Horn (2015).
21. Kalhenberg (1997); Kahlenberg and Potter (2012).
22. Arcidiacono et al. (2011); Arcidiacono and Lovenheim (2016).
23. Rojas (2007); Taylor (2010); Biondi (2014); Rogers (2012).

24. Dietrich (2015).
25. Berrey (2015b).
26. Brown-Nagin (2005).
27. Santoro and McGuire (1997).
28. Bacchi (1996).
29. Leonard (1989).
30. Clayton and Crosby (1992).
31. Chávez (1998).
32. Gee (1996).
33. Omi and Takagi (1996).
34. Wu and Wang (1996).
35. Takagi (1990).
36. Chin, Cho, Kang, and Wu (1996).
37. Kidder (2006).
38. Tsuang (1989).
39. Lavin, Alba, and Silberstein (1981).
40. Rossmann et al. (1975).
41. Lavin and Hyllegard (1996).
42. Gunderson (2003).
43. Clark (1972); Ballard (1973, 2011).
44. Biondi (2014).
45. O'Connor (2008).

APPENDIX B. RESEARCH METHODOLOGY

1. Fligstein and McAdam (2012).
2. Soule et al. (1999).

REFERENCES

Adarand Constructors, Inc. v. Peña, 515 U.S. 200 (1995).

Afrikan Student Union. (2017, May 11). "Demands." Afrikan Student Union Member.

Ahmed, S. (2012). *On Being Included: Racism and Diversity in Institutional Life.* Durham, NC: Duke University Press.

Allen, C. M. (2008). *Ending Racial Preferences: The Michigan Story.* Lanham, MD: Lexington Books.

Alon, S. (2015). *Race, Class, and Affirmative Action.* New York: Russell Sage Foundation.

Alon, S., and Tienda, M. (2007). "Diversity, Opportunity, and the Shifting Meritocracy in Higher Education." *American Sociological Review* 72(4), 487–511.

Amaker, N. (1988). *Civil Rights and the Reagan Administration.* Washington, DC: Urban Institute Press.

Anderson, J. (2001, March 15). "Not with a BAMN, but with a Moan." *Daily Californian* (Berkeley). http://archive.dailycal.org/article.php?id=4963.

Anderson, J. D. (2007). "Past Discrimination and Diversity: A Historical Context for Understanding Race and Affirmative Action." *Journal of Negro Education* 76(3), 204.

Anderson, S., Cavanagh, J., Collins, C., and Benjamin, E. (2006). *Executive Excess 2006: Defense and Oil Executives Cash In on Conflict.* Washington, DC: Institute for Policy Studies/United for a Fair Economy.

Anderson, T. H. (2004). *The Pursuit of Fairness: A History of Affirmative Action.* New York: Oxford University Press.

Andrews, E. L. (1995, February 22). "House Votes to Kill Program for Minorities." *New York Times*. https://www.nytimes.com/1995/02/22/us/house-votes-to-kill -program-for-minorities.html.

Apodaca, E. (2009). "Open Admissions: An Experiment That Became a Reality." *Enrollment Management Journal 4*(3), 96–103.

Applebome, P. (1995, March 17). "Entrepreneur Gets $30 Million to Establish For-Profit Schools." *New York Times*. https://www.nytimes.com/1995/03/17/us /entrepreneur-gets-30-million-to-establish-for-profit-schools.html.

Arcidiacono, P., Aucejo, E. M., Fang, H., and Spenner, K. I. (2011). "Does Affirmative Action Lead to Mismatch? A New Test and Evidence." *Quantitative Economics 2*(3): 303–333.

Arcidiacono, P., and Lovenheim, M. (2016). "Affirmative Action and the Quality-Fit Trade-Off." *Journal of Economic Literature 54*(1), 3–51. https:doi.org/10.1257 /jel.54.1.3.

Arenson, K. W. (1998a, May 7). "Pataki-Giuliani Plan Would Curb CUNY Colleges' Remedial Work." *New York Times*. http://www.nytimes.com/1998/05/07/nyregion /pataki-giuliani-plan-would-curb-cuny-colleges-remedial-work.html.

Arenson, K. W. (1998b, May 14). "Pataki's Push for Trustee at CUNY Is Questioned." *New York Times*. http://www.nytimes.com/1998/05/14/nyregion/pataki-s-push -for-trustee-at-cuny-is-questioned.html.

Arenson, K. W. (1998c, May 27). "CUNY to Tighten Admissions Policy at 4-Year Schools." *New York Times*. http://www.nytimes.com/1998/05/27/nyregion /cuny-to-tighten-admissions-policy-at-4-year-schools.html.

Arenson, K. W. (1998d, August 11). "Judge Halts CUNY Remedial Cutback Efforts." *New York Times*. http://www.nytimes.com/1998/08/11/nyregion/judge -halts-cuny-remedial-cutback-efforts.html.

Arenson, K. W. (1999, November 24). "Opponents of a Change in CUNY Admissions Policy Helped Pass a Compromise Plan." *New York Times*. http:// www.nytimes.com/1999/11/24/nyregion/opponents-of-a-change-in-cuny -admissions-policy-helped-pass-a-compromise-plan.html 2/3.

Arenson, K. W. (2000a, September 7). "Critics Urge Regents to Reject CUNY's Four-Year Master Plan." *New York Times*. https://www.nytimes.com/2000/09/07 /nyregion/critics-urge-regents-to-reject-cuny-s-four-year-master-plan.html.

Arenson, K. W. (2000b, September 19). "Remedial Program Refuses to Die: Revamped SEEK Remains Path for Poor Into CUNY." *New York Times*. https:// www.nytimes.com/2000/09/19/nyregion/remedial-program-refuses-to-die -revamped-seek-remains-path-for-poor-into-cuny.html.

Arenson, K. W. (2001, June 6). "With Badillo Gone, CUNY Is Likely to Stay on Course He Set." *New York Times*. https://www.nytimes.com/2001/06/06 /nyregion/with-badillo-gone-cuny-is-likely-to-stay-on-course-he-set.html.

Arenson, K. W. (2005, May 26). "Honors College Helps CUNY Lure Students Who Shunned It." *New York Times*. https://www.nytimes.com/2005/05/26/nyregion /cuny-finds-a-way-to-lure-the-brightest.html.

Arenson, K. W. (2006, August 10). "CUNY Reports Fewer Blacks at Top Schools." *New York Times*. https://www.nytimes.com/2006/08/10/education/10cuny.html.

ASHE. (2010). "Historical Origins of HBCUs." *ASHE Higher Education Report* 35(5), 5–9.

Assembly Concurrent Resolution No. 151 Relative to Public Higher Education. (1974). California State Assembly.

Assembly Concurrent Resolution No. 83 Relative to Postsecondary Education. (1984). California State Assembly.

Associated Press. (1996, November 8). "23 Arrested After Prop. 209 Protest in Berkeley Tower." *Los Angeles Times*. http://articles.latimes.com/1996-11-08 /news/mn-62509_1_san-diego-police.

Atkinson, R. C., and Pelfrey, P. A. (2004, September 29). "Rethinking Admissions: US Public Universities in the Post-Affirmative Action Age." Paper presented at the UK and US Higher Education Finance and Access Symposium, Oxford, England. https://escholarship.org/uc/item/2w60b2x4.

Attewell, P., Lavin, D., Domina, T., and Levey, T. (2009). *Passing the Torch: Does Higher Education for the Disadvantaged Pay Off Across the Generations?* New York: Russell Sage Foundation.

Audi, T., Scheck, J., and Lawton, C. (2008, November 5). "California Votes for Prop 8." *Wall Street Journal*.

Ayres, B. D. (1995, February 16). "Conservatives Forge New Strategy to Challenge Affirmative Action." *New York Times*. https://www.nytimes.com/1995/02/16/us /conservatives-forge-new-strategy-to-challenge-affirmative-action.html.

Ayres, B. D. (1995, April 10). "California's Democrats Avert Split Over Affirmative Action." *New York Times*. https://www.nytimes.com/1995/08/08/us/on-affirmativ e-action-wilson-s-moderate-path-veered-quickly-to-right.html.

Bacchi, C. L. (1996). *The Politics of Affirmative Action: "Women," Equality and Category Politics*. London: SAGE.

Badillo, H. (1992, Autumn). "Setting a High Standard: Herman Badillo on the Future of City University (City Journal Interview)." *City Journal*. https://www .city-journal.org/html/city-journal-interview-setting-high-standard-12674 .html.

Badillo, H. (2006). *One Nation, One Standard: An Ex-liberal on How Hispanics Can Succeed Just Like Other Immigrant Groups*. Annotated ed. New York: Sentinel.

Bailey, E. (1995, November 1). "Hunger Strikers Rally in Capitol." *Los Angeles Times*. http:articles.latimes.com/print/1995-11-01/news/mn-63700_1_hunger-strikers.

Balingit, M. (2019, March 18). "The Forgotten Minorities of Higher Education." *Washington Post*. https://www.washingtonpost.com/news/magazine/wp/2019 /03/18/feature/does-affirmative-action-help-or-hurt-asians-who-dont-fit-the -model-minority-stereotype/.

Ballard, A. B. (1973). *The Education of Black Folk: The Afro-American Struggle for Knowledge in White America*. New York: Harper & Row.

Ballard, A. B. (2011). *Breaching Jericho's Walls: A Twentieth-Century African American Life*. Albany: State University of New York Press.

Barrera, L. L. (1998). "Minorities and the University of Texas School of Law (1950–1980)." *Texas Hispanic Journal of Law and Policy 4*, 99–111.

Bastedo, M., Bowen, N. A., Glaesner, K. M., Kelly, J. L., and Bausch, E. (2017, November). *Policy Brief: What Is Holistic Review in College Admissions?* Ann Arbor: Center for the Study of Higher and Postsecondary Education, University of Michigan.

Bastedo, M., Howard, J. E., and Flaster, A. (2016). "Holistic Admissions After Affirmative Action: Does 'Maximizing' the High School Curriculum Matter?" *Educational Evaluation and Policy Analysis 38*(2), 389–409.

Baum, S., Kurose, C., and McPherson, M. (2013). "An Overview of American Higher Education." *The Future of Children 23*(1), 17–39.

Baumeister, C., and Kilian, L. (2016). "Forty Years of Oil Price Fluctuations: Why the Price of Oil May Still Surprise Us." *Journal of Economic Perspectives 30*(1), 139–160. https://doi.org/10.1257/jep.30.1.139.

Bell, D. A. J. (1978). "The Referendum: Democracy's Barrier to Racial Equality." *Washington Law Review 54*, 1.

Bell, D. A. J. (1979). "*Bakke*, Minority Admissions, and the Usual Price of Racial Remedies." *California Law Review 67*, 1.

Bell, D. A .J. (1980). "*Brown v. Board of Education* and the Interest-Convergence Dilemma." *Harvard Law Review 93*, 3.

Bell, D. A. J. (2003). "Diversity's Distractions." *Columbia Law Review 103*, 6.

Bell, J. M., and Hartmann, D. (2007). "Diversity in Everyday Discourse: The Cultural Ambiguities and Consequences of 'Happy Talk.' " *American Sociological Review 72*(6), 895–914.

Benson, J. F. (2007). "Election Fraud and the Initiative Process: A Study of the 2006 Michigan Civil Rights Initiative." *Fordham Urban Law Journal 34*, 3.

Berdahl, R. M. (1998, January 23). "After Proposition 209: Addressing the Fundamental Issues of Educational Inequity." Speech presented at the Commonwealth Club, San Francisco. http://chancellor.berkeley.edu/chancellors/berdahl/speeches/addressing-fundamental-issues-of-educational-inequity.

Berdahl, R. M. (2000, March 21). "Policies of Opportunity: Fairness and Affirmative Action in the 21st Century." Keynote Address at Case Western Reserve University, Cleveland, Ohio. https://chancellor.berkeley.edu/chancellors/berdahl/speeches/fairness-and-affirmative-action.

Bernstein, R. (1995, January 25). "Moves Underway in California to Overturn Higher Education's Affirmative Action Policy." *New York Times*. https://www.nytimes.com/1995/01/25/us/moves-under-way-california-overturn-higher-education-s-affirmative-action-policy.html.

Bernstein, E. M. (1998, January 17). "SUNY and CUNY Heads Differ in Reactions to Cuts." *New York Times*. http://www.nytimes.com/1996/01/17/nyregion/suny-and-cuny-heads-differ-in-reactions-to-cuts.html.

Berrey, E. (2011). "Why Diversity Became Orthodox in Higher Education, and How It Changed the Meaning of Race on Campus." *Critical Sociology* 37(5): 573–596.

Berrey, E. (2015a). *The Enigma of Diversity: The Language of Race and the Limits of Racial Justice*. Chicago: University of Chicago Press.

Berrey, E. (2015b). "Making a Civil Rights Claim for Affirmative Action: BAMN's Legal Mobilization and the Legacy of Race-Conscious Policies." *Du Bois Review: Social Science Research on Race 12*(2), 375–405.

"Best Public Universities in the United States 2018." (2018). Times Higher Education. https://www.timeshighereducation.com/student/best-universities/best-public-universities-united-states.

Biondi, M. (2014). *The Black Revolution on Campus*. Berkeley: University of California Press.

Birnbaum, R., and Goldman, J. (1971). *The Graduates: A FollowUp Study of New York City High School Graduates of 1970*. New York: Center for Social Research, City University of New York.

Biskupic, J. (2012, December 4). "Special Report: Behind U.S. Race Cases, a Little-Known Recruiter." Reuters. http://www.reuters.com/article/2012/12/04/us-usa-court-casemaker-idUSBRE8B30V220121204.

Black Action Movement. (1970–1987). Select Documents; Black Action Movement I (box 107), II (box 109), and III (box 22); President (University of Michigan) Records; Bentley Historical Library, University of Michigan. http://hdl.handle.net/2027.42/109663.

Black Student Union, University of Michigan. (2014). "Demands and Speech Given at the Steps of Hill Auditorium #BBUM." https://www.scribd.com/doc/200999679/Transcription-of-the-speech-given-at-the-steps-of-Hill-Auditorium-BBUM.

Blalock, H. (1967). *Toward a Theory of Minority-Group Relations*. New York: Wiley.

Blum, E. (2014, August 18). *Supreme Court of the United States Blog on Camera: Edward Blum*. https://www.youtube.com/watch?v=xZyR3Ty35Og&t=1s.

Boggs, J. (1963). *The American Revolution: Pages from a Negro Worker's Notebook*. New York: Monthly Review Press.

Bollinger, L. C. (2002, Fall). "Seven Myths About Affirmative Action in Universities." Speech presented at the Education and Law Symposium, Willamette University, Salem, OR. http://www.columbia.edu/cu/president/docs/communications/2002-2003/021016-SevenMyths.html.

Bollinger, L. C. (2007, June 1). "Why Diversity Matters." *Chronicle of Higher Education*. http://www.columbia.edu/cu/president/docs/communications/2006-2007/070601-why-diversity-matters-chronicle.html.

Bonilla-Silva, E. (2001). *White Supremacy and Racism in the Post-Civil Rights Era*. Boulder, CO: Lynne Rienner.

Bonilla-Silva, E. (2006). *Racism Without Racists: Color-Blind Racism and the Persistence of Racial Inequality in the United States*. 2nd ed. Lanham, MD: Rowman & Littlefield.

Boudreau, J. (1994, December 27). "Effort to Outlaw Affirmative Action Promoted in California." *Washington Post*. https://www.washingtonpost.com/archive /politics/1994/12/27/effort-to-outlaw-affirmative-action-promoted-in-california /a363f147-8186-4e1f-b831-c4ee12af2973/?utm_term=.feaedodd93bc.

Bound, J., and Turner, S. (2002). "Going to War and Going to College: Did World War II and the G.I. Bill Increase Educational Attainment for Returning Veterans?" *Journal of Labor Economics* 20(4), 784.

Bowen, W. G., and Bok, D. C. (2000). *The Shape of the River: Long-Term Consequences of Considering Race in College and University Admissions*. Princeton, NJ: Princeton University Press.

Bowler, S., and Donovan, T. A. (2001). *Demanding Choices: Opinion, Voting, and Direct Democracy*. Ann Arbor: University of Michigan Press.

Bowles, S., and Gintis, H. (2011). *Schooling in Capitalist America: Educational Reform and the Contradictions of Economic Life*. Reprint. Chicago: Haymarket Books.

Boyd, R. L. (2007). "Historically Black Colleges and Universities and the Black Business Elite." *Sociological Perspectives* 50(4), 545–560.

Bray, T. (2003, January 19). "Michigan Race Case Not Just a Right-Wing Affair." *San Francisco Chronicle*. http://www.sfgate.com/opinion/article/Michigan -race-case-not-just-a-right-wing-afair-2678884.php.

Breitman, G., LeBlanc, P., and Wald, A. (1996). *Trotskyism in the United States: Historical Essays and Reconsiderations*. Atlantic Highlands, NJ: Humanities Press International.

Brock, T. (2010). "Young Adults and Higher Education: Barriers and Breakthroughs to Success." *The Future of Children* 20(1), 109–132.

Brodkin Sacks, K. (1994). "The GI Bill: Whites Only Need Apply." In R. Delgado and J. Stefancic (eds.), *Critical White Studies: Looking Behind the Mirror*. Philadelphia: Temple University Press.

Broscheid, A. (2011). "Are Some U.S. Courts of Appeals More Liberal or Conservative Than Others?" *Law and Society Review* 45(1): 171–194.

Brown v. Board of Education of Topeka, 347 U.S. 483 (1954).

Brown, M. K., Carnoy, M., Currie, E., Duster, T., Oppenheimer, D. B., Schultz, M. M., and Wellman, D. (2005). *Whitewashing Race: The Myth of a Color-Blind Society*. Rev. ed. Berkeley: University of California Press.

Brown-Nagin, T. (2005). "Elites, Social Movements, and the Law: The Case of Affirmative Action." *Columbia Law Review* 105(5), 1436–1528.

Bureau of Labor Statistics. (2017). "Databases, Tables, & Calculators by Subject." https://data.bls.gov/timeseries/LNU04000000?years_option=all_years& periods_option=specific_periods&periods=Annual+Data.

Burdman, P. (1996, July 10). "Cal Chancellor to Resign: UC Berkeley Stunned by News He'll Quit by July '97" *San Francisco Chronicle*. https://www.sfgate.com /bayarea/article/Cal-Chancellor-to-Resign-UC-Berkeley-stunned-by-2974580 .php.

Burka, P. (1996, September). "Cheryl Hopwood: She Fought Affirmative Action at the University of Texas—And Won." *Texas Monthly.* http://www.texasmonthly .com/content/law-•-cheryl-hopwood.

Burnham, M. (2015). "The Long Civil Rights Act and Criminal Justice." *Boston University Law Review* 95(3), 687–712.

Bush v. Vera, 517 U.S. 952 (1996).

Cahn, R. (1977, April 13). "Quotas Are Completely out of Tune." Editorial. *New York Times.* https://www.nytimes.com/1977/04/13/archives/letters-on -college-admission.html.

"California Master Plan for Higher Education 2010 Review." (2010). University of California Office of the President. http://www.ucop.edu/acadinit/mastplan /mpsummary.htm.

California Postsecondary Education Commission. (1997). *Eligibility of California's 1996 High School Graduates for Admission to the State's Public Universities* (Report 97-9). Sacramento: California Postsecondary Education Commission. http:www.cpec.ca.gov/CompleteReports/1997Reports/97-10.pdf.

California State Auditor. (2016). *The University of California: Its Admissions and Financial Decisions Have Disadvantaged California Resident Students* (Report 2015-107). Sacramento: California State Auditor. http://www.auditor.ca.gov /reports/2015-107/summary.html.

California State Department of Education. (1960). *Master Plan for Higher Education in California 1960–1975.* Sacramento: California State Department of Education. http://www.ucop.edu/acadinit/mastplan/MasterPlan1960.pdf.

Calkins, L. (2002, February). "Samuel Codes Watson." *Michigan History* 86(1), 48–52.

Carbado, D. W., and Harris, C. I. (2012). "The New Racial Preferences." In D. Martinez HoSang, O. LaBennet, and L. Pulido (eds.), *Racial Formation in the Twenty-First Century.* Berkeley: University of California Press.

Carter, L. J. (1969). "University of Texas: On the Way Up—But Politics Still Intrude." *Science* 164(3884), 1150–1154. https://doi.org/10.1126/science.164.3884.1150.

Center for Individual Rights. (2011). "Cases." https://www.cir-usa.org/cases/.

Center for Individual Rights. (2011). "Mission." https://www.cir-usa.org/mission/.

Chan, J., and Eyster, E. (2003). "Does Banning Affirmative Action Lower College Student Quality?" *American Economic Review* 93, 858–872.

Chang, T., and Rose, H. (2010). "A Portrait of Underrepresented Minorities at the University of California 1994–2008." In E. Grodsky and M. Kurlaender (eds.), *Equal Opportunity in Higher Education: The Past and Future of California's Proposition 209.* Cambridge, MA: Harvard Education Press.

Chapa, J. (1997). *The Hopwood Decision in Texas as an Attack on Latino Access to Selective Higher Education Programs.* Los Angeles: UCLA Civil Rights Project. http://escholarship.org/uc/item/662513sp.

Charles, C. Z., Fischer, M. J., Mooney, M. A., and Massey, D. S. (2009). *Taming the River: Negotiating the Academic, Financial, and Social Currents in Selective Colleges and Universities.* Princeton, NJ: Princeton University Press.

Chávez, C. I., and Weisinger, J. Y. (2008). "Beyond Diversity Training: A Social Infusion for Cultural Inclusion." *Human Resource Management* 47(2), 331–350. https://doi.org/10.1002/hrm.20215.

Chávez, L. (1998). *The Color Bind: California's Battle to End Affirmative Action.* Berkeley: University of California Press.

Chetty, R., Friedman, J. N., Saez, E., Turner, N., and Yagan, D. (2017). "Mobility Report Cards: The Role of Colleges in Intergenerational Mobility" (Working Paper 23618). National Bureau of Economic Research, Cambridge, MA. http://www.nber.org/papers/w23618.

Chin, G. J., Cho, S., Kang, J., and Wu, F. H. (1996). "Beyond Self-Interest: Asian Pacific Americans Toward a Community of Justice." *Asian Pacific American Law Journal 4*, 129–162.

City College of New York. (n.d.). "About: Our History." https://www.ccny.cuny.edu/about/history.

City of Richmond v. J. A. Crosson Company, 488 U.S. 469 (1989).

City of Rome v. United States, 446 U.S. 156 (1980).

Clark, K. (1972). "The Advantages and Disadvantages of Open Admissions—And Some History." In *Open Admissions: The Pros and Cons.* Washington, DC: Council for Basic Education.

Clauset, A., Arbesman, S., and Larremore, D. B. (2015). "Systematic Inequality and Hierarchy in Faculty Hiring Networks." *Science Advances 1*(1), e1400005. https://doi.org/10.1126/sciadv.1400005.

Clayton, S. D., and Crosby, F. J. (1992). *Justice, Gender, and Affirmative Action.* Ann Arbor: University of Michigan Press.

Clinton, W. J. (1995, July). "Mend It Don't End It." Speech at the National Archives, Washington, DC. http://web.utk.edu/~mfitzge1/docs/374/MDE1995.pdf.

Coalition of Asian American Associations. (2015, May 15). "Complaint Against Harvard University and the President and Fellows of Harvard College for Discriminating Against Asian-American Applicants in the College Admissions Process" (submitted to the Office for Civil Rights, U.S. Department of Education and the Civil Rights Division, U.S. Department of Justice). *Chronicle of Higher Education.* http://www.chronicle.com/items/biz/pdf/Final%20Aisan%20Complaint%20Harvard%20Document%2020150515.pdf.

Coalition for Economic Equity v. Wilson, 107 F.3d 704 (9th Cir. 1997).

Cohen, A. M., and Kisker, C. B. (2009). *The Shaping of American Higher Education: Emergence and Growth of the Contemporary System.* 2nd ed. San Francisco: Jossey-Bass.

Cohen, C. (1995). *Naked Racial Preference.* Lanham, MD: Madison Books.

Cokorinos, L. (2003). *The Assault on Diversity: An Organized Challenge to Racial and Gender Justice.* Lanham, MD: Rowman & Littlefield.

Coleman, M. S. (2003, January 16). "Statement by University of Michigan President Mary Sue Coleman to U-M Board of Regents." University of Michigan. http://ns.umich.edu/Releases/2003/Jan03/r011603a.html.

Coleman, M. S. (2006, December). "We Will Not Be Deterred." Speech at the University of Michigan, Ann Arbor. http://ns.umich.edu/new/releases /1050.

Collins, S. M. (2011). "From Affirmative Action to Diversity: Erasing Inequality from Organizational Responsibility." *Critical Sociology 37*(5), 517–520. https:// doi.org/10.1177/0896920510380072.

Colorado Unity. (2008). "Promote Diversity, Protect Equal Opportunity: State Coalition Announces 'Decline to Sign' Campaign" (press release).

Colson, C. (2017, January 16). "MLK: A Great Conservative, Not a Liberal Firebrand." CNSNews.com. https://www.cnsnews.com/commentary/chuck -colson/mlk-great-conservative-not-liberal-firebrand.

Committee on Admissions, Enrollment, and Preparatory Education. (2002). "A Report to the Berkeley Faculty on Undergraduate Admission and Comprehensive Review: 1995–2002." Academic Senate, University of California Berkeley. http://academic-senate.berkeley.edu/sites/default/files/aepe_2002 _report.pdf.

Connerly, W. (1995a, May 3). "UC Must End Affirmative Action" *San Francisco Chronicle*.

Connerly, W. (1995b, Spring). "Pride and Prejudice." *Policy Review*. http://www .hoover.org/research/pride-and-prejudice.

Connerly, W. (2001, January 30). "One Nation, Indivisible." *Hoover Digest*, no. 1. https://www.hoover.org/research/one-nation-indivisible.

Council, J., and Robbins, M. A. (2002, March 15). "Name of the Game." *Texas Lawyer*. http://www.texaslawyer.com/id=900005372054/Name-of-the -Game.

Cowie, J. R. (2012). *Stayin' Alive: The 1970s and the Last Days of the Working Class*. New York: New Press.

Crenshaw, K. W. (2007). "Framing Affirmative Action." *Michigan Law Review First Impressions 105*, 123. http://www.michiganlawreview.org/firstimpressions /vol105/ crenshaw.pdf.

CUNY. (2014). "Macaulay Honors College at CUNY, Donations." City University of New York. http://www.cuny.edu/about/invest-in-cuny/news-redirect/ev /college-profiles/mhc.html.

CUNY Office of Institutional Research. (2014). "Student Data Book." City University of New York. http://www.cuny.edu/about/administration/offices/ira /ir/data-book.html.

CUNY Office of Institutional Research. (2015). "A Profile of Undergraduates at CUNY Senior and Community Colleges: Fall 2015." City University of New York. http://www2.cuny.edu/wp-content/uploads/sites/4/media-assets/ug_student _profile_f15.pdf.

CUNY University Faculty Senate. (1999). "CUNY: An Institution Affirmed, Response to the Report of the Mayor's Task Force 'CUNY: An Institution Adrift.'"

Daily Texan Editorial Board. (2012, January 26). "Preserving the Grounds of Protest." *Daily Texan.* http://www.dailytexanonline.com/2012/01/26/preserving -the-grounds-of-protest.

Dale, C. V. (2005). *Federal Affirmative Action Law: A Brief History* (Congressional Research Service no. RS22256). Washington, DC: Congressional Research Service, Library of Congress. http://fpc.state.gov/documents/organization /53577.pdf.

Davidson, C. (1992). *Race and Class in Texas Politics.* Reprint. Princeton, NJ: Princeton University Press.

Dávila, A. (2004). *Barrio Dreams: Puerto Ricans, Latinos, and the Neoliberal City.* Berkeley: University of California Press.

Decker, C. (1995, August 7). "Backers of Affirmative Action Face Tough Task." *Los Angeles Times.* http://articles.latimes.com/1995-08-07/news/mn -32427_1_affirmative-action-programs/2.

Delgado, R., and Stefancic, J. (2012). *Critical Race Theory: An Introduction.* New York: New York University Press.

D'Emilio, J. (2004). *Lost Prophet: The Life and Times of Bayard Rustin.* Chicago: University of Chicago Press.

Deslippe, D. (2012). *Protesting Affirmative Action: The Struggle Over Equality After the Civil Rights Revolution.* Baltimore: Johns Hopkins University Press.

Dettmer, D. (ed.). (2012). *The Texas Book Two: More Profiles, History, and Reminiscences of the University.* Austin: University of Texas Press.

Dietrich, D. R. (2015). "Racially Charged Cookies and White Scholarships: Anti–Affirmative Action Protests on American College Campuses." *Sociological Focus 48*, 105–125.

DiMaggio, P. J., and Powell, W. W. (1983). "The Iron Cage Revisited: Institutional Isomorphism and Collective Rationality in Organizational Fields." *American Sociological Review 48*(2), 147–160.

Dixson, A. D., and Rousseau, C. K. (2005). "And We Are Still Not Saved: Critical Race Theory in Education Ten Years Later." *Race Ethnicity and Education 8*(1), 7–27. http://doi.org/10.1080/1361332052000340971.

Doane, A. W. (2007). "The Changing Politics of Color-Blind Racism." *Research in Race and Ethnic Relations 14*, 181–197.

Doane, A. W., and Bonilla-Silva, E. (eds.). (2003). *White Out: The Continuing Significance of Racism.* New York: Routledge.

Dong, H. (2009). "Third World Liberation Comes to San Francisco State and UC Berkeley." *Chinese America: History & Perspectives*, 95–106.

Douglass, J. A. (1997). "A Brief on the Events Leading to SP1: Submitted to the Task Force on Governance, Panel 2 on Shared Governance." University of California Academic Senate. http://senate.universityofcalifornia.edu/reports/sp1rev.pdf.

Dreier, P. (2004, May 1). "Reagan's Legacy: Homelessness in America." Shelterforce. https://shelterforce.org/2004/05/01/reagans-legacy-homelessness -in-america/.

Du Bois, W. E. B. (1998). *Black Reconstruction in America, 1860–1880*. New York: Free Press.

Duggan, L. (2004). *The Twilight of Equality?: Neoliberalism, Cultural Politics, and the Attack on Democracy*. Boston: Beacon.

Duren, A. M., and Iscoe, L. (1979). *Overcoming: A History of Black Integration at the University of Texas at Austin*. University of Texas at Austin. https://www .utexas.edu/cola/depts/aads/_files/pdf/Duren%20Book%20%20Fall%202011 .pdf.

Elson, A. S. (2009). "Disappearing Without a Case—The Constitutionality of Race-Conscious Scholarships in Higher Education." *Washington University Law Review 86*(4). http://openscholarship.wustl.edu/cgi/viewcontent.cgi?article =1130&context=law_lawreview.

Embrick, D. G. (2011). "The Diversity Ideology in the Business World: A New Oppression for a New Age." *Critical Sociology 37*(5), 541–556. https://doi .org/10.1177/0896920510380076.

Eschen, P. M. V. (1997). *Race Against Empire: Black Americans and Anticolonialism, 1937–1957*. Rev. ed. Ithaca, NY: Cornell University Press.

Espenshade, T. J., and Radford, A. (2009). *No Longer Separate, Not Yet Equal: Race and Class in Elite College Admission and Campus Life*, Princeton, NJ: Princeton University Press.

Evenwol v. Abbott, 578 U.S. ____ (2016).

Figart, D. M., and Mutari, E. (2014). "Is the Casino Economy Creating Jobs?" *Challenge 57*(2), 91–108. https://doi.org/10.2753/0577-5132570207.

Firefighters v. City of Cleveland, 478 U.S. 501 (1986).

Firefighters Local Union No. 1784 v. Stotts. 467 U.S. 561 (1984).

Firestone, D. (1997, February 8). "Ex-assistant to Giuliani Will Head Housing Department." *New York Times*. https://www.nytimes.com/1997/02/08/nyregion /ex-assistant-to-giuliani-will-head-housing-dept.html.

Fischer, M. J. (2010). "A Longitudinal Examination of the Role of Stereotype Threat and Racial Climate on College Outcomes for Minorities at Elite Institutions." *Social Psychology of Education 13*(1), 19–40. https://doi.org/10.1007 /s11218-009-9105-3.

Fisher v. University of Texas, 645 F. Supp. 2d 587 (W.D. Tex. 2009).

Fisher v. University of Texas, 631 F.3d 213 (5th Cir. 2011).

Fisher v. University of Texas, 570 U.S.___ (2013).

Fisher v. University of Texas, 758 F.3d 633 (5th Cir. 2014).

Fisher v. University of Texas, 579 U.S.___ (2016).

Fiske, E. B. (1976, June 2). "Tuition Imposed at City U., Ending a 129-Year Policy: A 7-To-1 Approval; Kibbee Ordered to Set Fees Comparable with State U.'s." *New York Times*.

Fitzgerald, R. (2015, August 26). "U-M to Test New Way to Reach High-Achieving, Low-Income Students." *University of Michigan Record*. https://record.umich. edu/articles/u-m-test-new-way-reach-high-achieving-low-income-students.

Fligstein, N., and McAdam, D. (2012). A *Theory of Fields*. Oxford: Oxford University Press.

Flores, S. M., and Horn, C. L. (2015). *The Texas Top Ten Percent Plan: How It Works, What Are Its Limits, and Recommendations to Consider*. Princeton, NJ: Educational Testing Service.

Flores, S. M., and Oseguera, L. (2013). "Public Policy and Higher Education Attainment in a 21st Century Racial Demography: Examining Research from Early Childhood to the Labor Market." In M. Paulsen (ed.), *Higher Education: Handbook of Theory and Research*, 28: 513–560. Dordrecht, Netherlands: Springer.

Freeman, J. (2001). *Working-Class New York: Life and Labor Since World War II*. New York: The New Press.

Fried, C. (1990, October 4). "The Civil Rights Sham of 1990." *New York Times*. http://www.nytimes.com/1990/10/04/opinion/the-civil-rights-sham-of-1990 .html.

Frosch, D. (2008, April 1). "Colorado Petition Draws Charges of Deception." *New York Times*. http://www.nytimes.com/2008/04/01/us/01denver.html?_r=0.

Frost, J. (1998). "Berkeley Pledge." *Berkeleyan* (Berkeley, CA). http://www.berkeley .edu/news/berkeleyan/1998/0616/.

Fryer, R., Loury, G., and Yuret, T. (2008). "An Economic Analysis of Color-Blind Affirmative Action." *Journal of Law, Economics, and Organization* 24(2), 319–355.

Fusarelli, L. D. (2002). "The Political Economy of Gubernatorial Elections: Implications for Education Policy." *Educational Policy* 16(1), 139–160.

Gaertner, M., and Hart, M. (2013). "Considering Class: College Access and Diversity" *Harvard Law and Policy Review* 7(2), 367.

Gamble, B. S. (1997). "Putting Civil Rights to a Popular Vote." *American Journal of Political Science* 41(1), 245–269.

Ganz, M. (2010). *Why David Sometimes Wins: Leadership, Organization, and Strategy in the California Farm Worker Movement*. Reprint. New York: Oxford University Press.

Garfield, L. Y. (2005). "Back to *Bakke*: Defining the Strict Scrutiny Test for Affirmative Action Policies Aimed at Achieving Diversity in the Classroom." *Nebraska Law Review* 83, 631. https://papers.ssrn.com/abstract=1151955.

Garris, C. (2006). "Martin Luther King's Conservative Legacy." Heritage Foundation. https://www.heritage.org/report/martin-luther-kings-conservative-legacy.

Gayner, J. B. (1995, October 12). "The Contract with America: Implementing New Ideas in the U.S." Heritage Foundation. http://www.heritage.org/research /lecture/the-contract-with-america-implementing-new-ideas-in-the-us.

Gee, H. (1996). "Changing Landscapes: The Need for Asian Americans to Be Included in the Affirmative Action Debate." *Gonzaga Law Review* 32, 621.

Georgia v. United States, 411 U.S. 526 (1973).

Gilmore, J. (2000, February 7). "UC Berkeley's Berkeley Pledge Outreach Program Posts Significant Gains in K–12 Math and Literacy" (press release).

University of California Berkeley. http://www.berkeley.edu/news/media
/releases/2000/02/02-07-2000.html.

Gilmore, R. W. (2007). *Golden Gulag: Prisons, Surplus, Crisis and Opposition in Globalizing California*. Berkeley: University of California Press.

Giroux, H. A. (2014). *Neoliberalism's War on Higher Education*. Chicago: Haymarket Books.

Gladwell, M. (1995, March 25). "Proposed Education Cuts Protested in New York." *Washington Post*.

Glenn, A. (2010, March 30). " 'Open It Up or Shut It Down': The 1970 Black Action Movement Strike at Michigan." *Ann Arbor (MI) Chronicle*. http://annarborchronicle.com/2010/03/30/open-it-up-or-shut-it-down/.

Goldberg, D. T. (2008). *The Threat of Race: Reflections on Racial Neoliberalism*. Malden, MA: Wiley-Blackwell.

Goldberg, H. (1997, December). "The Abolition of Affirmative Action at UC Berkeley." Solidarity. http://www.solidarity-us.org/site/node/1976.

Goodman, J. (2008, May 5). "No Affirmative Action Vote in Missouri." *Governing*. http://www.governing.com/blogs/politics/No-Affirmative-Action-Vote.html.

Gordon, E. W., and Wilkerson, D. A. (1966). "Compensatory Education for the Disadvantaged, Programs and Practices—Preschool Through College." New York: College Entrance Examination Board. https://eric.ed.gov/?id=ED011274.

Graham, H. D. (1990). *The Civil Rights Era: Origins and Development of National Policy, 1960–1972*. Oxford: Oxford University Press.

Graham, J. (1999, September 23). "Latins Miffed by Badillo Talk on Immigrants." *New York Post*. http://nypost.com/1999/09/23/latins-miffed-by-badillo-talk-on -immigrants/.

Gramsci, A. (1971). *Selections from the Prison Notebooks*. Edited by Q. Hoare and G. N. Smith. New York: International Publishers.

Granovetter, M. (1995). *Getting a Job: A Study of Contacts and Careers*. Chicago: University of Chicago Press.

Gratz v. Bollinger, 122 F. Supp. 2d 811 (E.D. Mich. 2001).

Gratz v. Bollinger, 539 U.S. 244 (2003).

Graves, N. (1999, January 26). "Remedial Classes Cut Again by CUNY." *New York Post*. http://nypost.com/1999/01/26/remedial-classes-cut-again-by-cuny/.

Green, E. L., Apuzzo, M., and Benner, K. (2018, July 3). "Trump Officials Reverse Obama's Policy on Affirmative Action in Schools." *New York Times*. https://www.nytimes.com/2018/07/03/us/politics/trump-affirmative-action-race -schools.html.

Greenberg, S. B. (1996). *Middle Class Dreams: The Politics and Power of the New American Majority*. Rev. updated ed. New Haven, CT: Yale University Press.

Greenland, F. R., Chen, A. S., and Stulberg, L. M. (2010, June 4). "Beyond the Open Door: The Origins of Affirmative Action in Undergraduate Admissions at Cornell and the University of Michigan." Paper presented at the Policy History Conference, Columbus, OH.

Grodsky, E. (2007). "Compensatory Sponsorship in Higher Education." *American Journal of Sociology 112*(6): 1662–1712. https://doi.org/10.1086/512707.

Grodsky, E., and Kurlaender, M. (eds.). (2010). *Equal Opportunity in Higher Education: The Past and Future of California's Proposition 209.* Cambridge, MA: Harvard Education Press.

Grove City College v. Bell, 465 U.S. 555 (1984).

Grutter v. Bollinger, 137 F. Supp. 2d 874 (E.D. Mich. 2001).

Grutter v. Bollinger, 539 U.S. 306 (2003).

Guerrero, A. (2002). *Silence at Boalt Hall: The Dismantling of Affirmative Action.* Oakland: University of California Press.

Guinier, L., and Torres, G. (2003). *The Miner's Canary: Enlisting Race, Resisting Power, Transforming Democracy.* Cambridge, MA: Harvard University Press.

Gunderson, C. (2003). "The Struggle for CUNY: A History of the CUNY Student Movement, 1969–1999." Unpublished thesis. http://macaulay.cuny .edu/eportfolios/hainline2014/files/2014/02/Gunderson_The-Struggle-for -CUNY.pdf.

Gurin, P., Lehman, J. S., Lewis, E., Dey, E. L., Hurtado, S., and Gurin, G. (2004). *Defending Diversity: Affirmative Action at the University of Michigan.* Ann Arbor: University of Michigan Press.

Hall, S. (1980). "Race, Articulation, and Societies Structured in Dominance." In *Sociological Theories: Race and Colonialism.* Paris: UNESCO.

Hall, S. (1988). "Gramsci and Us." Chap. 10 in *The Hard Road to Renewal: Thatcherism and the Crisis of the Left.* London: Verso. https://www.versobooks.com /blogs/2448-stuart-hall-gramsci-and-us.

Hall, S., and Grossberg, L. (1996). "On Postmodernism and Articulation: An Interview with Stuart Hall." In D. Morley and K. Chen (eds.), *Stuart Hall: Critical Dialogues in Cultural Studies,* London: Routledge.

Hall, S., and O'Shea, A. (2013). "Common-Sense Neoliberalism." *Soundings: A Journal of Politics and Culture 55,* 8–24.

Haney-Lopez, I. (2007). " 'A Nation of Minorities': Race, Ethnicity, and Reactionary Colorblindness." *Stanford Law Review 59*(4), 985–1063.

Haney-Lopez, I. (2013). *Dog Whistle Politics: How Coded Racial Appeals Have Reinvented Racism and Wrecked the Middle Class.* Oxford: Oxford University Press.

Hannah-Jones, N. (2013, March 18). "A Colorblind Constitution: What Abigail Fisher's Affirmative Action Case Is Really About." ProPublica. http://www .propublica.org/article/a-colorblind-constitution-what-abigail-fishers -affirmative-action-case-is-r.

Harris, A. L., and Tienda, M. (2010). "Minority Higher Education Pipeline: Consequences of Changes in College Admissions Policy in Texas." *Annals of the American Academy of Political and Social Science 627*(1), 60–81.

Harris, A. L., and Tienda, M. (2012). "Hispanics in Higher Education and the Texas Top 10 Percent Law. *Race and Social Problems 4*, 57–67.

Harris, S. A. (1997, April 29). "UC Students Storm Sproul Hall in Prop. 209 Protest." *San Francisco Chronicle.* http://www.sfgate.com/news/article/UC -students-storm-Sproul-Hall-in-Prop-209-protest-3123314.php.

Hartocollis, A. (2016, January 4). "As Justices Weigh Affirmative Action, Michigan Offers an Alternative." *New York Times.* https://www.nytimes .com/2016/01/05/us/affirmative-action-supreme-court-michigan.html.

Harvey, D. (2009). *A Brief History of Neoliberalism.* Oxford: Oxford University Press.

Hauptman, A. M. (1999). "Financing Remediation at CUNY on a Performance Basis: A Proposal" (DRR-2055-1). RAND, New York. http://www.nyc.gov/html /records/rwg/cuny/pdf/randdrr-2055-1.pdf.

Haurwitz, R. K. M. (2005, March 31). "Faulkner Argues for Altering Top 10 Percent Law." *Austin American-Statesman.* http://www.texastop10.princeton.edu/publicity /general/AustinAmericanStatesman033105.pdf.

Hebel, S. (2002, March 1). "A New Look for CUNY: Tough Admissions Policies Have Drawn Good Students, but Turned Some Immigrants Away." *Chronicle of Higher Education.*

Helfland, H. (2002). *The Campus Guides: University of California Berkeley.* New York: Princeton Architectural Press.

Henary, B. (2002, September 23). "On the Right Side of the Law." *Weekly Standard.* http://staging.weeklystandard.com/Content/Public/Articles/000/000/001 /692xnozx.asp.

Herbers, J. (1970, February 19). "Panetta's Ouster Linked to Policy." *New York Times.* https://www.nytimes.com/1970/02/19/archives/panettas-ouster-linked -to-policy-nixon-shift-following-stand-by.html.

Herbert, B. (2000, March 27). "In America; Contracts for Cronies." *New York Times.* https://www.nytimes.com/2000/03/27/opinion/in-america-contracts-for -cronies.html.

Hertog Foundation. (n.d.). "About." http://hertogfoundation.org/about.

Hertog Scholars Program. (2011). "Brochure." http://macaulay.cuny.edu/hertog /wp-content/uploads/2011/11/MHC_hertog_booklet_092811.pdf.

Hevesi, D. (1995, June 14). "CUNY Seeks to Bar Remedial Courses Beyond First Year." *New York Times.* http://www.nytimes.com/1995/06/14/nyregion/cuny -seeks-to-bar-remedial-courses-beyond-first-year.html.

Hilliard, T. (2018, August). "Excelsior Scholarship Serving Very Few New York Students." Center for an Urban Future. https://nycfuture.org/research /excelsior-scholarship.

Hinrichs, P. (2012). "The Effects of Affirmative Action Bans on College Enroll-ment, Educational Attainment, and the Demographic Composition of Universities." *Review of Economics and Statistics 94*, 712–722.

Hinsdale, B. A. (2010). *History of the University of Michigan.* Charleston, SC: Nabu Press.

Hinton, E. K. (2016). *From the War on Poverty to the War on Crime: The Making of Mass Incarceration in America.* Cambridge, MA: Harvard University Press.

Hirschman, D., and Berrey, E. (2017). "The Partial Deinstitutionalization of Affirmative Action in U.S. Higher Education, 1988 to 2014." *Sociological Science 4,* 449–468.

Hirschman, D., Berrey, E., and Rose-Greenland, F. (2016). "Dequantifying Diversity: Affirmative Action and Admissions at the University of Michigan." *Theory and Society 45*(3), 265–301.

Hochschild, J. L. (1999). "Affirmative Action as Culture War." In M. Lamont (ed.), *The Cultural Territories of Race: Black and White Boundaries,* 343–368. Chicago: University of Chicago Press; New York: Russell Sage Foundation.

Honan, W. B. (1995, February 8). "SUNY Chancellor Warns of Big Tuition Increases If Budget Cuts Are Made." *New York Times.* http://www.nytimes .com/1995/02/08/us/suny-chancellor-warns-of-big-tuition-increases-if-budget -cuts-are-made.html?pagewanted=print.

Hopwood v. Texas, 861 F. Supp. 554 (W.D. Tex. 1994).

Hopwood v. Texas, 78 F.3d 932 (5th Cir. 1996).

Horn, C. L., and Flores, S. M. (2003). *Percent Plans in College Admissions: A Comparative Analysis of Three States' Experiences.* Cambridge, MA: Harvard University. http://civilrightsproject.ucla.edu/research/college-access/admissions /percent-plans-in-college-admissions-a-comparative-analysis-of-three-states 2019-experiences/horn-percent-plans-2003.pdf.

Hochschild, A. R. (2016). *Strangers in Their Own Land: Anger and Mourning on the American Right.* New York: The New Press.

Huber, E., and Stephens, J. D. (2001). *Development and Crisis of the Welfare State: Parties and Policies in Global Markets.* Chicago: University of Chicago Press.

Impoco, J. (1995, March 20). "California Dreams of the White House." *U.S. News & World Report.*

The Internationalist. (1999, February). "Smash Racist Purge of CUNY—Fight for Open Admissions, Free Tuition!" http://www.internationalist.org/cuny0299. html.

Irving, C. (1999, Spring). "Texas' Demographic Challenge: New Programs Attempt to Substitute for Race-Based Admissions Policies." *National Crosstalk.* Center for Public Policy and Higher Education. http://www.higher education.org/crosstalk/ct0499/news0499-texas.shtml.

James, A. (2008, February 7). "Coalition Warns About Dishonest Affirmative Action Signature Gathering in Missouri." *St. Louis American.* http:// www.stlamerican.com/news/local_news/article_3c242fba-17e2-500a-832a -5d694264b232.html?mode=jqm.

Jencks, C., and Phillips, M. (1998). *The Black-White Test Score Gap.* Washington, DC: Brookings Institution Press.

Jenson, J. (2013). *Changing Perspectives on Social Citizenship: A Cross-Time Comparison*. Oxford: Oxford University Press.

Jett v. Dallas Independent School District, 491 U.S. 701 (1989).

Johnson v. Transportation Agency, Santa Clara City, 480 U.S. 616 (1987).

Johnson, J. (1988, March 17). "Reagan Vetoes Bill That Would Widen Federal Rights Law." *New York Times*.

Johnson, L. B. (1965, June). "To Fulfill These Rights." Commencement address at Howard University, Washington, DC. http://www.lbjlib.utexas.edu/johnson /archives.hom/speeches.hom/650604.asp.

Johnson, L. B. (1966, March 3). "Remarks Upon Signing the 'Cold War GI Bill' (Veterans Readjustment Benefits Act of 1966)." American Presidency Project. http://www.presidency.ucsb.edu/ws/?pid=27461.

Jones, C. (1995, June 27). "CUNY Adopts Stricter Policy on Admissions." *New York Times*.

Jones, D. K., Bradley, K. W. V., and Oberlander, J. (2014). "Pascal's Wager: Health Insurance Exchanges, Obamacare, and the Republican Dilemma." *Journal of Health Politics, Policy and Law* 39(1), 97–137.

Kahlenberg, R. D. (1997). *The Remedy: Class, Race, and Affirmative Action*. New York: Basic Books.

Kahlenberg, R. D., and Potter, H. (2012). *A Better Affirmative Action: State Universities That Created Alternatives to Racial Preferences*. Washington, DC: Century Foundation. https://www.tcf.org/assets/downloads/tcf-abaa.pdf.

Karabel, J. (1989). *Freshman Admissions at Berkeley: A Policy for the 1990s and Beyond*. Berkeley: University of California. http://academic-senate.berkeley.edu /committees/aepe/freshman-admissions-berkeley-policy-1990s-and-beyond.

Karabel, J. (1999). "The Rise and Fall of Affirmative Action at the University of California." *Journal of Blacks in Higher Education, 77*(1), 15–26.

Karabel, J. (2005). *The Chosen: The Hidden History of Admission and Exclusion at Harvard, Yale, and Princeton*. Boston: Mariner.

Katznelson, I. (2005). *When Affirmative Action Was White: An Untold History of Racial Inequality in Twentieth-Century America*. New York: Norton.

Kerr, C. (2001). *The Uses of the University*. Cambridge. MA: Harvard University Press.

Kidder, W. C. (2006). "Negative Action Versus Affirmative Action: Asian Pacific Americans Are Still Caught in the Crossfire." *Michigan Journal of Race and Law 11*, 605.

Kim, R. (1995). "Affirmative Action Groups Clash Over Tactics, Non-student Participation Raises Hackles." *Daily Californian* (Berkeley). web.archive .org/web/20040305002725/http://archive.dailycal.org/archive/09.25.95/groups .txt.

King, M. L., Jr. (1961, February 4). "The President Has the Power . . . Equality Now." *The Nation*. http://www.thekingcenter.org/archive/document/nation -president-has-power-equality-now#.

King, M. (2002, October 11). "Capitol Chronicle: Hopwood Lawyer Steven Wayne Smith Aspires to Supreme Heights." *Austin Chronicle.* http://www.austin chronicle.com/news/2002-10-11/104692/.

Klar, S. (2014). "A Multidimensional Study of Ideological Preferences and Priorities Among the American Public." *Public Opinion Quarterly 78*, 344–359.

Koffman, D., and Tienda, M. (2008). "Missing in Application: The Texas Top 10 Percent Law and Campus Socioeconomic Diversity" (Texas Higher Education Opportunity Project Working Paper). Princeton University, Princeton, NJ.

Kolbert, E. (1989, May 3). "Cuomo Blocks a Rise in SUNY and CUNY Tuition." *New York Times.* https://www.nytimes.com/1989/05/03/nyregion/cuomo-blocks -a-rise-in-suny-and-cuny-tuition.html.

Koury, R. (1995, August 31). "Berkeley Students Rally for Affirmative Action, Some Blockade Office in Peaceful Protest." *San Jose Mercury News.*

Krauthammer, C. (1995, May 26). "Myth of the Angry White Male." *Washington Post.*

Kroll, A. (2013, February 5). "Exposed: The Dark-Money ATM of the Conservative Movement." *Mother Jones.* http://www.motherjones.com/politics/2013/02 /donors-trust-donor-capital-fund-dark-money-koch-bradley-devos.

Kroll Associates. (2015). *University of Texas at Austin—Investigation of Admissions Practices and Allegations of Undue Influence.* New York: Kroll Associates. https://www.utsystem.edu/sites/default/files/news/assets/kroll-investigation -admissions-practices.pdf.

La Voz de Berkeley Newswire. (1996, November 8). "UC Berkeley Students Continue to Occupy Campanile Tower." Driftline. http://www.driftline.org /cgi-bin/archive/archive_msg.cgi?file=spoo . . . al.archive/marxism-general _1996/96-11-15.074&msgnum=21&start=2708.

Ladson-Billings, G. (2005). "The Evolving Role of Critical Race Theory in Educational Scholarship." *Race Ethnicity and Education 8*(1), 115–119. http://doi.org /10.1080/1361332052000341024.

Lamis, A. P. (ed.). (1999). *Southern Politics in the 1990s.* Baton Rouge: Louisiana State University Press.

Larson, J., and Menendian, S. (2008). *Anti-affirmative Action Ballot Initiatives.* Columbus: Kirwan Institute for the Study of Race and Ethnicity, Ohio State University. http://www.kirwaninstitute.osu.edu/reports/2008/12_2008 _AntiAffirmativeActionBallotInitiatives.pdf.

Lavin, D. E., Alba, R. D., and Silberstein, R. A. (1981). *Right Versus Privilege: The Open Admissions Experiment at the City University of New York.* New York: Free Press.

Lavin, D. E., and Hyllegard, D. (1996). *Changing the Odds: Open Admissions and the Life Chances of the Disadvantaged.* New Haven, CT: Yale University Press.

Laycock, D. (2001). "*Hopwood v. Texas*: The Background." Tarlton Law Library, Jamail Center for Legal Research, University of Texas School of Law. http:// tarltonguides.law.utexas.edu/content.php?pid=98968&sid=772237.

Leadership Conference on Civil Rights. (2009). *Restoring the Conscience of a Nation: A Report on the U.S. Commission on Civil Rights*. Washington, DC: Leadership Conference on Civil Rights Education Fund.

Left Spot. (2006, September 29). "Some Thoughts on the History of CUNY SLAM." http://leftspot.com/blog/?q=cunyarticle.

Leonard, J. S. (1989). "Women and Affirmative Action." *Journal of Economic Perspectives 3*(1), 61–75.

Lewin, T. (2006, October 31). "Race Preferences Vote Splits Michigan." *New York Times*. https://www.nytimes.com/2006/10/31/us/31michigan.html.

Lewis, E., and Cantor, N. (2016). *Our Compelling Interests: The Value of Diversity for Democracy and a Prosperous Society*. Princeton, NJ: Princeton University Press.

Lewis, N. A. (1992, July 1). "The 1992 Campaign; Selection of Conservative Judges Insures a President's Legacy." *New York Times*. https://www.nytimes.com/1992/07/01/us/the-1992-campaign-selection-of-conservative-judges-insures-a-president-s-legacy.html.

Lin, N. (1999). "Social Networks and Status Attainment." *Annual Review of Sociology 25*, 467–487.

Lipson, D. N. (2007). "Embracing Diversity: The Institutionalization of Affirmative Action as Diversity Management at UC-Berkeley, UT-Austin, and UW-Madison." *Law and Social Inquiry 32*(4), 985–1026.

Lipson, D. N. (2011). "The Resilience of Affirmative Action in the 1980s: Innovation, Isomorphism, and Institutionalization in University Admissions." *Political Research Quarterly 64*(1), 132–144.

Liptak, A. (2012, October 10). "Justices Weigh Race as Factor at Universities." *New York Times*. http://www.nytimes.com/2012/10/11/us/a-changed-court-revisits-affirmative-action-in-college-admissions.html.

Litolff, E. H., III. (2007). "Higher Education Desegregation: An Analysis of State Efforts in Systems Formerly Operating Segregated Systems of Higher Education." PhD diss., Louisiana State University, Baton Rouge. https://digitalcommons.lsu.edu/cgi/viewcontent.cgi?article=4133&context=gradschool_dissertations.

Liu, A. (2008). "Affirmative Action and Negative Action: How Jian Li's Case Can Benefit Asian Americans." *Michigan Journal of Race and Law 13*, 391–432.

Loeb, P. (1994). *Generation at the Crossroads : Apathy and Action on the American Campus*. New Brunswick, NJ: Rutgers University Press.

Long, M., Saenz, V., and Tienda, M. (2010). "Policy Transparency and College Enrollment: Did the Texas Top Ten Percent Law Broaden Access to the Public Flagships?" *Annals of the American Academy of Political and Social Science 627*(1), 82–105.

Long, M. C., and Tienda, M. (2008). "Winners and Losers: Changes in Texas University Admissions Post-Hopwood." *Educational Evaluation and Policy Analysis 30*(3), 255–280.

Looney, A., and Yannelis, C. (2015). *A Crisis in Student Loans? How Changes in the Characteristics of Borrowers and in the Institutions They Attended Contributed to Rising Loan Defaults.* Washington, DC: Brookings Institution. https://www.brookings.edu/wp-content/uploads/2015/09/LooneyTextFall15BPEA.pdf.

Lopez v. Monterey County, 525 U.S. 266 (1999).

Lorance v. AT&T Technologies, Inc., 490 U.S. 900 (1989).

Los Angeles Times. (1989, April 7). "UC Berkeley Apologizes for Policy That Limited Asians."

Lowe, L. (2015). *The Intimacies of Four Continents.* Durham, NC: Duke University Press.

Lungren v. Superior Court of Sacramento County, 48 Cal. App. 4th 435, 55 Cal. Rptr. 2d 690 (1996). http://law.justia.com/cases/california/court-of-appeal/4th/48/435.html.

Mac Donald, H. (1994, Summer). "Downward Mobility." *City Journal.* http://www.city-journal.org/story.php?id=1425.

Mac Donald, H. (1996, Summer). "Disturbing Admissions." *City Journal.* https://www.city-journal.org/html/disturbing-admissions-12301.html.

Mac Donald, H. (1998, Winter). "CUNY Could Be Great Again." *City Journal.* http://www.city-journal.org/html/8_1_cuny_could.html.

Macaulay Honors College. (2018). "About Macaulay: Fast Facts." https://macaulay.cuny.edu/about-macaulay/.

MacLachlan, A. J. (2007). "Report on Academic Outreach and Support for Diversity After Proposition 209." Commissioned report for the Warren Institute, Boalt Law School. Berkeley, CA.

Maeroff, G. I. (1974, June 7). "Effects of Open Admissions Stir New Dispute at City U." *New York Times.*

Maharidge, D. (1995, December). "California Schemer: What You Need to Know About Pete Wilson." *Mother Jones.* http://www.motherjones.com/politics/1995/11/california-schemer-what-you-need-know-about-pete-wilson.

Malveaux, J. (2004). "Know Your Enemy: The Assault on Diversity." *Black Issues in Higher Education 21*, 32–33.

Maney, G. M., Kutz-Flamenbaum, R. V., Rohlinger, D. A., and Goodwin, J. (2012). *Strategies for Social Change.* Minneapolis: University of Minnesota Press.

Manning, A., Hartmann, D., and Gerteis, J. (2015). "Colorblindness in Black and White: An Analysis of Core Tenets, Configurations, and Complexities." *Sociology of Race and Ethnicity 1*(4), 532–546.

Maramba, D. C., Sulé, V. T., and Winke-Wagner, R. (2015). "What Discourse on the Texas Top Ten Percent Plan Says About Accountability for Diversity." *Journal of Higher Education 86*(5), 751–776.

Marshall, T. H. (1950). *Citizenship and Social Class: And Other Essays.* Cambridge: Cambridge University Press.

Martin v. Wilks, 490 U.S. 755 (1989).

Massey, D. S., Charles, C. Z., Lundy, G., and Fischer, M. J. (2006). *The Source of the River: The Social Origins of Freshmen at America's Selective Colleges and Universities*. Princeton, NJ: Princeton University Press.

Massie, M. (2004). "Litigators and Communities Working Together: *Grutter v. Bollinger* and the New Civil Rights Movement." *Berkeley Women's Law Journal* 19(2), 318–323.

Matthews, J. (1990, October 2). "Bias Against Asians Found in Admissions to UCLA; U.S. Says Whites Were Favored for Math." *Washington Post*.

Mayer, J. (2017). *Dark Money: The Hidden History of the Billionaires Behind the Rise of the Radical Right*. Reprint. New York: Anchor.

McCarthy, M. (1995, April 16). "Casey May Enliven Presidential Race." *Buffalo News*. https://buffalonews.com/1995/04/16/casey-may-enliven-presidential-race.

McFadden, R. D. (1993, June 29). "CUNY Board Gives Backing to a Redesign." *New York Times*. http://www.nytimes.com/1993/06/29/nyregion/cuny-board-gives-backing-to-a-redesign.html.

McKinley, J. C., Jr. (1989, May 2). "Tuition Protests Spread to Most CUNY Campuses." *New York Times*. http://www.nytimes.com/1989/05/02/nyregion/tuition-protests-spread-to-most-cuny-campuses.html.

McLaurin v. Oklahoma State Regents, 339 U.S. 637 (1950).

McMillan-Cottom, T. (2017). *Lower Ed: The Troubling Rise of For-Profit Colleges in the New Economy*. New York: New Press.

McNeil, L. (2000). *Contradictions of School Reform: Educational Costs of Standardized Testing*. New York: Routledge.

McPhee, M. (2008, April 24). "Group Challenges Affirmative-Action Initiative." *Denver Post*. http://www.denverpost.com/ci_9041278.

Meachum, J. M. (1995, March 6). "Undecided: Will California's 'Lead Dog' Run?" *Newsweek* 125(10).

Meachum, R. (1975, February 21). "Students End Ad. Bldg. Sit In." *Michigan Daily* (Ann Arbor).

Meyer, D. S., and Staggenborg, S. (2012). "Thinking About Strategy." In G. M. Maney, R. V. Kutz-Flamenbaum, D. A. Rohlinger, and J. Goodwin (eds.), *Strategies for Social Change*. Minneapolis: University of Minnesota Press.

Meyers, B. (1999). "In Defense of CUNY." In R. Martin (ed.), *Chalk Lines: The Politics of Work in the Managed University*. Durham, NC: Duke University Press.

Michigan Civil Rights Commission. (2006). "Report of the Michigan Civil Rights Commission Regarding the Use of Fraud and Deception in the Collection of Signatures for the Michigan Civil Rights Initiative Ballot Petition." https://www.michigan.gov/documents/PetitionFraudreport_162009_7.pdf.

Michigan Daily. (1990, November 13). "Unwanted Activists: Revolutionary Workers League Irks 'U' Groups." Ann Arbor. https://news.google.com/newspapers?nid=2706&dat=19901113&id=AOFQAAAAIBAJ&sjid=6xoNAAAAIBAJ&pg=5758,3466018&hl=en.

Michigan Daily. (2001, September 27). "Sectarian Sojourn: BAMN Must Work Well with Others or Take Trotskyite Philosophy Elsewhere." Ann Arbor. http://www.michigandaily.com/content/sectarian-sojourn-bamn-must-work-well-others-or-take-trotskyite-philosophy-elsewhere.

Micklethwait, J., and Wooldridge, A. (2004). *The Right Nation: Conservative Power in America*. New York: Penguin.

Milliken v. Bradley, 418 U.S. 717 (1974).

Missouri Census Data Center. (2018). "Population Estimates by Age, Race [California]." https://census.missouri.edu/population-by-age/.

Missouri ex rel. Gaines v. Canada, 305 U.S. 337 (1938).

Molina, J. (1996, Fall). "CSUN Students Tell BAMN to 'Go Home.'" *Daily Sundial* (Northridge, CA). web.archive.org/web/20040624183934/http://sundial.csun.edu/sun/96f/093096ne3.htm.

Moll, R. (1986). *The Public Ivys*. New York: Penguin.

Moore, W. L., and Bell, J. M. (2011). "Maneuvers of Whiteness: 'Diversity' as a Mechanism of Retrenchment in the Affirmative Action Discourse." *Critical Sociology* 37(5), 597–613. https://doi.org/10.1177/0896920510380066.

Morris, G. S. (1995). *Head of the Class: An Oral History of African-American Achievement in Higher Education and Beyond*. New York: Twayne.

Mouw, T. (2003). "Social Capital and Finding a Job: Do Contacts Matter?" *American Sociological Review* 68, 868–898.

Movement for Black Lives. (2016). "Reparations." https://policy.m4bl.org/reparations/.

Murray v. Pearson, 169 Md. 478, 182 A. 590 (1936).

Murray, M. E. (2002). "Whatever Happened to G.I. Jane?: Citizenship, Gender, and Social Policy in the Postwar Era." *Michigan Journal of Gender and Law* 9, 91.

Musgrove, G. D. (2012). *Rumor, Repression, and Racial Politics: How the Harassment of Black Elected Officials Shaped Post–Civil Rights America*. Athens: University of Georgia Press.

National Advisory Commission on Civil Disorders. (1968). *Report of the National Advisory Commission on Civil Disorders*. New York: Bantam.

National Center for Education Statistics. (2015). "Table 306.50, Total Fall Enrollment in Degree-Granting Postsecondary Institutions, by Control and Classification of Institution, Level of Enrollment, and Race/Ethnicity of Student: 2015." https://nces.ed.gov/programs/digest/d16/tables/dt16_306.50.asp.

National Center for Education Statistics. (2016). "Table 104.20, Percentage of Persons 25 to 29 Years Old with Selected Levels of Educational Attainment, by Race/Ethnicity and Sex: Selected Years, 1920 Through 2016." https://nces.ed.gov/programs/digest/d16/tables/dt16_104.20.asp.

National Center for Education Statistics. (2017a). "Table 326.10, Graduation Rate from First Institution Attended for First-Time, Full-Time Bachelor's Degree-Seeking Students at 4-Year Postsecondary Institutions, by Race/Ethnicity, Time to Completion, Sex, Control of Institution, and Acceptance

Rate: Selected Cohort Entry Years, 1996 Through 2009." https://nces.ed.gov/programs/digest/d16/tables/dt16_326.10.asp.

National Center for Education Statistics. (2017b). "Table 326.20, Graduation Rate from First Institution Attended Within 150 Percent of Normal Time for First-Time, Full-Time Degree/Certificate-Seeking Students at 2-Year Postsecondary Institutions, by Race/Ethnicity, Sex, and Control of Institution: Selected Cohort Entry Years, 2000 Through 2012." https://nces.ed.gov/programs/digest/d16/tables/dt16_326.20.asp.

National Institute on Money in State Politics. (2015a). "Proposition 107: Bans Discrimination & Preferential Treatment (Arizona, 2010)."

National Institute on Money in State Politics. (2015b). "Proposition 109: Right to Hunt and Fish (Arizona 2010)."

New York State. (2017a). "New York's Promise to Students: Ever Upward Summary." https://www.ny.gov/sites/ny.gov/files/atoms/files/ExcelsiorScholarship_OnePagers.pdf.

New York State. (2017b). "Tuition-Free Degree Program: The Excelsior Scholarship." https://www.ny.gov/programs/tuition-free-degree-program-excelsior-scholarship.

New York Times. (1996, March 27). "The Twin Crises at CUNY."

Newfield, C. (2011). *Unmaking the Public University: The Forty-Year Assault on the Middle Class*. Cambridge, MA: Harvard University Press.

Newfield, J. (1965, May 20). "Campus Across the River: Cause Without a Rebel." *Village Voice*.

Newman, N. (1995, September/October). "Affirmative Action, the UC Regents, and the Explosion of Campus Activism." *Independent Politics*. http://www.nathannewman.org/other/aa-indp.html.

Newman, N. (2003, March 15). "Hijacking the Affirmative Action Movement." *Progressive Populist* 9(5). http://www.populist.com/03.05.newman.html.

Nguyen Barry, M., and Dannenberg, M. (2016). *Out of Pocket: The High Cost of Inadequate High Schools and High School Student Achievement on College Affordability*. Washington, DC: Education Reform Now. https://edreformnow.org/wp-content/uploads/2016/04/EdReformNow-O-O-P-Embargoed-Final.pdf.

Niu, S. X., Sullivan, T. A., and Tienda, M. (2008). "Minority Talent Loss and the Texas Top 10 Percent Law." *Social Science Quarterly* 89(4), 831–845.

Obasogie, O. K. (2013). *Blinded by Sight*. Palo Alto, CA: Stanford University Press.

O'Connor, A. (2008). "The Privatized City: The Manhattan Institute, the Urban Crisis, and the Conservative Counterrevolution in New York." *Journal of Urban History* 34(2), 333–353.

Olivas, M. A. (2013). *Suing Alma Mater: Higher Education and the Courts*. Baltimore: Johns Hopkins University Press.

Olson, K. W. (1973). "The G.I. Bill and Higher Education: A Success and Surprise." *American Quarterly* 25(5), 596–610.

Omi, M., and Takagi, D. Y. (1996). "Situating Asian Americans in the Political Discourse on Affirmative Action." *Representations*, no. 55, 155–162.

Omi, M., and Winant, H. (2015). *Racial Formation in the United States*. 3rd ed. New York: Routledge.

One America Initiative. (1997). "One America—Summer of Unity and Liberation (SOUL)." The White House. http://clinton5.nara.gov/Initiatives/OneAmerica /Practices/pp_19980729.6584.html.

Onishi, N. (2012, October 16). "California Ballot Initiatives, Born in Populism, Now Come from Billionaires." *New York Times*. https://www.nytimes.com /2012/10/17/us/politics/california-ballot-initiatives-dominated-by-the-very -rich.html.

Onkst, D. H. (1998). "'First a Negro . . . Incidentally a Veteran': Black World War Two Veterans and the G. I. Bill of Rights in the Deep South, 1944–1948." *Journal of Social History 31*(3), 517–543.

"Opportunity Programs." (n.d.). City University of New York. http://www2 .cuny.edu/financial-aid/federal-and-state-grants/opportunity-programs/.

Orlans, H. (1992). "Affirmative Action in Higher Education." *Annals of the American Academy of Political and Social Science 523*(1), 144–158.

Painter, N. I. (2006). *Creating Black Americans: African-American History and Its Meanings, 1619 to the Present*. New York: Oxford University Press.

Paolucci, A. (1970, September 26). "Chaos in 'Open Enrollment.'" Editorial. *New York Times*.

Parents Involved in Community Schools v. Seattle School District No. 1, 551 U.S. 701 (2007).

Parker, T. L., and Richardson, R. (2005). "Ending Remediation at CUNY: Implications for Access and Excellence." *Journal of Educational Research and Policy Studies 5*(2), 1–22.

Patillo, M. (2013). *Black Picket Fences*. 2nd ed. Chicago: University of Chicago Press.

Patterson v. McLean Credit Union, 491 U.S. 164 (1989).

Patton, S. (2012). "From Cellblock to Campus, One Black Man Defies the Data." *Chronicle of Higher Education*.

Paul, N. (1990). "*Wards Cove Packing Co. v. Atonio*: The Supreme Court's Disparate Treatment of the Disparate Impact Doctrine." *Hofstra Labor and Employment Law Journal 8*(1), 127–165. http://scholarlycommons.law.hofstra.edu/hlelj/vol8 /iss1/3.

Perkins, L. M. (2012.). "The First Black Talent Identification Program: The National Scholarship Service and the Fund for Negro Students, 1947–1968." In M. Gasman and R. L. Geiger (eds.), *Higher Education for African Americans Before the Civil Rights Era, 1900–1964*. New Brunswick, NJ: Transaction.

Perry, B. A. (2007). *The Michigan Affirmative Action Cases*. Lawrence: University Press of Kansas.

Plessy v. Ferguson, 163 U.S. 537 (1896).

Plestis, V. (2011, August 3). "Tuition Hikes, Aid Cuts Threaten to Put CUNY Out of Reach." *Gotham Gazette* (New York). http://www.gothamgazette.com /index.php/education/797-tuition-hikes-aid-cuts-threaten-to-put-cuny-out -of-reach.

Polletta, F. (2006). *It Was Like a Fever: Storytelling in Protest and Politics.* Chicago: University of Chicago Press.

Polletta, F., Chen, P. C. B., Gardner, B. G., and Motes, A. (2011). "The Sociology of Storytelling." *Annual Review of Sociology 37*(1), 109–130.

Powell, L. F. (1971). "Confidential Memorandum: Attack on American Free Enterprise System." http://law2.wlu.edu/deptimages/Powell%20Archives/Powell MemorandumTypescript.pdf.

Powell, W. W., and DiMaggio, P. J. (eds.). (2012). *The New Institutionalism in Organizational Analysis.* Chicago: University of Chicago Press.

Powers, B. (2012, October 10). "Bill Powers: An Admissions Policy That Prizes Diversity." *Wall Street Journal.* http://www.wsj.com/articles/SB10000872396390 4440047045780321641472092262.

PricewaterhouseCoopers. (2015). *A Marketplace Without Boundaries? Responding to Disruption.* London: PricewaterhouseCoopers. http://www.pwc.com/gx/en /ceo-survey/2015/assets/pwc-18th-annual-global-ceo-survey-jan-2015.pdf.

Purdum, T. S. (1995, July 20). "President Shows Fervent Support for Goals of Affirmative Action." *Washington Post.*

Pusser, B. (2004). *Burning Down the House: Politics, Governance, and Affirmative Action at the University of California.* Albany: State University of New York Press.

Regents of the University of California v. Bakke, 436 U.S. 265 (1978).

Renfro, S., and Armour-Garb, A. (1999, June). "Open Admissions and Remedial Education at the City University of New York" New York: Mayor's Advisory Task Force on the City University of New York. http://www.nyc.gov/html /records/rwg/cuny/html/admissions.html

Reno v. Bossier Parish School Board, 528 U.S. 320 (2000).

Revolutionary Worker. (1996, November 17). "California Protests Answer Passage of Prop 209: Students Fight for Real Equality." http://revcom.us/a/firstvol/882 /prop1.htm.

Rhoads, R. A., Saenz, V., and Carducci, R. (2005). "Higher Education Reform as a Social Movement: The Case of Affirmative Action." *Review of Higher Education 28*(2), 191–220.

Robinson, C. (2000). *Black Marxism: The Making of the Black Radical Tradition.* Chapel Hill: University of North Carolina Press.

Robinson, N. (2003). "Undergraduate Access to the University of California After the Elimination of Race-Conscious Policies." Office of the President, University of California. http://ucop.edu/student-affairs/_files/aa_final2.pdf.

Rockwell, P. (1995). "University of California Regents and Conflict of Interest." *In Motion Magazine.* http://www.inmotionmagazine.com/rock2.html.

Roff, S. S., Cucchiara, A. M., and Dunlap, B. J. (2000). *From the Free Academy to CUNY: Illustrating Public Higher Education in New York City, 1847–1997*. New York: Fordham University Press.

Rogers, I. H. (2011). "The Black Campus Movement: The Case for a New Historiography." *The Sixties: A Journal of History, Politics, and Culture* 4(2), 171–186. https://doi.org/10.1080/17541328.2011.625195.

Rogers, I. H. (2012). *The Black Campus Movement: Black Students and the Racial Reconstitution of Higher Education, 1965–1972*. New York: Palgrave Macmillan.

Rojas, F. (2007). *From Black Power to Black Studies: How a Radical Social Movement Became an Academic Discipline*. Baltimore: Johns Hopkins University Press.

Romo, H. D., and Falbo, T. (1995). *Latino High School Graduation: Defying the Odds*. Austin: University of Texas Press.

Roosevelt, F. D. (1943, July 28). "Fireside Chat." American Presidency Project. http://www.presidency.ucsb.edu/ws/?pid=16437.

Rorabaugh, W. J. (1989). *Berkeley at War: The 1960s*. New York: Oxford University Press.

Rossmann, J. E., Astin, H. S., Astin, A. W., and El-Khawas, E. H. (1975). *Open Admissions at City University of New York: An Analysis of the First Year*. Englewood Cliffs, NJ: Prentice-Hall.

Roush, A. (2012, November 2). "TXEXplainer: Why Top 10 Percent Is Now Top 7." *Alcalde*. http://alcalde.texasexes.org/2012/11/txexplainer-why-top-10-percent-is -now-top-7/.

Royster, D. (2003). *Race and the Invisible Hand: How White Networks Exclude Black Men from Blue-Collar Jobs*. Berkeley: University of California Press.

Sack, K. (1995, June 3). "Albany's Budget: The Impact; Plan Will Leave Mark on Every Resident." *New York Times*. https://www.nytimes.com/1995/06/03/nyregion /albany-s-budget-the-impact-plan-will-leave-mark-on-every-resident.html.

Saltonstall, D. (1997, October 10). "Baruch Prez Offers RX for a Troubled City U." *New York Daily News*. http://www.nydailynews.com/archives/news/baruch-prez -offers-rx-troubled-city-u-article-1.779962.

San Antonio Independent School District v. Rodriguez, 411 U.S. 1 (1973).

Sander, R., and Taylor, S. (2012). *Mismatch: How Affirmative Action Hurts Students It's Intended to Help, and Why Universities Won't Admit It*. New York: Basic Books.

Santoro, W. A., and McGuire, G. A. (1997). "Social Movement Insiders: The Impact of Institutional Activists on Affirmative Action and Comparable Worth Policies." *Social Problems* 44(4), 503–519.

Satija, N., and Watkins, M. (2017, August 21). "UT System Oil Money Is a Gusher for Its Administration—And a Trickle for Students." *Texas Tribune*. https:// www.texastribune.org/2017/08/21/ut-system-oil-money-gusher-its -administration-and-trickle-students/.

Savage, C. (2012, January 17). "Affirmative Action Foe Is Facing Allegations of Financial Misdeeds." *New York Times*. https://www.nytimes.com/2012/01/18 /us/ward-connerly-faces-allegations-of-fiscal-misdoing.html.

Saxon, W. (1999, January 6). "Henry Paolucci, 77, Scholar and a Leader in the Conservative Party." *New York Times*. https://www.nytimes.com/1999/01/06 /nyregion/henry-paolucci-77-scholar-and-a-leader-in-conservative-party .html.

Scherer, R. (1995, March 29). "Cuts Stir New Wave of Student Protests." *Christian Science Monitor*. http://www.csmonitor.com/1995/0329/29011.html.

Schmidt, B. C., Badillo, H., Brady, J. V., Mac Donald, H., Ohrenstein, M., Roberts, R. T., and Schwartz, R. (1999). *The City University of New York: An Institution Adrift*. New York: City of New York. http://home.nyc.gov/html/records/rwg /cuny/pdf/adrift.pdf.

Schmidt, P. (2012, January 4). "New Hampshire Ends Affirmative-Action Preferences at Colleges." *Chronicle of Higher Education*. http://chronicle.com /article/New-Hampshire-Ends/130196/.

School Desegregation: Hearings Before the Subcommittee on Civil and Constitutional Rights of the House Committee on the Judiciary, 97th Cong., 1st Sess. (1981).

Schuette v. Coalition to Defend Affirmative Action (BAMN), 572 U.S.___ (2014).

Selingo, J. (2001, August 3). "U. of California Regents Adopt Admissions Plan." *Chronicle of Higher Education*. http://www.chroniclecareers.com/article /U-of-California-Regents-Adopt/12954/.

Shabazz, A. (2004). *Advancing Democracy: African Americans and the Struggle for Access and Equity in Higher Education in Texas*. Chapel Hill: University of North Carolina Press.

Shaw, M. P. (2016). "Bans on Affirmative Action in States with a History of State-Sponsored Discrimination." In E. Frankenburg, L. M. Garcers, and M. Hopkins (eds.), *School Integration Matters: Research-Based Strategies to Advance Equity*. New York: Teachers College Press.

Shaw, M. P. (2017). "The Impact of Affirmative-Action Bans in States with a History of State-Sponsored Discrimination in Higher-Education." PhD diss., Harvard Graduate School of Education, Cambridge, MA. https://dash.harvard .edu/bitstream/handle/1/33797228/SHAW-QUALIFYINGPAPER-2017.pdf ?sequence=1.

Sheet Metal Workers v. EEOC, 478 U.S. 421 (1986).

Shelby County v. Holder, 570 U.S. 2 (2013).

Sherman, M. (2012, October 11). "Texas Affirmative Action Plan in Trouble at Court." Associated Press. http://bigstory.ap.org/article/texas-affirmative-action -plan-trouble-court.

Shinar, A. (2013). "Dissenting from Within: Why and How Public Officials Resist the Law." *Florida State University Law Review 40*(3), 601–657.

Siegel, R. (2000). "Discrimination in the Eyes of the Law: How Color Blindness Discourse Disrupts and Rationalizes Social Stratification." *California Law Review 88*, 77–118.

Simon, S. (2008, January 19). "Affirmative Re-action." *Los Angeles Times*. http:// articles.latimes.com/2008/jan/19/nation/na-affirmative19.

Simpson, I. (2017, April 18). "Georgetown University Renames Buildings to Atone for Slavery Ties." Reuters. https://www.reuters.com/article/us -washingtondc-georgetown-slavery/georgetown-university-renames-buildings -to-atone-for-slavery-ties-idUSKBN17K2AR.

Sipuel v. Board of Regents of University of Oklahoma, 332 U.S. 631 (1948).

Skrentny, J. D. (1996). *The Ironies of Affirmative Action: Politics, Culture, and Justice in America*. Chicago: University of Chicago Press.

Skrentny, J. D. (2001). "Republican Efforts to End Affirmative Action: Walking a Fine Line." In M. Landy, M. Levin, and M. Shapiro (eds.), *Seeking the Center: Politics and Policymaking at the New Century*, 132–171. Washington, DC: Georgetown University Press.

Slevin, P. (2008, March 26). "Affirmative Action Foes Push Ballot Initiatives." *Washington Post*. http://www.washingtonpost.com/wp-dyn/content/article /2008/03/25/AR2008032502401.html.

Smith, J. (2010, February 20). "Utah Legislature: Anti-affirmative Action Measure Sinking Fast in Utah House." *Deseret News* (Salt Lake City). http:// www.deseretnews.com/article/700010743/Utah-Legislature-Anti-affirmative -action-measure-sinking-fast-in-Utah-House.html?pg=all.

Smith, N. (1996). *The New Urban Frontier: Gentrification and the Revanchist City*. London: Routledge.

Smith, P., and Parrish, L. (2014). "Do Students of Color Profit from For-Profit College? Poor Outcomes and High Debt Hamper Attendees' Futures." Center for Responsible Lending. http://www.responsiblelending.org/student-loans /research-policy/CRL-For-Profit-Univ-FINAL.pdf.

Soares, J. A. (2011). *SAT Wars: The Case for Test-Optional College Admissions*. New York: Teachers College Press.

Solomon, A., and Hussey, D. (1998, April 21). "Enemies of Public Education." *Village Voice*.

Soule, S. A., McAdam, D., McCarthy, J. and Yang, S. (1999). "Protest Events: Cause or Consequence of State Action? The U.S. Women's Movements and Federal Congressional Activities, 1956–1979." *Mobilization*. 4(2): 239–256.

South Carolina v. Katzenbach, 383 U.S. 301 (1966).

St. Louis Post-Dispatch Editorial Board. (2008, April 14). "Carpetbaggers Wanted." *St. Louis Post-Dispatch*. http://www.stltoday.com/news/opinion/columns/the -platform/carpetbaggers-wanted/article_2dcc75da-a505-56eb-895c -1675daba9b99.html.

Staggs, B. (1998, January 4). "Student Life: Headlines from the Fall Semester; Infighting at Berkeley Over Style of Protests." *New York Times*. http://www .nytimes.com/1998/01/04/education/student-life-headlines-f...ester-infighting -berkeley-over-style-protests.html?pagewanted=print.

Stahl, J. (2016). *Right Moves: The Conservative Think Tank in American Political Culture Since 1945*. Chapel Hill: University of North Carolina Press.

Stall, B., and Morain, D. (1996, November 6). "Prop. 209 Wins, Bars Affirmative Action." *Los Angeles Times.* http://articles.latimes.com/1996-11-06/news /mn-62738_1_affirmative-action.

Steck, H. (2006). "Contested Futures: Public Policy and the State University of New York." In R. F. Pecorella and J. M. Stonecash (eds.), *Governing New York State.* Albany: State University of New York Press.

Steensland, B., and Wright, E. L. (2014). "American Evangelicals and Conservative Politics: Past, Present, and Future." *Sociology Compass 8*(6), 705–717. https://doi.org/10.1111/soc4.12175.

Stefancic, J., and Delgado, R. (1996). *No Mercy: How Conservative Think Tanks and Foundations Changed America's Social Agenda.* Philadelphia: Temple University Press.

Stein, H. (2006, Spring). "A Preemptive Surrender: Michigan Republicans Are AWOL in the Fight Against Racial Preferences." *City Journal.* https://www.city -journal.org/html/preemptive-surrender-12937.html.

Steinberg, S. (1974). *Academic Melting Pot: Catholics and Jews in American Higher Education.* New York: McGraw-Hill.

Steinberg, S. (1995). *Turning Back: The Retreat from Racial Justice in American Thought and Policy.* Boston: Beacon.

Steinberg, S. (2003, Summer). "Nathan Glazer and the Assassination of Affirmative Action." *New Politics 9*(3), 9–21.

Steinberg, S. (2018, February). "Revisiting Open Admissions." *Clarion: Newspaper of the Professional Staff Congress, City University of New York.* https://www.psc -cuny.org/clarion/december/2018-0.

Stohr, G. (2004). *A Black and White Case: How Affirmative Action Survived Its Greatest Legal Challenge.* Princeton, NJ: Bloomberg.

Stronach v. Virginia State University, 577 F. Supp. 2d 788 (E.D. Va. 2008).

Stulberg, L. M., and Chen, A. S. (2014). "The Origins of Race-Conscious Affirmative Action in Undergraduate Admissions: A Comparative Analysis of Institutional Change in Higher Education." *Sociology of Education 87*(1), 36–52. http://doi.org/10.1177/0038040713514063.

Subways, Suzy. (2008). "A Culture of Resistance: Lessons Learned from the Student Liberation Action Movement." *Upping the Anti: A Journal of Theory and Action,* no. 8. http://uppingtheanti.org/journal/article/08-a-culture-of -resistance1/.

Subways, Suzy. (2010, October). "'We Shut the City Down': Six Former Student Liberation Action Movement (SLAM) Members Reflect on the Mass Direct Actions Against the 2000 RNC in Philadelphia" (pamphlet).

Subways, Suzy. (2015, March 23). "'It Was Electrifying': Organizers Reflect on the March 23, 1995 CUNY Protest 20 Years Later." SLAM! Herstory Project. https:// slamherstory.wordpress.com/2015/03/23/it-was-electrifying-organizers -reflect-on-the-march-23-1995-cuny-protest-20-years-later/.

Svrluga, S. (2015, November 9). "U. Missouri President, Chancellor Resign Over Handling of Racial Incidents." *Washington Post*. https://www.washingtonpost .com/news/grade-point/wp/2015/11/09/missouris-student-government-calls -for-university-presidents-removal/.

Sweatt v. Painter, 339 U.S. 629 (1950).

Takagi, D. Y. (1990). "From Discrimination to Affirmative Action: Facts in the Asian American Admissions Controversy." *Social Problems* 37(4), 578–592.

Taliaferro, T. (2015, June). "Powers Takes His Leave." *Alcalde*. https://alcalde .texasexes.org/2015/04/powers-takes-his-leave/.

Tarrow, S. G. (2011). *Power in Movement: Social Movements and Contentious Politics*. 3rd ed. Cambridge: Cambridge University Press.

Taylor, K.-Y. (2016). *From #BlackLivesMatter to Black Liberation*. Chicago: Haymarket Books.

Taylor, P., and Balz, D. (1995, September 30). "Gov. Wilson Quits Presidential Race." *Washington Post*. https://www.washingtonpost.com/archive/politics /1995/09/30/gov-wilson-quits-presidential-campaign/e1c2bcb9-27f3-433d -b579-e892d4338f63/?utm_term=.4f5204a36dde.

Taylor, U. (2010). "Origins of African American Studies at UC-Berkeley." *Western Journal of Black Studies* 34(2), 256–265.

Taylor, V., and Van Dyke, N. (2004). " 'Get Up, Stand Up': Tactical Repertoires of Social Movements." In D. A. Snow, S. A. Soule, and H. Kriesi (eds.), *The Blackwell Companion to Social Movements*, 262–293. Hoboken, NJ: Blackwell.

Teles, S. M. (2008). *The Rise of the Conservative Legal Movement: The Battle for Control of the Law*. Princeton, NJ: Princeton University Press.

Texas Education Agency. (n.d.). "State Graduation Requirements." https:// tea.texas.gov/graduation.aspx.

Texas Higher Education Coordinating Board. (1997). *Alternative Diversity Criteria: Analyses and Recommendations. A Report by Advisory Committee on Criteria for Diversity*. Austin: Texas Higher Education Coordinating Board. http://archive.org/details/ERIC_ED408908.

Texas House of Representatives. (1997). *Daily Journal for the 75th Legislature*. http://www.journals.house.state.tx.us/hjrnl/75R/html/.

Thelin, J. R. (2011). *A History of American Higher Education*. 2nd ed. Baltimore: Johns Hopkins University Press.

Thomas, G. (2015). *The Founders and the Idea of a National University: Constituting the American Mind*. New York: Cambridge University Press.

Thompson, J. P., and Tobias, S. (2000). "The Texas Ten Percent Plan." *American Behavioral Scientist* 43(7), 1121–1138.

Thorne, B. (2012, March 5). "Supreme Court Case on Affirmative Action Questions Ruling with Flint Ties." MLive Media Group. https://www.mlive.com /news/flint/index.ssf/2012/03/supreme_court_case_on_affirmat.html.

Tien, C.-L. (1995). "Affirming Affirmative Action." In G. A. Lew (ed.), *Perspectives on Affirmative Action and Its Impact on Asian Pacific Americans.* Los Angeles: LEAP Asian Pacific American Public Policy Institute.

Tien, C.-L. (1996, July). "Recollections on Affirmative Action." *Chinese American Forum 12*(1), 6–9.

Tienda, M., Alon, S., and Niu, S. (2010). "Affirmative Action and the Texas Top 10 Admissions Law: Balancing Equity and Access to Higher Education." *Sociétés Contemporaines 79,* 19–39.

Tienda, M., Leicht, K. T., Sullivan, T., Maltese, M., and Lloyd, K. (2003). "Closing the Gap?: Admissions and Enrollments at the Texas Public Flagships Before and After Affirmative Action." Texas Higher Education Opportunity Project, http://theop.princeton.edu/reports/wp/closing_the_gap.pdf.

Tienda, M., and Niu, S. X. (2006). "Capitalizing on Segregation, Pretending Neutrality: College Admissions and the Texas Top 10 Percent Law." *American Law and Economics Review 8*(2), 312–346.

Tilly, C. (1978). *From Mobilization to Revolution.* New York: McGraw-Hill.

Tilly, C. (2005). *Popular Contention in Great Britain 1758–1834.* London: Paradigm.

Toldson, I.A.(2013)."MoreBlackMeninJailThaninCollege?Wrong."*TheRoot.*http://www.theroot.com/more-black-men-in-jail-than-in-college-wrong-1790895415.

Toldson, I., and Lewis, C. D. (2012). *Challenge the Status Quo: Academic Success Among School-Age African-American Males.* Washington, DC: Congressional Black Caucus Foundation.

"Top Public Schools—National Universities." (n.d.). *U.S. News & World Report.* https://www.usnews.com/best-colleges/rankings/national-universities/top-public.

Torche, F. (2011). "Is a College Degree Still the Great Equalizer? Intergenerational Mobility Across Levels of Schooling in the US." *American Journal of Sociology 117*(3), 763–807.

Treschan, L., and Mehrotra, A. (2012). *Unintended Impacts: Fewer Black and Latino Freshmen at CUNY Senior Colleges After the Recession.* New York: Community Service Society. http://b.3cdn.net/nycss/2e01feab246663d4a8_lhm6b94lq.pdf.

Tsuang, G. W. (1989). "Assuring Equal Access of Asian Americans to Highly Selective Universities." *Yale Law Journal 98,* 659.

Tuomey, J. (1995, October 30). "Thousands Rally for Affirmative Action." *The Militant.* http://www.themilitant.com/1995/5940/5940_27.html.

Tushnet, M. (1994). *Making Civil Rights Law: Thurgood Marshall and the Supreme Court, 1936–1961.* Oxford: Oxford University Press.

UC Berkeley Office of Planning and Analysis. (2017a). "B2. Enrollment by Racial/Ethnic Category." *Common Data Set 2012–2013.* Berkeley: UC Berkeley Office of Planning and Analysis.

UC Berkeley Office of Planning and Analysis. (2017b). "Common Data Set." https://opa.berkeley.edu/campus-data/common-data-set.

UCLA Undergraduate Admission. (2017). "Admission Statistics." http://www.admission.ucla.edu/prospect/stat.htm.

University of California Office of Institutional Research and Academic Planning (2018a). "CSS Third Week Enrollment File." https://www.universityofcalifornia.edu/infocenter/fall-enrollment-glance.

University of California Office of Institutional Research and Academic Planning (2018b). "Fall Enrollment at a Glance." http://www.universityofcalifornia.edu/infocenter/fall-enrollment-glance.

University of California Office of Institutional Research and Academic Planning (2018c). "Freshmen and Transfer Admissions by Residency and Ethnicity." http://www.universityofcalifornia.edu/infocenter/admissions-residency-and-ethnicity

U.S. Bureau of the Census (2018). "Population Estimates by Age, Race [California]" https://www.census.gov/quickfacts/ca.

U.S. Bureau of the Census (2018). "Population Estimates by Age, Race [Texas]" https://www.census.gov/quickfacts/tx.

Uhlig, M. A. (1987, September 17). "Ohrenstein: A Career That Began with Reform." *New York Times*.

United States v. Paradise, 480 U.S. 149 (1987).

University of Michigan. (2016). *Many Voices, Our Michigan: Diversity, Equity and Inclusion Strategic Plan* (Executive Summary). Ann Arbor: University of Michigan.

University of Michigan Office of the Registrar. (2017). "Ethnicity Reports." http://ro.umich.edu/enrollment/ethnicity.php.

University of Texas at Austin. (n.d.). "Admission Decisions." https://admissions.utexas.edu/apply/decisions.

University of Texas at Austin Office of Admissions. (2004). "Proposal to Consider Race and Ethnicity in Admissions." https://www.utexas.edu/student/admissions/about/admission_proposal.pdf.

University of Texas at Austin Office of Institutional Reporting, Research, and Information Systems (2017). "Common Data Set." https://reports.utexas.edu/common-data-set.

U.S. Census. (2006). "Michigan." https://web.archive.org/web/20060715161518/http://quickfacts.census.gov/qfd/states/26/ 2622000.html.

Van Deburg, W. L. (1992). *New Day in Babylon: The Black Power Movement and American Culture, 1965–1975*. Chicago: University of Chicago Press.

Vassar, E. (2015). "Support for the Nominations of Lewis Powell and William Rehnquist." Richard Nixon Foundation. http://nixonfoundation.org/2015/03/support-nominations-lewis-powell-william-rehnquist/.

Verhovek, S. H. (1996, March 23). "For 4 Whites Who Sued University, Race Is the Common Thread." *New York Times*. http://www.nytimes.com/1996/03/23/us/for-4-whites-who-sued-university-race-is-the-common-thread.html.

Vitale, A. (1995, October). "Coalition and Its Discontents: A Sociology Student Assesses the Cuts Fight." *The Advocate*.

"Vote Yes on 2: Michigan Civil Rights Initiative" (2006). Print Campaign Advertisement. Retrieved from: https://archive.li/nMmI8.

Waitrovich, A. (2017). "Jacqueline Brady Joins PGIM Real Estate's Americas Business Development Team." https://irei.com/news/jacqueline-brady-joins -pgim-real-estates-americas-business-development-team/.

Walker, A. (1992, May 9). "Has CUNY Unofficially Abolished Open Admissions?" *New York Amsterdam News.*

Wallace, A., and Lesher, D. (1995, July 21). "UC Regents, in a Historic Vote, Wipe Out Affirmative Action." *Los Angeles Times.* http://articles.latimes.com/1995-07-21/news /mn-26379_1_regents-vote-affirmative-action-university-of-california-regents.

Walsh, M. (1990, October 10). "Bias Against Asians at U.C.L.A. Found by Education Department." *Education Week.* http://www.edweek.org/ew/articles/1990 /10/10/10370004.h10.html.

Wang, L.-C. (1993). "Higher Education Policy." In *The State of Asia Pacific America: Policy Issues to the Year 2020.* Los Angles: LEAP Asian Pacific American Public Policy Institute and UCLA Asian American Studies Center.

Wang, L. (1997, Spring). "Chronology of Ethnic Studies at U.C. Berkeley." Newsletter of the Department of Ethnic Studies, UC Berkeley.

Wards Cove Packing Co. v. Atonio, 490 U.S. 642 (1989).

Ware, L. B. (2001). "Setting the Stage for *Brown*: The Development and Implementation of the NAACP's School Desegregation Campaign, 1930–1950." *Mercer Law Review 52*(2), 631–673.

Warikoo, N. K. (2016). *The Diversity Bargain: And Other Dilemmas of Race, Admissions, and Meritocracy at Elite Universities.* Chicago: University of Chicago Press.

Washington v. Seattle School District No. 1, 458 U.S. 457 (1982).

Washington Post. (2017). "DOJ Job Posting Seeking Lawyers to Investigate and Litigate 'Cases Related to Intentional Race-Based Discrimination' in College Admissions: Detail Opportunity, Office of the Assistant Attorney General." http://apps.washingtonpost.com/g/documents/national/doj-job-posting -asks-lawyers-to-investigate-and-litigate-cases-related-to-intentional-race -based-discrimination-in-college-admissions/2516/.

Washington Post Editorial Board. (2017, January 15). "Martin Luther King Jr. Was a True Conservative." https://www.washingtonpost.com/opinions/martin -luther-king-jr-was-a-true-conservative/2017/01/15/b0f465e4-d9c6-11e6-9a36 -1d296534b31e_story.html.

Watanabe, T. (2016a, June 23). "How UCLA Is Boosting Campus Diversity, Despite the Ban on Affirmative Action." *Los Angeles Times.* http://www.latimes.com /local/california/la-me-ucla-diversity-20160620-snap-story.html.

Watanabe, T. (2016b, July 6). "UCLA, UC Berkeley Boost Admissions of Californians, Including Blacks and Latinos." *Los Angeles Times.* http://www.latimes .com/local/lanow/la-me-uc-admissions-20160706-snap-story.html.

Watkins, M. (2017, June 27). "Man Behind Fisher Affirmative Action Case Files New Lawsuit Against UT-Austin." *Texas Tribune.* https://www.texastribune .org/2017/06/27/man-behind-fisher-case-files-new-lawsuit-challenging -affirmative-actio/.

Webster, N. (2007). *Analysis of the Texas Ten Percent Plan*. Columbus: Kirwan Institute for the Study of Race and Ethnicity, Ohio State University. http://kirwaninstitute.osu.edu/reports/2007/08_2007_DemMerit_AnalysisofTX TenPercent.pdf.

WeTheProtestors. (2015). "The Demands." https://thedemands.org.

Whitford, E. (2017, April 12). "Cuomo's Tuition-Free College Plan Could Turn Into a Lottery If Funding Falls Short." *Gothamist*. http://gothamist.com/2017/04/12 /cuomo_tuition_lottery.php.

Whitney, K. M. (2006). "Lost in Transition: Governing in a Time of Privatization." In W. G. Tierney (ed.), *Governance and the Public Good*. Albany: State University of New York Press.

Wilkinson, J. H. (1979). *From Brown to Bakke: The Supreme Court and School Integration*. New York: Oxford University Press.

Williams, L. (2001, November 27). "W. Glenn Campbell, Confidant of Reagan." *San Francisco Chronicle*.

Wilson, W. J. (2012). "Race and Affirming Opportunity in the Barack Obama Era. *Du Bois Review: Social Science Research on Race* 9(1), 5–16.

Winant, H. (1994). *Racial Conditions: Politics, Theory, Comparisons*. Minneapolis: University of Minnesota Press.

Women's City Club of New York. (1975). *The Privileged Many: A Study of the City University of New York's Open Admissions Policy, 1970–1975*. New York: Women's City Club of New York.

Woo, E. (1988, November 18). "U.S. Probing Possible Asian Bias at UCLA, UC Berkeley." *Los Angeles Times*. http://articles.latimes.com/1988-11-18/news/mn -452_1_uc-berkeley.

Wu, F. H., and Wang, T. H. (1996). "Beyond the Model Minority Myth: Why Asian Americans Support Affirmative Action." *Guild Practitioner 53*, 35–47.

Wygant v. Jackson Board of Education, 476 U.S. 267 (1986).

Wynn, N. A. (1976). *The Afro-American and the Second World War*. New York: Holmes & Meier.

XIV Foundation (2012). "XIV Foundation, About Us." Retrieved from: http://www .xivfoundation.org.

"Yes on Proposal 2" (2006). Television Campaign Advertisement. Retrieved from: https://www.youtube.com/watch?v=AmK2SWWGkBY.

Yosso, T. J., Parker, L., Solórzano, D. G., and Lynn, M. (2004). "From Jim Crow to Affirmative Action and Back Again: A Critical Race Discussion of Racialized Rationales and Access to Higher Education." *Review of Research in Education 28*, 1–25.

Zeveloff, N. (2008, November 7). "After Colorado Loss, Ward Connerly May Pull the Plug on Affirmative-Action Bans." *Colorado Independent*. http://www.colora- doindependent.com/14617/ward-connerly-may-pull-the-plug.

INDEX

CPSIA information can be obtained
at www.ICGtesting.com
Printed in the USA
LVHW032112310120
645499LV00001B/2

9 780231 183093